*To the fans who, for decades,
have been tirelessly litigating this issue with their voices,
keyboards—and occasionally their fists.*

SLUGFEST

INSIDE THE EPIC
FIFTY-YEAR BATTLE BETWEEN

MARVEL AND DC

REED TUCKER

SPHERE

First published in the US by Da Capo Press, an imprint of Perseus Books, LLC,
a subsidiary of Hachette Book Group, Inc.

First published in Great Britain in 2017 by Sphere

1 3 5 7 9 10 8 6 4 2

A CIP catalogue record for this book
is available from the British Library.

ISBN 978-0-7515-6897-4

Printed and bound in Great Britain by
Clays Ltd, St Ives plc

Editorial production by Lori Hobkirk at the Book Factory.
Print book interior design by Cynthia Young.

Papers used by Sphere are from well-managed forests
and other responsible sources.

Sphere
An imprint of
Little, Brown Book Group
Carmelite House
50 Victoria Embankment
London EC4Y 0DZ

An Hachette UK Company
www.hachette.co.uk

www.littlebrown.co.uk

CONTENTS

PROLOGUE

My first glimpse of true comic book culture came when a friend took me to a shop called Dave's Comics in Richmond, Virginia, in the mid eighties.

Dave's was located in a strip mall down the street from a university. For millennials and others of a certain age who have lived nearly their entire lives when superheroes have existed inside the mainstream, for whom visiting a funny bookstore means turning up to a clean, well-lit pseudo-macchiato bar run by hipsters, it's difficult to convey how underground and marginalized comic books used to be.

Dave's Comics sat literally at the end of an alley bookended by a chemical-smelling hair salon on one side and dumpsters on the other. The store was tiny—two hundred square feet, maybe. The space looked like it had once been a storage closet for the mall's maintenance equipment before the owner one day had a brainstorm that he could hose it down and rent it out for a few bucks.

The new comics were displayed in two modest, shoulder-high wooden racks, and in those days the entire weekly output from DC and Marvel could fit into a couple of dozen slots. These days you'd probably need the whole mall.

The rest of the store was filled—buried, really—with back stock stored in long white cardboard boxes piled on top of each other and containing God knows how many wonders.

If all this sounds like a fun place for a kid to spend a day, it wasn't. Dave's had a strict no-browsing rule in order to safeguard the condition of the wares, and the owner and his staff were militant about it. Like Michigan-militia militant. Start flipping through a random box, and you'd get yelled at with a quickness. If you wanted a particular back issue, you had to timidly ask for it, forcing the clerk to sigh loudly, get up from behind the cash register, and start yanking unmarked boxes from the stacks, straining to remove and return at least three before he found the correct one.

Dave's Comics eventually moved to another location in the mall that offered pristine amenities the original didn't—such as ventilation. The shop, before closing in 2015 after the unexpected death of its owner, appears to have done well for itself over the years. And like a lot of comic stores, its growth was probably driven in part by an expanded customer base, as more and more readers realized, in the words of a jillion clichéd newspaper headlines, "comics aren't just for kids anymore."

I came to that same conclusion while still a kid. I can remember being at a bookstore in 1986 and spotting a display beside the cash register sporting the most bad-ass image of Batman I'd ever seen.

The cashier saw me staring and, completely unsolicited, said, "You should buy that. It'll change your life."

I did buy it, and that book was Frank Miller's *The Dark Knight Returns*, aka the single-coolest thing Western civilization has ever produced. (Your mileage may vary.)

I knew immediately this was a different kind of comic—and not just because it cost an allowance-draining $12.95. For one, it looked like a proper book and was printed on sturdy paper that didn't seem to dissolve as you turned the pages. The art was graphic and kinetic, and the hero presented within those pages was dark and violent, a frightening shadowy figure who dangled criminals from rooftops and snapped legs with powerful roundhouses. This Batman bore little resemblance to the one whose adventures I'd seen on Saturday morning cartoons. This felt dangerous and adult. Even the costume was darker and lacked the goofy yellow oval on his chest emblem.

It was lost on me at the time, but *The Dark Knight Returns* was a true milestone in comic book history. It was one of the most influential and important advances in the revolution that was then sweeping through the medium, putting a more sophisticated spin on superheroes. And I happened to have the good fortune to be at the perfect age to benefit from that revolution.

In the America I was born into, comic books were considered almost exclusively kiddie fare. They were something to be read for a few years before you inevitably outgrew them, somewhere around age eleven. Then you would move on to other hobbies, like trying to convince someone in the grocery store parking lot to buy you beer, a younger reader would replace you, and the cycle would continue.

It took until basically my lifetime for this pattern to be broken. Just as I was on the way toward becoming an adult and leaving superheroes behind, superheroes instead came with me.

With the publication of more mature titles, including *Watchmen* and *Saga of the Swamp Thing*, as well as the recent spate of comic-sourced TV shows and movies, the material has grown up. As a result, my generation became the first who didn't need to age out of superheroes. Head to any comic convention nowadays, and you'll find loads of full-grown adults, browsing the booths and jousting with plastic swords while wearing bright-red Deadpool costumes. It's probably still not a great look for a Tinder profile, but in terms of the cultural mainstream, these people have never been more in.

The superhero industry is now worth billions of dollars, and as was the case more than fifty years ago, Marvel and DC remain the only major players—the Coke and Pepsi of spandex—continuing to battle each other like Batman and the Joker.

Not that I'd ever personally characterize either company as the villain. I've got no dog in the Marvel vs. DC fight. I don't read comics from either these days, instead preferring independently published, nonsuperhero titles such as *Saga, Criminal, Queen & Country*, and *The Walking Dead*.

If I have any bias, it's for the Marvel movies, which I think it's safe to say are objectively better than those from DC. At least when it comes to DC's recent output. For ten years I covered movies for the *New York Post*—a cushy gig that allowed me to see films for free during work hours—and let's just say that when it came to *Batman v Superman: Dawn of Justice*, I'd have rather been sitting in the office. I don't think that makes me a Marvel homer. It just makes me a person with eyes.

Rabid fans in both camps have endlessly debated the question of which is better, Marvel or DC, for literally decades, and I'm not sure this book is going to settle that argument. It may never be settled. I fully expect that at the 2045 San Diego Comic-Con, attendees will still be getting into slap-fights debating whether the Green Lantern featured in the seventh and latest cinematic reboot could beat up the tenth onscreen version of Wolverine.

And would we fans have it any other way? So much of what makes the comic book world fun is the passion and the enthusiasm of the fans, not to mention those who work in the industry. The competition between Marvel and DC is fuel for that fire. Without this rivalry the comic book industry would be a lot less interesting. And boring is something that gets old quickly to adult and child alike.

INTRODUCTION

*T*his is a story about innovation.

As much as readers might like to romanticize the comic book business, it's still just that: a business. Art Spiegelman, the Pulitzer prize-winning cartoonist behind *Maus*, called comics "the bastard offspring of art and commerce." And money (measured in part by sales) is still one of the most critical components in every single one of those bagged and boarded issues you've lovingly stored in your closet—if not to the talent involved, then certainly for their corporate masters in the corner offices.

And as with any business, innovation is everything. It's the key to success, and a single groundbreaking leap forward can shake up an industry, blaze new trails, and reverberate in the industry for years or even decades to come. It can literally change the world. Apple did it with the iPhone, George Lucas did it with *Star Wars*, and Taco Bell did it with its transcendent Doritos Locos Taco.

More often than not, the company with the best ideas is the one that comes out on top.

The superhero landscape today is really a product of two massive innovations: one by DC some eighty years ago and another by Marvel almost sixty. Both breakthroughs were so fresh, so game changing that the comics industry—and, ultimately, Robert Downey Jr.'s career—would never the same again.

These innovations helped each publisher cement its identity and, at the time, gain a crucial edge on the competition. The ripples from both leaps still define the comics industry.

As difficult as it might be to imagine now, with Marvel's complete and utter stranglehold on global pop culture through its movie studio, the publisher was once a superhero also-ran.

For much of the twentieth century it was DC, then known as National, that was the undisputed leader in the spandex game, having created the genre with the 1938 publication of Joe Shuster and Jerry Siegel's Superman strip. For a long time DC had the most money, the best talent, and comfortable offices inside a Midtown Manhattan skyscraper clad in gold. Its titles sold millions of copies every year, and its iconic characters were familiar to nearly everyone in America.

Superman, Batman, Wonder Woman—DC had them all. It was the industry's blue chip, the Ford to everyone else's Packard.

In the late fifties Marvel Comics was just a ragged little shop with basically one employee. Its single-room office was down the hall from a porno mag. It had been founded as Timely in the 1930s and, in an underwhelming vote of confidence regarding its brand strength, had operated under a few different names in the decades to follow.

During the 1950s and early 1960s its output consisted mostly of second-tier titles, including various war, monster, and Western anthologies as well as long-forgotten romance books, including *My Girl Pearl*.

It was being run by a middle-aged, wannabe novelist who had toiled in the comic business since he was seventeen, churning out hundreds of stories, but had somehow failed to distinguish himself. Burnt out and sensing the futility of his career, he finally resolved to do something he should have done years earlier had he any hope of earning a decent wage and a modicum of self-respect: turn off the lights, close his office door behind him, and walk away from the comics business for good. But like an aging detective in a bad cop movie, he couldn't retire until he gave it one last shot.

That wannabe novelist was Stan Lee, and that final shot was his and Jack Kirby's *Fantastic Four* #1.

With its publication in August 1961 and the subsequent release of a wave of equally revolutionary books, upstart Marvel changed the superhero business forever and quickly established itself as the edgier, hipper alternative to stodgy old DC.

DC was blindsided by the challenge, and ever since the publisher has been playing catch-up, trying to capture some of Marvel's cool and struggling to make its fleet of aged characters relevant to contemporary readers. Sometimes it has succeeded. Other times it has stumbled.

For much of DC's life larger corporations have owned the publisher, and as such the bureaucracy, sluggishness, and other problems that stereotypically go hand in hand with corporate life have hampered it. Corporations rarely break ground. They rarely push boundaries or spark revolutions, especially when it comes to creative pursuits.

And nothing better exemplifies DC's corporate cluelessness—its bumbling pursuit of Marvel—than what happened in the mid-1960s.

By the middle of the decade DC was taking serious fire as Marvel's tiny stable of titles was showing increasing success month after month. As improbable as it seemed at the time, Marvel was gaining on mighty DC. You can imagine the executives' mouths hanging open in wonderment at the idea of this impertinent little company daring to siphon off some of its sales.

The DC brass certainly had cause for concern. Marvel still didn't come close to outselling its rival in terms of total units, but its books did have a better sell-through percentage—meaning it had a lower percentage of the number of copies that were returned to the publisher, unsold from store racks. Any title that suffered more than a 50 percent return rate was in trouble. Readers were snatching up about 70 percent of the Marvel books, while DC was hovering closer to the 50 percent break-even mark.

Up on the tenth floor of DC's Lexington Avenue headquarters—a bland, corporate spread with little adornment to remind people this was a company churning out fun, four-color superhero books—the suits were agitated. Something had to be done.

So DC did what any big company does when facing declining sales and potential ruin: it called a meeting.

At this and a series of subsequent sit-downs, Vice President Irwin Donenfeld, Editorial Director Carmine Infantino, and Superman Editor Mort Weisinger, along with a baffled staff, gathered to try to figure out the secret to Marvel's success. What did Marvel have that DC didn't? they wondered. How could this nothing publisher possibly be within sniffing distance of DC?

But they were worried.

"I recall they were at a loss to understand why they were trailing in sales," says John Romita Sr., then an artist on DC's romance titles. "We were sure DC was the benchmark of comics quality."

One of the editors grabbed a stack of Marvel's recent output, including the *Fantastic Four* and *The Avengers*, and the books were spread across a conference room table or their covers were tacked on a board alongside DC's offerings. The gathered forces studied the product and tentatively took stabs at ideas.

"At DC there was a tendency sometimes to resist learning from the competition because it was the competition," says Mark Evanier, a screenwriter and former DC freelancer. "And when they did learn, they frankly learned the wrong things."

One strong theory to explain Marvel's popularity was that it must have something to do with the covers. The hypothesis certainly jibed with Donenfeld's belief that "good, intriguing covers were about all that mattered" in the comic book business.

Perhaps it had something to do with how much red Marvel was using, someone offered. Could the kids be attracted to red?

Another staffer noticed how many word balloons were stuffed on the front of Marvel mags. Maybe that was what readers were responding to?

"They agreed that the covers were 'garish,' with trashy logos and word balloons," Romita Sr. says.

Infantino, who still swore that Marvel would be out of business in a few months, just grumbled.

Finally the books were opened and the interior art quickly analyzed. The figures were not particularly handsome; the faces looked grotesque. And who's this strange-looking being over here? And what's with this bizarre machine?

Understandably, Marvel's interiors repelled the brass. The art was blockier and more experimental than at DC, where the books were drawn in a safe, polished house style. DC's editors considered Marvel's art, especially that of Jack Kirby, Steve Ditko, and Dick Ayers, to be raw and childlike. And perhaps therein lay its appeal.

"They thought maybe the readers liked bad art because it's crude, like a kid would draw," says Jim Shooter, Marvel's former editor-in-chief who worked at DC in the 1960s. "'Maybe we should tell the artists to draw worse.' That's a quote. I heard that."

Ultimately DC brainstormed a lot of ideas in those meetings, and the publisher tested a few half-baked modifications, including altering the coloring style in certain titles or changing panel shapes in a desperate attempt to copy Marvel.

None of it worked.

"They found all these fatuous, self-deceiving explanations," says Roy Thomas, a writer and editor who briefly worked at DC in 1965 before jumping to Marvel.

What Infantino, Donenfeld, and the others missed in that conference room back in the 1960s was that Marvel was beating them for reasons that had nothing to do with the amount of red or the number of word balloons on its covers. It had nothing to do with coloring or panel shapes either.

According to Stan Lee, the company's surge boiled down to one simple thing: "We were smarter than they were," he says.

Marvel's on-the-street intelligence was certainly better. Lee had gotten wind of the DC strategy meetings and the changes that came out of them, and he took great glee in countering his rival, move for move. When DC decided to load up its covers with more word balloons in an attempt to emulate Marvel, Lee responded by making his covers less wordy. When DC started splashing red on its covers, Lee stopped altogether.

"It didn't make any difference in the sales," Lee said in 2000. "It must have driven them crazy. We played this little game for months. . . . They never caught on."

Compare, for example, *Fantastic Four* #15, cover date June 1963, to issues of the series that came a few years later. The front of #15 is crowded with eighty-three words, including five verbose speech bubbles as well as the classic header, "The world's greatest comic magazine." By the mid-1960s the magazine's covers had become more poster-like, with a single, stirring image and limited text. "Lo, there shall be an ending!" proclaims #43 (October 1965) over a Kirby illustration of the Four lying defeated in their destroyed headquarters.

Meanwhile, over at DC, a book such as *Wonder Woman* #159, released in late 1965, is chockablock full of captions in a misguided attempt to copy the earlier Marvel style. The illustration of the heroine occupies a small sliver on the cover's left side, and the rest of the magazine's front is overrun with exclamation mark–filled text boxes and booming headlines such as, "Now! At last! For the first time since the Golden Age of comics!"

As Lee had figured out, due in part to the hundreds of fan letters flooding into the company's headquarters, covers had little to do with Marvel's success. The real draw was that the comic book company was offering a product unlike anything else on the stands. Not that those in charge at DC would ever know it. The execs failed to do the single-most important thing you're supposed to do with a comic book.

"The older guys wouldn't lower themselves to read the competition," says former DC production manager Bob Rozakis, who joined the company in 1973. Donenfeld, National's then head and the son of its co-founder, once claimed the only comic he read was *Sugar and Spike*, a humorous, kiddie book about cartoon toddlers.

But Rozakis and so many other young people across America were devouring Marvel comics every month, loving the new take on superheroes Lee and his artists delivered.

The kids were certainly plugged in, but the execs above them were out of touch. Most were born around the time zeppelin travel was in vogue, and you might toss around the word *gentlemen* to describe them. They dressed conservatively and thought conservatively.

"[DC publisher] Carmine Infantino used to refer to us as 'the kids,' but we, 'the kids,' were actually reading the Marvel books, and we knew there was a whole different idea, a different feel to the books," Rozakis says. "But Carmine was like, 'Well, we don't need to listen to the kids.' He thought we were just fanboys who liked comic books and were only there so we could get them for free."

"I was in several meetings with Mort [Weisinger] and a few people," Shooter says. "They were holding up the Marvel comics and ridiculing them. There was an issue of *X-Men* with a picture of [winged hero] Angel—a full-page shot—and the caption was all about the glory of flying. And their attitude was, 'What's the big deal?' Superman flies all the time.' I'm like, 'Don't you get it? He flies all the time, and no one gives a damn.' One guy held up a *Spider-Man* and said, 'They've got two pages of Peter Parker talking to his aunt. The kids are going to be bored out of their minds.' Nope."

"Nope" is right.

Marvel's new approach to storytelling changed not only the comic book business but also the way superheroes were handled in general—an approach that still provides the template today that has made superheroes a multibillion, multimedia cash cow.

Marvel's ascendency also touched off a battle with DC that has raged for decades. For more than a half century Marvel and DC have faced off across newsstands and spinner racks, rivals in the billion-dollar superhero business. The two companies basically own North American comic-book publishing and have spent the last fifty years clawing for market share and trying to kneecap each other in ways both above board and below. At stake is not just sales but cultural relevancy and the hearts of millions of fans.

The war has at times gotten ugly, playing out in the pages of the magazines, with editors trading insults in the letters columns and parodying—or blatantly borrowing—the other company's characters. Battles have also been fought in the real world, as DC and Marvel have tried to outfox each other with price wars and creative marketing schemes.

And as in any war, you better pick a side. Comic readers are often fiercely loyal to one team, which naturally sets them in opposition to the other. Inside dusty comic stores, at conventions, and in online forums, debates have been raging for decades about the superiority of each publisher.

The debate is hardly trivial. Quite possibly the most revealing question you can ask a comic book fan is, "Marvel or DC?" The answer is as telling, as integral to his personality as which Beatle he prefers or his favorite flavor of ice cream. The two companies were shaped by different eras, have different publishing philosophies, and stand for two completely different worldviews.

DC was born in the thirties, Marvel's major heroes not until some twenty-five years later.

If DC represented Eisenhower's America, Marvel was like John F. Kennedy's. The publisher was younger, cooler, and possibly sleeping with your girlfriend. The modern-day Marvel that arrived in 1961 quickly shook up the comics industry in a way that mirrored the dramatic cultural and political upheavals the entire country was experiencing.

Marvel represented change. It was counterculture, the scruffy underdog to DC's establishment. Its covers announced adventures for "The New Breed of Comic Reader."

"I think the Marvels are great for a very conceited reason," an Ohio University student named Barry Jenkins wrote in a swinging 1966 *Esquire* article. "A person has to have intelligence to read them. I feel that comic book reading goes through three stages. First, the actual comic figures of talking dogs, pigs and ducks. Then, as a person gets older, he moves up to the world of 'real' people. (As exemplified by [DC].) Finally, if he has the capacity [*sic*], he moves into the relm [*sic*] of Marvels."

Even forgiving Barry's not-quite-college-level spelling, he was onto something. Marvel books were smarter and different for the time—just as Stan Lee had claimed.

Beginning with the Fantastic Four and then continuing with the Hulk, Spider-Man, the X-Men, Iron Man, and many more, writer-editor Lee and his talented cocreators, including Kirby and Steve Ditko, set out to change the way superhero stories were told. And at the time that meant doing them differently from the gold standard of capes, DC.

The storytelling approach proved popular with readers, including educated, college-age ones, a demographic that was not big comic buyers at the time. It wasn't long before Marvel did what once seemed unthinkable: it overtook mighty DC in sales. The poles in the comics world reversed, and suddenly the former underdog became the top dog. Marvel never looked back.

Now in the twenty-first century DC is also trailing Marvel in the multibillion-dollar movie world. The company is deploying a similar strategy to the one that has made Marvel so dominant at the multiplex, unleashing a long string of films featuring solo characters as well as team-ups like *The Justice League*.

DC has certainly published its share of great individual projects over the years. *Sandman*, *Watchmen*, *The Dark Knight Returns*, and *Saga of the Swamp Thing* all expanded the medium's boundaries and were among the most influential graphic novels ever to see print. But as a brand DC has often lagged behind Marvel, not just in market share but also in intangible measures, such as buzz and relevance. Though it's hardly from a lack of trying. Could DC's multimedia strategy, which includes a string of successful TV series as well as the company's ambitious movie slate, finally put the company back on top?

This is the story of the fifty-year battle between the two companies—some of it driven by DC's desire to copy Marvel, some of it driven by Marvel's desire to copy DC, and some of it—the most fun stuff, let's be honest—driven by pure gamesmanship and spite. Loosen your mask, drop your cape at the dry cleaners, and let's begin.

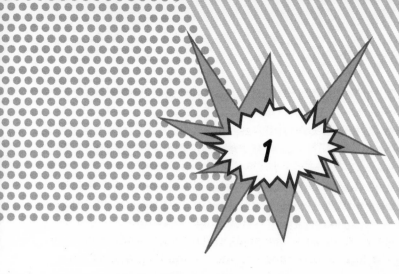

DC Becomes the Industry's Eight-Hundred-Pound Gorilla

"All of a sudden it hits me—I conceive of a character like Samson, Hercules, and all the strong men I ever heard of rolled into one. Only more so."

—Jerry Siegel, cocreator of Superman

Walking into DC's offices in 1960, visitors would have been forgiven for thinking they'd mistakenly turned up at an insurance company.

The spacious digs on the tenth floor of New York's Grolier Building at 575 Lexington Avenue exuded a particular blandness, as though someone forgot, "Hey, we're doing superheroes here." They were clean and comfortable—the building with its gold anodized aluminum facade had just been constructed—but did not accrue major points in the personality department. A row of offices lined one wall, surrounding a middle production area. Flat file cabinets holding the original art pages were scattered about.

"They could have been any kind of office," recalled Steve Mitchell, who toured DC as a teenager and would go on to work in the production department. "Very few reminders that comics were published there were in evidence. Sure, each editor had a corkboard with their latest covers, but otherwise not much else. If you've watched the fourth season of the TV show *Mad Men*, the DC offices had similar frosted glass walls seated in metal frames."

"It was a very traditional company," says Mike Friedrich, a fan-turned-pro who began writing for DC in the late sixties. "They kind of aped corporate culture."

One of the nods to that conventional culture was that everyone wore a suit and tie—absolutely everyone. The kids who were enjoying the fun, colorful books about space explorers and masked heroes probably had no inkling they were produced by men dressed for a job interview at IBM.

"Even the people in the production department were wearing ties when they were cutting up balloons and whiting letters out and all the stuff they did," Friedrich says. The janitor probably shopped at Brooks Brothers.

Jim Shooter, a Pittsburgh boy wonder who began writing stories for the company in 1965 when he was just thirteen, visited 575 Lexington in 1966 to discuss business. His editor insisted on meeting the young scribe at a nearby hotel first to make certain Shooter was properly dressed and wouldn't "embarrass" anyone.

When Shooter was allowed inside, what he found was a stifling environment populated by "dignified" people tiptoeing around, speaking in "solemn voices" as though they were discussing mutual funds or something.

And what of the men being strangled by this neckwear on a daily basis? DC's editors were hardly the scruffy, art-school dropouts one might expect in a business whose foundation was ink and Bristol board. Instead, they were middle-aged careerist types whom one might mistake on the subway for a bank branch manager. They had wives and houses and mortgages and belonged to professional organizations. These were serious men, respectable men whose passing would later be noted by the *New York Times*.

"The editors had this great little gentleman's club," the late artist-editor Joe Orlando, who joined DC in 1968, said in 1998. "Every day a two-hour lunch. They wore leather patches on the elbows of their tweed jackets, sucked on empty pipes, and debated the liberal issues of that day."

They lorded over their fiefdoms from on high, each controlling a stable of titles—sometimes for decades. One freelancer who worked for DC in the sixties recalled that he was required to buy his editor a Christmas present, not the other way around.

Arguably the most powerful of the bunch at the time was Mort Weisinger, who was in charge of DC's best-selling Superman family of books, which also included *Superman's Girlfriend Lois Lane* and *Superman's Pal Jimmy Olsen.*

Weisinger had been born in the Bronx in 1915 and had gotten into publishing through sci-fi fandom. He joined DC in 1941 and would ultimately stay for nearly thirty more years. He was steady. He was Yale educated and intelligent. He was also a world-class jerk.

The stories of his abuse number in the dozens if not hundreds. If you ever met him, you probably have one worth telling. Shooter, who wrote for Weisinger in the sixties, says the editor treated him like "dirt" and hurled slurs at him, such as "retard." One boy who took the DC office tour claimed he rode the elevator down with the editor, and Weisinger proceeded to jokingly tell him about an exciting upcoming story in the Lois Lane title. Lane, in yet another desperate attempt to figure out if Superman and Clark Kent were one and the same, concocts a crazy scheme to feel Superman's balls to see if they match Kent's.

A telling—almost certainly apocryphal—story involves Weisinger's funeral in 1978. As is the tradition at Jewish farewells, the attendees were invited to stand and speak about the good qualities of the deceased. The offer was greeted with silence. Finally someone in the back of the room stood and said, "His brother was worse."

Despite his foul temperament, Weisinger was able to consistently moonlight for prestigious publications outside the comics industry, and he penned a trashy beach novel called *The Contest.* He liked to brag that he had received $125,000 for the movie rights alone, and the man never seemed to be hurting for money. He drove a huge white Cadillac, and his old mansion in Great Neck, the same ritzy New York City suburb that was once home to F. Scott Fitzgerald, is now worth $3.2 million.

Weisinger's childhood friend, Julius Schwartz, also served as a longtime DC editor and in 1960 ran a slate of titles that included Westerns and sci-fis. As teenagers Schwartz and Weisinger had met at a sci-fi group called the Scienceers, and the duo later published a sci-fi fanzine. As adults they opened the first literary agency specializing in science fiction and fantasy, repping Ray Bradbury, H. P. Lovecraft, and Leigh Brackett (cowriter of *The Empire Strikes Back*), among other genre names.

Schwartz, known affectionately as "Uncle Julie," could be grouchy and demanding. He was hands-on and often sat with writers, working out stories. In his forty-two years at DC he played a part in numerous significant moments and ultimately became one of the most important people ever in the biz.

"Julie Schwartz made a point of being crusty and a curmudgeon," says Joe Rubinstein, an inker who has worked for Marvel and DC since the 1970s. "That was Julie's way. It was somewhere in the Bible or the Talmud: don't show them love—it'll make them soft."

Robert Kanigher lasted nearly as long as Schwartz did at DC, having gotten into the comics biz in 1945. By 1960 he was in charge of the company's war books as well as *Wonder Woman*. Pictures from the era reveal a professor-ish man with a full head of black hair, wearing a smart suit and gripping a pipe. He enjoyed mountain climbing and skiing, once calling it "intoxicating." He was a literary man who liked to reference Dante and El Greco in interviews.

Like Weisinger, Kanigher could be abusive. He was notoriously difficult to get along with and had a volcanic temper. Stories abound of him tearing into someone who criticized his writing or an artist who dared to make a small change to his script. He is rumored to have given one penciler a full-on nervous breakdown.

Kanigher, Weisinger, and Schwartz made up the core of DC's editorial staff in 1960—just one year before the dawn of the so-called Marvel age of comics—and they represented an old-fashioned mentality that would, in a few short years, find itself woefully out of step with the changing times. They had different values and priorities from the younger generations. DC's brass grew up during the Great Depression, which had imprinted on them a respect for work and the firm that employed you. In short, they were company men.

"That was the attitude particularly among Depression-era guys," says Mark Evanier, who broke into comics in 1969 working as Jack Kirby's assistant. "The company put bread and butter on your table, and all those guys who grew up in the Depression had a very, very strong orientation about who pays you your paycheck at the end of the week. It was like you didn't mock your company like you didn't mock your father."

It wasn't just DC's editors who were particularly unprogressive. Conservatism was in the company's blood. It was baked in from the company's very start. DC had been founded in part as a way for its shady founders to purify their image. And then the publisher came of age during an ugly era when comic books were facing constant attacks from moralists, and the industry was desperate to purge any hint of impropriety from its pages in hopes of placating the critics and keeping the lights on.

DC's beginnings go back to 1935 when a former US Cavalry officer and pulp writer named Major Malcolm Wheeler-Nicholson created *New Fun Comics*. The black-and-white tabloid was notable in that it was the first comic book to include original material. Publishers had been reprinting flimsy collections of Sunday funnies since at least the 1920s, but *New Fun Comics* is considered the first modern comic book.

Wheeler-Nicholson's company, called National Allied Publications, released five more issues before it ran out of money. In need of funds, the major teamed up with a company called Independent News. The publishing and distribution venture had been launched in 1932 by a Jewish immigrant, Harry Donenfeld, and his business manager, Jack Liebowitz. Donenfeld was fast talking and rumored to have mob connections. Liebowitz was a buttoned-up numbers man.

Donenfeld had been in the magazine business since the 1920s, and he'd earned his money by backing a series of racy pulps.

His magazines and those like it came under fire in the early 1930s. A group calling itself the New York Citizens Committee on Civic Decency launched a campaign against the smut, and in 1934 Donenfeld got into serious hot water after publishing a photo of a naked woman, a sliver of pubic hair exposed, in *Pep!*

It was within this hostile social environment that Donenfeld and Liebowitz struck a deal with Wheeler-Nicholson to fund more comics. Independent News was looking to diversify away from its girlie-heavy portfolio and expand into more innocent publishing arenas. Comic books seemingly offered just that.

The new venture was called Detective Comics, Inc., and it would later lend its name to the consolidated publishing company. The first title released under the new partnership was March 1937's *Detective Comics* #1. The issue offered several short stories, including one featuring lawman Speed Saunders battling a villain named Cap'n Scum and another starring private eye Slam Bradley, created by Jerry Siegel and Joe Shuster.

Wheeler-Nicholson, still suffering from cash-flow issues, was forced out in 1938, and Donenfeld and Liebowitz took control of *Detective* as well as two other titles, *More Fun* and *New Adventure*.

The company would soon expand with June 1938's *Action Comics* #1, the debut of Superman.

This was the one that started it all—and Donenfeld paid just $130 for the rights. This was the book that gave us the superhero archetype as we now know it and marked the start of an American art form. Creators Siegel and Shuster deftly combined the fast-paced adventure of Sunday comic strips, such as Tarzan, with the costumed crime-fighting heroics of pulp characters, such as the Shadow, and out came something new and exciting, something kids and adults across America were willing to plunk down 10 cents to read. Superman was an innovation that would change the publishing and entertainment industries forever, and it would help put its publisher, DC, atop the spandex heap.

The Superman of 1938 was a far more down to earth (literally) hero than the one he would later evolve into. His powers were limited. He couldn't fly, instead having the power only to leap one-eighth of a mile. He had enhanced strength but was far from invulnerable. An artillery shell was said to be able to pierce his skin.

The kinds of cases he chose to tackle were equally earthbound. In his early appearances he tossed a wife-beating husband against a wall, tangled with a corrupt judicial system, and broke up a lynch mob. Superman acted less like the heartland-born do-gooder he would later become and more like that activist hippie who lived down the hall from you in the college dorm.

Superman—and the flood of four-color heroes that would soon follow—racked up massive sales by delivering inexpensive escapist entertainment at a bleak time when the nation was hobbled by the Great Depression, battered by the Dust Bowl, and teetering on the brink of war. They provided power fantasies for the many Americans who were feeling powerless.

DC printed 202,000 copies of *Action Comics* #1 and sold 64 percent of a print run—an astonishing success. The brass, however, wasn't sure which of *Action*'s eight stories was driving sales, so in *Action Comics* #4, a survey was included asking readers to rank their top five. An overwhelming 404 of the 542 responses named the Man of Steel as their favorite.

The superhero—and especially Superman—was clearly becoming a cash cow. Sales of *Action Comics* climbed month by month, and by 1940 DC was moving 1.3 million an issue, with companion title *Superman* selling 1.4 million. Stores were also flooded with merchandise, including shirts, soap, pencil sets, belts, and watches.

Superman's first appearance was followed the next year by Batman—a dark vigilante created by Bob Kane and Bill Finger and made his debut in 1939's *Detective Comics* #27.

The third member of DC's so-called Trinity, Wonder Woman, appeared in 1941. She was created by William Moulton Marston, a Harvard-educated psychologist who imagined a "feminine character with all the strength of Superman plus all the allure of a good and beautiful woman," as he wrote at the time.

The happy days wouldn't last long.

Just two years removed from the debut of *Action Comics* #1, a serious existential challenge to DC and the medium of comic books itself was brewing. In 1940 a newspaper writer named Sterling North published an editorial in the *Chicago Daily News* entitled "A National Disgrace," attacking the "poisonous" effects of a fast-growing new medium: comic books.

It marked one of the first national salvos against comic books and helped launch a protracted war that would rage for fourteen more years and culminate in nothing short of federal government hearings.

In his editorial North claimed to have examined 108 books available on the newsstand and found, to his horror, that at least 70 percent contained "material that no respectable newspaper would accept." He went on to report, "Superman heroics, voluptuous females in scanty attire, blazing machine guns, hooded 'justice' and cheap political propaganda were to be found on almost every page."

Other critics soon piled on, including Fredric Wertham, a New York City–based psychiatrist who blamed comics for bad behavior he'd seen among his young patients.

The backlash reached its climax when, in April 1954, a Senate Subcommittee on Juvenile Delinquency convened a hearing on the medium's evils.

The publishers didn't wait around for the committee's findings to be released that next March. In the fall of 1954 the industry produced its own code of conduct by which nearly all the comic book companies agreed to abide. The lengthy list of rules governed everything from magazine titles to depictions of violence to costume appearances.

Many publishers were unable to adapt, and within three years of the Code's adoption twenty-four of the twenty-nine original subscribing members had gone out of business. In 1952 some 630 titles·had hit newsstands. That number had dropped to just 250 in 1956—a staggering 252 percent fall. The comic book business was being slowly strangled to death.

DC was one of the few publishers that managed to weather the crisis, due in part to its family-friendly rep. In the summer of 1941 it had formed an in-house editorial advisory board to ensure its content met "whole-some" moral standards. Post-Code, Irwin Donenfeld, Harry's son and DC's then editorial director, traveled the country speaking to PTA groups and appearing on TV programs to talk about how comics helped teach kids to read.

The era helped establish DC even more firmly as the class of the field, far different from the schlocky publishers—with their cheap production, amateurish art, and fly-by-night existences—that had once populated the industry.

"DC was part of National Periodical Publications, a real company," says former DC writer Jim Shooter. "They had a mentality that they were a cut above. DC has always clung to the pretense that they were classy, and they stuck with that for a long time."

This haughty attitude that crystalized in DC's early years would be one of the reasons the publisher would have trouble adapting to changing tastes and times in the coming decades and part of the reason why it still lags to this day.

"The thing that allowed DC to survive the fifties and the Senate sub-committee was Liebowitz and Donenfeld and [editor] Whit Ellsworth going for clean, accessible storytelling and characters so that you didn't mind if a six-year-old was reading the comics," says comics historian and former DC editor Bob Greenberger. "It then kept them stuck," he says—stuck in a defensive posture and a conservative mindset.

One of the reasons DC's trinity of Superman, Batman, and Wonder Woman have become such iconic characters is that, unlike their peers, they've been in continuous publication since their debuts. Their longevity has been truly remarkable and speaks not only to the appeal of the characters but also to the stability of their publisher, DC. (As well as to the amount of money being raked in from themed merchandise, but that's a story for a bit later.)

The marathon run these characters have had has not always been a given. The comic book industry is cyclical, with genres and characters fall-ing in and out of favor like a pair of high-waisted jeans. Westerns are hot for a few years, then they're gone. Romance comics are all the rage, then you can't give away a copy of *Flaming Love*. The same has been true of superheroes.

Some ten years after Superman first appeared, audiences began to get a bit bored by the whole idea of superpowers, and the genre faltered. Titles across the market got the axe, including some at DC. The adventures of the ring-wielding hero Green Lantern came to an abrupt halt in 1949, and in 1951 DC swung the axe on the Justice Society of America, a super-team composed of the publisher's roster of World War II–era characters, including Hawkman, Hour-Man, and Doctor Fate.

As anyone who reads comic books knows, however, a hero never really stays dead for long.

But it wouldn't be magical chicanery or some interdimensional deus ex machina that would revive the superheroes; it would be down to another tried-and-true device of the genre: recycling old ideas.

Even with the anticomics crusade crippling the market, DC was in need of fresh material, but DC head Jack Liebowitz was cautious about releasing new titles, fearing that canceling a series after just a few issues would create panic among readers and distributors. Irwin Donenfeld came up with a novel solution: a series to be called *Showcase*, in which each issue would feature a new character. It was a smart way to cheaply test new concepts without having to invest in the launch of a brand-new title.

DC's editors would take turns producing issues of *Showcase*, and Weisinger handled the debut. He floated an idea for a story about firefighters, in no small part because it offered a chance for a potentially appealing cover image.

"DC had all these little lists circulating about what covers sold, and they'd argue about it in editorial meetings," Evanier says. "Weisinger believed that fire on covers was commercial and that kids had an interest in firefighters."

Turns out, not so much. "*Showcase* #1 was a spectacular flop," Evanier says. "It sold so badly, they couldn't believe it, and all the other editors jumped on Weisinger and mocked him." (From that point on, Weisinger would rarely stray from the safe, reliable world of Superman.)

Issue #2 featured a Native American hero from Kanigher, and #3 another Kanigher-penned tale about Navy frogmen. Those two, like #1, bombed.

By *Showcase* #4 the responsibility fell to Schwartz. The idea he tossed out at an editorial meeting would change the history of superheroes and launch the so-called Silver Age of comics. He suggested reviving the Flash, a speedster whose popularity, like nearly every other costumed hero, had tailed off during the late forties and early fifties. His solo title had been canned in 1949. Schwartz's coeditors were skeptical.

"I pointed out that the average comic book reader started reading them at age 8 and gave them up at the age of 12," the late Schwartz wrote in his autobiography, *Man of Two Worlds.* "And since more than four years had already passed, there was a whole new audience out there who really didn't know that the Flash had flopped, and maybe they might give it a try."

To draw the strip Schwartz tapped Carmine Infantino, a Brooklyn-born artist who'd gotten his start in the business as a teenager. Infantino's smooth pencil style would come to define DC in later years, due in part to his success on the Flash.

The original Flash had first appeared in 1940's *Flash Comics* #1, written by Gardner Fox and drawn by Harry Lampert. He was Jay Garrick, a college student who'd gained superspeed after exposure to heavy water.

Showcase #4 featured a new spin on the character. He was now Barry Allen (named after talk show hosts Barry Gray and Steve Allen), a police scientist who gains his powers after lightning strikes a shelf full of chemicals. Kanigher wrote the story and introduced the fun detail that the hero's red costume—newly designed by Infantino—would magically pop out of Allen's ring.

The October 1956 issue shocked National with its success. It sold 59 percent of a 350,000-print run. A sequel was quickly scheduled, and the Flash returned eight months later in *Showcase* #8, then again in #13 and #14. The subsequent issues also sold well, and the character was promoted to his own title. *The Flash* debuted in 1959, though as issue #105 instead of issue #1, picking up on the numbering from the character's previous 1949 series.

Even though the Flash had a legacy number on its cover, the contents were obviously something fresh, and audiences responded. The character's reintroduction ushered in a new superhero craze that led to a second explosion of superhero titles—a big bang that would help trigger the rebirth of Marvel Comics a few years later.

"The Flash jump-started the whole superhero business again, and went a long way in saving the comic book business from extinction," Infantino wrote. "DC followed with Green Lantern and then the whole group of superheroes. . . . So the Flash started the superhero party all over again, changing the course of the entire industry."

DC would soon also unveil revamped versions of the Atom and Hawkman. By 1960 the company was enjoying profitable sales on its titles and was virtually unchallenged in the superhero realm. Certainly not by the company that would become Marvel, which had by the end of the fifties spiraled into has-been status.

"Back then both of the companies were family-owned businesses that have just gone through an existential crisis that almost killed them, with the political situation in the fifties and the collapse of their distribution system," Friedrich says. "There was not much competition. They were part of a beleaguered industry that was trying to survive together."

That situation would soon change with Marvel's emergence as a superhero company once again.

Mighty Marvel
Comes Out Swinging

"The fact is that Marvel Comics are the first comic books in history in which a post-adolescent escapist can get personally involved. For Marvel Comics are the first comic books to evoke, even metaphorically, the Real World."

—*The Village Voice*, April 1, 1965

For much of its early life Marvel was the equivalent of a bad bar cover band. The company was less the "house of ideas," as it would come to be known, than "the house of other people's ideas."

"We were a company of copycats," Stan Lee would say of the company he first joined in 1940 as an errand boy.

Marvel's founder, Brooklyn-born Martin Goodman, got his start producing low-rent magazines, just like the men who founded DC. By the 1930s his empire had ballooned to dozens of different publishing entities. (It sounds impressive, but it was actually a tax dodge.) Much of his business would revolve around so-called sweat mags, such as *Swank* and *Stag*, but his companies also vomited forth dozens of Western, jungle, and detective pulp titles.

Goodman released his first comic book in 1939 under his Timely imprint, and *Marvel Comics* #1, like many books hitting the stands during those years, was designed to draft off the success of DC's Superman. The book introduced the first of the publisher's superheroes: Carl Burgos's combustible android, the Human Torch, and flying merman Sub-Mariner, from Bill Everett.

"We tried to outdo Superman," the late Everett said of Sub-Mariner in 1971.

Those two characters have remained relevant to this day (though with fluctuating levels of popularity), but little else from those earliest days has. Goodman tried to build on the success of *Marvel Comics* #1 by churning out a list of less-enduring superheroes, including the Phantom Bullet, the Blue Blaze, and the Blonde Phantom. When the sales of comic books about costumed heroes dipped in the late forties, he moved on to other genres.

"Marvel was built on the idea of 'Let's see what's selling for other people and imitate it,'" says comic writer and historian Evanier. "That was the history of [Marvel founder] Martin Goodman. He was notorious for it, and he owned up to it all the time."

The Marvel honcho once reportedly summed up his business strategy as, "If you get a title that catches on, then add a few more, you're in for a nice profit."

That particular philosophy might be good for the bottom line, but when it comes to creating a quality product, it leaves much to be desired. Just ask anyone who sat through that second movie about an asteroid on a collision course with earth or the second movie about a killer volcano.

Throughout the forties and fifties Marvel jumped from fad to fad, with little originality or leadership in evidence. When crime comics began to take off, Marvel gave readers *Lawbreakers Always Lose* and *All-True Crime*. If Looney Tunes and funny animals were the thing, it pushed out *Daffy*—er, *Wacky Duck*. When B-Westerns got hot in Hollywood, Marvel rolled out *Whip Wilson* and *The Arizona Kid*. The company even published a title called *Homer the Happy Ghost* that bore more than a passing resemblance to *Casper the Friendly Ghost*.

Few of these books were memorable or had any lasting impact. They existed simply to exist—to plug a slot in the newsstand in the hopes that someone might stumble along and pick up one based on the subject matter alone.

Because of its leading-from-behind style of doing business, Marvel for many years lacked a strong identity. It had no unifying tone or theme running through its line of titles. Its magazines' covers often had no particular design aesthetic, identifiable trade dress, or easily recognizable logo.

The company was the worst kind of imitator. Which brings us to one of the greatest ironies in the history of comics. The copycat notorious for lazily following trends and knocking off other companies suddenly, in 1961, became the most original name in superheroes.

And it did it by knocking off another company.

Marvel's great leap forward would launch it in an exciting new direction and set it on the path to becoming the multibillion-dollar entity we know today. And it would resurrect a company whose best days were behind it.

Goodman's troubles would date back to 1951 when he dumped his distributor (the middle man responsible for getting his magazines to stores) and launched his own. He called it Atlas News Company, and from 1951 until 1956 handling distribution himself allowed Goodman to unleash a tidal wave of books, releasing more titles than any other company in the industry.

By the mid fifties, though, Atlas was in the red. (Whether the losses were a result of the shrinking market or some bookkeeping shenanigans is unclear.) Goodman shuttered Atlas, and in the summer of 1956 he signed a five-year deal with distributor American News Company.

The decision would prove catastrophic for Goodman. A few months later, in May 1957, American News Company would abruptly close up shop, leaving Goodman with no way to get his books to the stands.

Goodman was forced to lay off his entire comic book staff, with the exception of Lee. It wasn't long before DC, sensing that Atlas was fatally wounded, ghoulishly came sniffing around. In a deal that looks insanely lowball by today's hyperinflated superhero market, DC offered to buy Atlas's characters—Captain America, Sub-Mariner, and the Human Torch—for $15,000 (about $126,000 in today's dollars). Goodman considered the offer, but in the end he passed. What was $15,000 to a millionaire like him?

Imagine how different the world would be today had that deal gone through. We'll never know. Goodman held on to his titles and turned his attention to his immediate problem: finding a new distributor willing to accept his account and prevent his business from spiraling into oblivion. In a matter of months Atlas/Timely—or whatever name Goodman was using that week—had gone from one of the most prolific publishers in the market to one of the least.

Goodman had to act. The good news was that by the next month he'd found a distributor willing to accept his account. The bad news was that this distributor happened to be Independent News, the company started by Donenfeld. The reason Independent was willing to handle a direct competitor's books had little to do with altruism; instead, it and sister company DC were concerned about appearing to be a monopoly, and agreeing to distribute Goodman's line was a way to dispel those charges. Without the new distribution deal, Marvel would have likely died in the 1950s.

Regardless of motivations, Independent must have relished sticking it to its main competitor. The terms of the distribution deal it lorded over its rival were draconian, allowing Marvel to release only eight titles a month.

"We didn't want the competition," DC head Liebowitz wrote in his unpublished memoir.

Goodman opted to make the most of the limitation and instead of publishing eight monthly titles, chose to release sixteen bimonthlies. The first wave of books bearing the "IND" symbol denoting its distributor arrived on stands in the summer of 1957. The initial round included *Gunsmoke Western*, *Kid Colt Outlaw*, *Love Romances*, and *Marines in Battle*, among others. The second batch included *World Fantasy*, *Two-Gun Kid*, *Strange Tales*, and *Navy Combat*.

The next year, in 1958, Goodman's company published only ninety-six comics, the fewest since 1944. And superheroes were not on its menu. Beyond a failed attempt to revive the genre in the midfifties, the company that would become Marvel had mostly given up on costumed heroes. Captain America was put on ice in 1949. The Sub-Mariner's solo book was deep-sixed the same year.

The publisher no longer presented much competition for mighty National. By 1960 DC's top title was selling some 810,000 copies, while Marvel's bestseller, *Tales to Astonish*, barely moved 163,000.

And that's when Goodman fell backward into his greatest success by relying on his old copycat ways.

Over at DC the Flash had been rebooted in 1956, and the superhero genre was suddenly hot again. It didn't take long for competitors to sit up and take notice, and Atlas/Marvel was certainly one of those who did.

Multiple versions of what happened next have been propagated, and the one you believe will probably depend on how cynical you are.

The official version goes like this: One day in 1961 Goodman was playing a friendly game of golf with DC's Jack Liebowitz when Liebowitz began bragging about the sales of his new *Justice League of America*, a title launched in 1960 that combined the company's marquee heroes—Superman, Batman, Wonder Woman, Aquaman, and the Flash—into one powerful super team. (Both men later insisted they never played golf together.)

Another version finds Goodman hitting the links with the head of his distributor, Independent News. Still another circulated by the freelancers of the day has the crafty Goodman learning the sales information from spies planted within Independent.

Whatever the case, the outcome was the same. Goodman returned to his offices at Madison Avenue and 60th Street and ordered Lee to dream up a new team of heroes to compete with DC's.

"[Goodman] said, 'Hey, maybe there's still a market for superheroes. Why don't you bring out a team like the Justice League. We could call it the *Righteous League* or something,'" Lee recalled in 1977. "I worked for him, and I had to do what he wanted, so I was willing to put out a team of superheroes. But I figured I'll be damned if I'm just going to copy [DC]."

Lee had joined Goodman's company in 1940 as a teenager, performing whatever tedious jobs needed doing around the office, including proofreading, fetching coffee, and running errands. He was made editor in 1941 and had remained ever since, despite having aspirations to become a great novelist. Comics were hardly a prestige business at the time and were considered trashy by some and downright disreputable by others. When strangers asked him what he did for a living, the embarrassed Lee had taken to answering vaguely that he was in "publishing."

As DC's Superman had continued to gain in stature through the years—even landing his own cartoon in 1941—Lee had been stuck shoveling stories into Goodman's forgettable magazines, like coal into a furnace. From 1941 to 1961 Lee penned hundreds of quickly dashed-off tales in numerous genres, from romance to Western, all with little job satisfaction.

"Martin felt in those days that our readers were very, very young children or else older people who weren't too bright or they wouldn't be reading comics," Lee said in an audio commentary to the 2006 book *Stan Lee's Amazing Marvel Universe*. "I don't think Martin really had a great deal of respect for the medium, and therefore, I was told not to get stories that were too complex, not to dwell on too much dialogue or too much characterization."

So when Goodman asked for a new superhero team to compete with DC's *Justice League*, Lee was determined to do something outside the norm of regular superhero stories, something closer to what he might like to read.

For this undertaking he had the good sense to tap Jack Kirby as his collaborator. Kirby should need no introduction, but just in case: Born in 1917. Grew up on New York's rough-and-tumble Lower East Side. Self-taught artist with a unique visual style. Would go on to cocreate much of the Marvel Universe and is considered by many to be the most influential illustrator the medium has ever seen.

Kirby had been kicking around the comic industry for years. He'd co-created Captain America for Marvel in 1940 before defecting to DC in 1941. He'd returned to Marvel in the late fifties after having a nasty legal falling-out with one of DC's editors over royalties for a syndicated news-paper strip. DC's loss was Marvel's gain.

"DC did not see Jack Kirby as the major comic book figure that he was," former Marvel editor-in-chief Roy Thomas says. "He was just some guy who they'd blackballed because he got in a lawsuit with one of their top editors. He wouldn't have gone to Marvel other than that, because he was getting more money at DC. So DC kind of killed itself, in that it put Stan and Jack together."

Upon arrival at Marvel Kirby spent much of his time producing B-rate monster stories such as "The Creature from Krogarr." In 1961 Kirby and Lee would team up for a new kind of superhero story, and the results would be far more memorable.

What they came up with was a team of adventurers who gain fantasti-cal powers after flying into space and being bombarded by cosmic rays. Scientist Reed Richards, aka Mr. Fantastic, gains the ability to stretch his body like rubber. His girlfriend, Sue Storm, has the power to turn invisi-ble and takes the nickname the Invisible Girl. Her brother, Johnny Storm (the Human Torch), finds himself able to burst into flames, and Reed's friend Ben Grimm (the Thing) is transformed into an orange, rocky monster.

It sounds pretty standard, and the setup had some echoes of a book Kirby had done for DC in 1957, *Challengers of the Unknown*, about a group of four adventurers who survive a plane crash and tackle missions.

But *The Fantastic Four*, which hit newsstands in August 1961, had a crucial difference from that DC title as well as most every other superhero title that had come before.

"We tried to inject all kinds of realism, as we call it, into the stories," Lee said in a 1968 radio interview. "We say to ourselves, just because you have a superpower, that doesn't mean you might not have dandruff, or trouble with girls, or have trouble paying your bills."

Kirby and Lee attempted to instill these larger-than-life characters with a bit of humanity, for the first time giving superheroes real-world problems and anxieties. They became more three-dimensional.

"These are real people who just happen to have superpowers, as opposed to super powered people who are trying to be real," longtime Marvel artist and writer John Byrne told *Comics Feature* in 1984.

In the Fantastic Four's world, powers did not necessarily lead to happiness; if anything, they were the source of more trouble. The Four react to their newfound abilities like a scene straight out of a body-horror flick. The Thing is miserable being trapped in his rocky, orange form. Sue is terrified when she begins disappearing.

Another innovative touch: the characters squabble with one another like two kids on a long car trip.

"To keep it all from getting too goody-goody, there is always friction between Mr. Fantastic and the Thing, with Human Torch siding with Mr. F," Lee wrote in his original 1961 typewritten synopsis for the book.

In issue #2 the Thing tussles with both Reed and Johnny, as Sue pleads, "We'll just destroy ourselves if we keep at each other's throats! Don't you see?"

This new way of handling superheroes was revolutionary in large measure because it was completely different from what DC—who had invented the superhero and basically owned the market in 1961—was doing.

"I doubt you can imagine the sheer impact that single comic possessed back there in the comic-starved wastelands of 1961," Alan Moore, the great British comic writer behind *Watchmen*, declared of *Fantastic Four* #3 in a 1983 essay. "To someone who had cut his teeth upon the sanitized niceness of the *Justice League of America*, this was heady stuff indeed."

DC's heroes were blander, steadier, and less likely to be consumed by their emotions. They had fewer human foibles and little characterization beyond do-gooder, and as a result, they felt more like cardboard cutouts than living, breathing people.

"If you go back to early DC Comics like *World's Finest*, where you've got Superman and Batman and Wonder Woman—and [1970s Marvel writer] Steve Gerber said this—you can switch the tails of the balloon among characters, and it makes no difference," says David Anthony Kraft, a writer and editor at Marvel in the seventies. "They all talk exactly the same because they're not like really alive, they're not characters."

It wasn't just the dialogue that set Marvel apart from its competitor; DC's pantheon was generally composed of more powerful, godlike, and flawless members.

"There's something fundamental about the environment in which these heroes were imagined," says Joan Hilty, a DC editor from 1995 to 2010. "All of DC's heroes are royalty. Superman is the last son of an alien planet. Batman in a super-rich guy. Wonder Woman is a princess. Green Lantern is a top-line fighter pilot. Aquaman is the king of the sea. All of these heroes came out of the 1930s and '40s during World Wars and a desire to find archetypes that could save entire countries. DC characters are too perfect and pegged to a different time."

The heroes' alter egos also represented law, order, and mainstream values. Jim Corrigan, the Spectre, is a cop. Katar Hol, Hawkman, is also a cop but on an alien world. Barry Allen, the Flash, works as a police scientist. Ray Palmer, the Atom, is a university professor. Clark Kent, Superman, helps to right societal wrongs with his typewriter, working as a journalist at the *Daily Planet*.

The worlds they lived in were clean and tidy. DC had previously taken the exciting step of assembling its heroes into a superteam, driving young readers into a slobbering frenzy, only to deliver a story in which the group spends time debating the rules of meeting etiquette. Robert's Rules of Order was their greatest supervillain. The first appearance of DC's Justice Society of America in 1940 finds Hawkman, the Flash, Green Lantern, and the rest on the cover . . . sitting serenely around a table as if they're about to discuss that quarter's P/E ratio.

Back during the 1954 Senate subcommittee hearings, DC adviser Dr. Lauretta Bender was asked if she thought Superman was a good influence.

"A good influence," she replied affirmatively. "The children know that Superman will always come out on the right side."

And by the 1960s that was increasingly becoming a problem. DC's antiseptic heroes were well suited for the conservative forties and fifties, a time when McGraw-Hill produced a workplace educational video entitled

"The Trouble with Women" and Elvis Presley was allowed to be shown on TV only from the waist up.

But by the following decade America was changing. An unpopular war in Vietnam was escalating, changing many Americans' notions of its country's righteousness. Civil rights protests were flaring across the country. East Germany slapped up the Berlin Wall, and nuclear confrontation with the Soviet Union seemed closer than ever. America was retreating from the relative safety of the fifties and moving into a more volatile age. And certain readers were in search of a modern brand of storytelling that felt more sophisticated, more of the moment.

Lee and his collaborators, whether through good sense or sheer luck, managed to introduce a different kind of hero at a time when America was entering into a period of historic social upheaval. Who wants to read about a gee-whiz cop hero when you can see the real police every night on the news beating African Americans in the streets? How can you not roll your eyes at a Superman story in which the hero uses his virtually unlimited power to figure out how many jelly beans a mystery jar contains?

Fantastic Four was an immediate success. Lee and Kirby's new style of superhero struck a nerve, particularly among more mature and seasoned readers.

"Great art, terrific characters, and a more adult approach to the stories than any other mag," reader Len Blake wrote in a letter published in *Fantastic Four* #4. "You are definitely starting a new trend in comics—stories about characters who act like real people, not just lily-white do-gooders who would insult the average reader's intelligence."

Clearly Marvel was onto something, and in the months that followed, Lee and his collaborators would unveil more heroes within the groundbreaking mold of the *Fantastic Four*. They were often regular people on whom—to quote a famous phrase—"great responsibility" had been imposed, and they were left struggling with their new abilities and how best to use them.

The Hulk, introduced by Lee and Kirby in 1962, was scientist Bruce Banner who had been blasted by a gamma ray bomb after rushing to save a teenager who'd mistakenly wandered onto the test field. He then spontaneously began transforming into an angry monster who could smash anything in his wake. As with the Fantastic Four characters, Banner is conflicted about his newfound powers, breaking down in tears in the debut issue over what he's become.

Spider-Man made his debut in *Amazing Fantasy* #15, cover dated August 1962. The character was a collaboration between Lee and Steve Ditko, a frequent freelancer for Marvel whose style veered toward the oddball. His characters were gawky and weird, making him the perfect choice for developing the story of nerdy Peter Parker, a hapless high school brainiac who gets bitten by a radioactive spider and gains superstrength and agility. Though the teen's new status hardly solves all his problems.

"Sometimes, I hate my Spider-Man powers," the hero whined in one early issue. "Sometimes I wish I were just like any normal teen-ager."

Legend has it that Goodman loathed spiders and initially balked at publishing the story before finally allowing it to run in *Amazing Fantasy*, a title that was set to be canceled anyway.

By 1963 Marvel also had Ant-Man, Thor, and mystical sorcerer Dr. Strange in its bullpen. Iron Man, debuting in March 1963, provided a test for this modern way of storytelling. As Lee tells it, he wanted to create a character whom readers of the day would find, on the surface, unappealing. And what could be more unappealing at the height of the Cold War than a wealthy, arrogant weapons manufacturer?

Like the heroes who came before him, Iron Man (written by Stan's brother Larry Lieber and drawn by Don Heck) also took off.

"Marvel's success was about storytelling and putting a mirror up to the real world for not just kids but a growing group of adults who were tired of the DC traditional characters saying the same things as they did in the forties and the fifties, 'Good Grief!'" John Romita Sr. says.

What Lee and his gang had done—as counterculture newspaper the *Village Voice* suggested in a 1965 article—was bring the antihero to comics.

"How can a character as hopelessly healthy as Superman compete with this living symbol of the modern dilemma, this neurotic's neurotic, Spider-Man, the super-anti-hero of our time?" Sally Kempton asked in the piece about the growing "cult" of Marvel.

The antihero concept that Marvel co-opted had been bubbling up in literature for at least a decade, starting with 1951's *The Catcher in the Rye* and continuing with 1957's beat classic *On the Road*. It was a concept that proved particularly appealing for the morally muddy times. Marvel's heroes were not the clean, square-jawed heroes of old. They didn't even always act heroically. In fact, Marvel's first wave of 1960s characters seemed to have more in common with the monsters that had populated the company's books just a few years before.

"DC Comics came from a time historically where heroes came from the pulps—Doc Savage and The Shadow. These heroes were born good guys. They had shiny teeth; they had good aspirations when they were younger," says Neal Adams. Adams began drawing books for DC in 1967 and became one of the defining artists of the era as well as one of the most important behind-the-scenes forces in the industry.

Marvel upended the traditional template by casting morally questionable guys in the lead. Peter Parker is a social outcast who decides to become Spider-Man only after his inaction to catch a robber leads to the murder of his beloved uncle. Dr. Strange is an arrogant surgeon who learns humility—and the ways of magic—after losing the use of his hands in an accident. And the Hulk? He's a literal monster.

"All these characters are assholes," Adams says. "They're bad guys. They're not heroes. All the characters at Marvel began as monster stories, and they somehow find their way to doing good stuff in their lives."

Marvel's superhero books were written from the inside out, with a focus on characterization, emotion, and the heroes' inner turmoil.

"Marvel's stories were completely unstructured," former Marvel and DC writer Mike Friedrich says. "They were all over the map, emotion driven and character driven. DC's talked to you about plots and conflict and resolutions and all the traditional English analysis of creating stories."

To give a favorite Stan Lee example of DC's plot-driven style of storytelling: a mystery would arise that Batman would be required to solve. A clue would be planted. Batman would pick up on that clue and, by the last page, solve the mystery. The end. It was all very neat and tidy.

Marvel's new line began growing in leaps and bounds. The publisher sold some 18.9 million magazines in 1960. By 1964 that number had exploded to 27.7 million.

"Marvels sell fast! Marvels sell out!" a 1965 trade ad touted. "When fans EYE them, they BUY them!"

But the limitations of its distribution deal with Independent continued to hamstring Marvel. Goodman and Lee were unable to introduce solo titles for their increasingly popular heroes, and the characters were instead forced to share space in a single title. Captain America and Iron Man went halvsies in *Tales of Suspense*, for example.

Goodman's poor distribution deal did have one silver lining that became apparent only in retrospect. It allowed a lone editor, Stan Lee, to oversee an entire line of comic books, imposing a singular vision and voice on every title. In that sense, if you liked one Marvel magazine, chances are you'd like another. Marvel was finally emerging as a cohesive brand.

"Stan had an intention to build a company, to build an entity that would be called Marvel Comics," says Denny O'Neil, a former DC and Marvel writer-editor and a fifty-year industry veteran. "There was never any such intention from DC. They published forty titles a month but without any intention to make them uniquely DC titles."

At DC each of the editors was like his own separate brand.

"From the 1940s through the 1960s DC's editors were independent fiefdoms, never reading each others' books and rarely using each other's talent," former DC editor Bob Greenberger says.

As a result, each editor's books had a look and feel that might differ from those of the guy down the hall.

Marvel was different. Because Lee had been in charge of this newly emerging superhero line from its inception, he was able to build something special.

A coherent universe.

And that Marvel universe proved to be a huge selling point for the company through the 1960s and beyond.

The concept that heroes lived in the same world was not new, of course. The industry's first superhero crossover occurred in 1940's *Marvel Mystery Comics* #8. There, the publisher's two original characters, the Human Torch and Sub-Mariner, fought each other atop the Brooklyn Bridge. The story was so epic that it spilled over into the next issue.

DC also published the occasional crossover, although the editors were notoriously territorial and didn't like lending their characters to editors working on other books.

Batman and the Man of Steel teamed up on the comic book pages in 1952's *Superman* #76, and the company's World War II heroes also appeared side by side in the *Justice Society of America* during the 1940s. But in terms of a cohesive universe, DC didn't really have one.

Neither did Marvel. But that all changed with 1962's *Fantastic Four* #4. In that groundbreaking issue Johnny Storm encountered a mysterious man at a homeless shelter who turned out to be the Sub-Mariner. With that simple plot twist Lee and Kirby not only blew the minds of those old enough to remember the faded Golden Age figure but also introduced the idea that the Fantastic Four were not the only super-powered characters inhabiting this world.

Lee and Kirby also had the good sense to make that four-color world look as much like ours as possible. They set the Fantastic Four and the adventures of subsequent heroes in New York City, as opposed to the fictionalized Metropolises or Central Citys of DC's titles.

The real-life setting helped to ground Marvel's stories—future Marvel artist John Byrne has admitted that when reading the *Fantastic Four* as a kid in Canada, he thought they might be real—and this allowed for greater continuity among the titles. Soon the Incredible Hulk was slugging it out with the Thing, and Spidey was attempting to join the Fantastic Four in *The Amazing Spider-Man* #1. In perhaps the biggest twist of them all, Captain America was revived in 1964's *Avengers* #4, having spent the previous decades frozen in a block of ice. He was soon integrated into the contemporary Marvel universe, becoming one of its most important figures. Compare that to DC's 1960s revival of the Justice Society of America, which quarantined the veteran heroes in an alternate universe to the one inhabited by DC's contemporary names.

Marvel also pioneered the idea of stories continuing stories. By 1962 Lee was becoming increasingly overworked and no longer had the time to craft tight, self-contained stories. As a cheat, he took one story and stretched it out over several issues, leaving a cliffhanger at the end of each. The idea flew in the face of standard industry practices because the haphazard nature of comic book distribution meant a customer could never be sure he would be able to find consecutive issues at his local newsstand.

But the new format did not cause readers to abandon Marvel; in fact, they were being drawn deeper into this burgeoning fictional world, in some cases buying every title the company produced.

Readers were also digging the art, much of which Kirby handled. His line work was craggy, his figures somewhat boxy, and their fingers were squared off on the ends, giving the books a rawer quality than those of Marvel's competitors.

"Only a few short months later, I couldn't really look at Infantino or [Gil] Kane or [Curt] Swan or any of the other DC artists of that period without feeling that there was something missing," Alan Moore wrote of discovering early Marvel. "A lack of grittiness or something."

Beyond offering a unique artistic look, Kirby helped establish Marvel's visual style. His way of telling stories would soon become the default at the publisher, and Lee would use Kirby's pages as a guide to show other artists what to do. Kirby became so important to Marvel that colorist Stan Goldberg used to joke that when he and inker Frank Giacoia would go to lunch with Kirby, the two men would stand on either side of the star artist as they crossed the street in order to protect Kirby from oncoming traffic.

Kirby's art was like a silent movie that plucked out only the most dramatic moments. Everything was turned up to eleven. Even the simplest actions had to be exaggerated. Nothing was done halfway. If someone was throwing a punch, the artist would draw the conclusion of a follow-through so powerful that it looked as though it would yank the arm from its socket. When a character was angry, every tendon in his body strained.

Marvel's art conveyed a sense of movement and drama that few other books had at the time.

"The thing that appealed to me about Marvel was, first, its sense of dynamism," writer Peter Gillis, who wrote Marvel's *Defenders* and *Dr. Strange* in the seventies and eighties, said in 1985. "I picked up a *Tales of Suspense* with a ten-page Captain America story drawn by Jack Kirby, and there was more excitement in that one story than in practically all the DC Comics I'd read up to that point."

"It's a simple thing, but even today, I don't think DC fully understands it," Lee said in 2000.

If Marvel's art was a double espresso, DC's was like a pleasant green tea. The publisher favored a cleaner, more technically correct style than what Kirby, Ditko, and the others were doing for Marvel.

DC artists were forced to work within an established house style that governed the page layout as well as the look of the artwork. Editor Julie Schwartz's motto was, "If it's not clean, it's worthless."

Carmine Infantino and the other favored DC artists at the time were no doubt extremely talented men. The art they produced was beautiful. It was correctly referenced and anatomically accurate. It just lacked a certain flare, a certain energy, a certain danger that would get readers' hearts racing.

Marvel was more experimental, more edgy.

"Marvel is a cornucopia of fantasy, a wild idea, a swashbuckling attitude, an escape from the humdrum and prosaic," Lee would write, summing up what Marvel was all about. "It's . . . a literate celebration of unbridled creativity, coupled with a touch of rebellion and an insolent desire to spit in the eye of the dragon."

By the mid sixties the spitting would start going DC's way.

The Rivalry Catches Fire

"In the beginning, it was just the two of us in the office. DC was so big, and we were the little guys. They had Batman and Superman. It's just night and day, a little company to a huge company."

—Flo Steinberg, Stan Lee's former assistant

*B*y 1962 DC's boat had sprung a leak and was taking on water. The company was beginning to sink—it just didn't know it yet.

While the executives remained blissfully ignorant, two prescient staffers attempted to sound the alarm.

Bob Haney and Arnold Drake had both been writing for the publisher since the mid-1950s. Haney was large man—he came into the world at a whopping eleven pounds—and had grown up in one of the Depression-era shantytowns known as Hoovervilles near Philadelphia. He had worked most notably on DC's war comics. Drake was a New York City native and an observant Jew. He'd been writing on DC's sci-fi and mystery anthologies.

One night while working late the pair decided to sneak to the other side of 575 Lexington Avenue, where Independent News was located, to flip through (and possibly steal) a few of the magazines DC's sister company was distributing.

And that's when—just a few months removed from the publication of *Fantastic Four* #1—they got their first inkling that the industry was about to be turned upside down.

"We were looking at this Marvel stuff and saying, 'Look at this stuff!'" the late Haney said in 1997. "Kirby was doing this great stuff, and Stan Lee was editing and writing it. And we said, 'This is terrific stuff! This is real far-out, wing-dingy comics!'"

Although both writers were in their mid- to late thirties at the time, something about Marvel's hip, youthful energy set them abuzz. Drake and Haney grabbed a few magazines and later went in to see DC's publisher, Irwin Donenfeld. They confidently pushed the Marvel books his way and told the executive to take a look. This, the writers claimed, was "great stuff," and Donenfeld better recognize that something new was happening in the business.

Donenfeld was dismissive. He didn't see what Haney and Drake had seen. "We do $100 million a year and they do $35 million," the publisher said defensively.

"What was happening was the Marvel revolution, and we pointed it out to him," Haney said. "And he didn't recognize it. So then DC sales began to really drop. . . . Here was General Motors no longer selling every car they could turn out."

The giant was stumbling. DC's sales reached their height in 1963 and began to decline in 1964. Marvel's, however, would continue to climb through the decade.

The problem DC would soon face was not how many comics overall it was selling but what percentage. At the time comics were treated like other periodicals. The publisher produced a large print run, which the distributor delivered to newsstands and other outlets. The books were put on sale for a fixed amount of time, and at the end of that period the covers were stripped from whatever hadn't been sold and returned for credit. In most cases a significant number of copies from the print run went unsold and were eventually pulped, costing the publisher in wasted printing, paper, and administrative costs.

In 1962, when Drake and Haney were warning Donenfeld about DC's potential challenger, the executive had good reason to feel invincible. DC released 343 individual comics that year, the most of anyone in the business (a title it would hold until 1973). *Superman* was the number-one title overall, and DC hogged seven of the other spots in the top ten. On the surface the publisher appeared dominant. Underneath, the numbers would begin to reveal another story.

DC was tops only because it printed far more titles. The problem was, the publisher's sell-through rate, the percentage of the print run consumers were actually buying, was shakier compared to Marvel's. It was as clear an indication as any that their rival's readership was smaller but far more enthusiastic.

"Marvel was doing very well," DC's Carmine Infantino said in a 2000 interview. "We knew it because DC—Independent News—was handling Marvel at the time and their numbers were coming in. Marvel had books like *Spider-Man* coming in at 70, 80, even 85 percent sales. And we had books coming in at 40, 41, 42 percent. Something was wrong, and [DC's executives] didn't know how to fix it."

Marvel was becoming so popular—and profitable for its distributor— that in 1963 Independent News acquiesced to an expansion of titles. Marvel was now allowed ten to fourteen books a month.

Superheroes were in vogue, so Goodman asked Lee to create more of them. Lee initially teamed with Sub-Mariner creator Bill Everett for a brand-new character. But when Everett fell behind on the art chores, Lee was forced to go to plan B. Taking a page from DC's playbook, Lee tossed together members of the company's existing superhero roster into one powerful team, just like the Justice League. Using existing characters saved him and artist Jack Kirby from having to come up with brand-new ones and allowed the issue to be completed more quickly so it made it to the printer in time.

The Avengers #1, cover dated September 1963, featured Iron Man, Ant-Man, Thor, the Wasp, and the Hulk joining forces to defeat Loki— another preexisting character who'd been introduced in Thor's title the year before.

Marvel's other new title that month had even more in common with one of DC's—a lot more. The similarities were so eerie, so draw-droppingly unbelievable that conspiracy theories quickly sprouted and persist to this day.

The X-Men debuted in the summer of 1963, and—no shock here—it was written by Lee and penciled by Kirby. It was about the wheelchair-bound Professor X who ran a Westchester-based school for gifted youngsters. The Beast was an athletic, ape-like brainiac, Marvel Girl possessed the power of telekinesis, Cyclops could blast an energy beam from his eyes, Iceman controlled the cold, and Angel could soar through the air on his birdlike wings. The twist here was that these heroes hadn't acquired their power through cosmic rays or some scientific accident; they'd been born with them via a gene mutation.

Lee pitched Goodman on the series he called "The Mutants." Goodman rejected the title, reasoning that kids wouldn't have any idea what a mutant even was. Lee walked out of that meeting thinking, "This demonstrates how some people in big positions are idiots," as he recounted at the 2016 New York Comic Con. So Lee went with *The X-Men* instead—the X standing for "extra," as in the kids' abilities.

The cover to issue #1 promised "The Strangest Super-Heroes of All!" Only they weren't. DC had beat Marvel to it.

Three months earlier Marvel's rival had released *My Greatest Adventure* #80, which featured the first appearance of a new team called the Doom Patrol. The artist was Bruno Premiani, and the writer was none other than Arnold Drake—that is, one of the few at DC who seemed to be paying attention to what was going on at Marvel. As such, it was probably no coincidence that the Doom Patrol came the closest to feeling like a Marvel book that DC produced at the time.

"One of the only guys who ever addressed the stylistic challenge [from Marvel] was Arnold Drake," says Paul Kupperberg, a former DC writer and editor who would reboot the Doom Patrol in 1977. "*Doom Patrol*, if you read it now, was a pretty sophisticated book for its time. It had heady continuity and that Marvel interaction between characters. Arnold saw what was going on."

The Doom Patrol was born when Murray Boltinoff, another of DC's long-serving, pipe-smoking editors, decided to change up *My Greatest Adventure*. The anthology, which told a diverse range of stories from sci-fi to monster, had been floundering, so Boltinoff attempted to boost sales by injecting the flavor of the minute: superheroes. He asked Drake for ideas.

Over a single weekend Drake, with help from his buddy Haney, brainstormed a group that, as Drake described it, would attempt to move the superhero more into the real world and say, "They've got problems too. You don't live without problems."

The story found a wheelchair-bound genius, known as the Chief, gathering a team of misfits to fight crime and right wrongs. Actress Rita Farr, test pilot Larry Trainor, and race car driver Cliff Steele are all survivors of bizarre accidents that have granted them special powers. After inhaling volcanic gases in the African jungle, Farr becomes able to shrink and grow her body, taking on the name Elasti-Girl. Trainor (aka Negative Man) is exposed to cosmic radiation while flying a plane high in the atmosphere and is suddenly able to project from his body a being of negative energy. Steele is horribly mangled during an auto race, and his brain is transferred into a mechanical body, turning him into Robotman.

Like the members of Marvel's Fantastic Four, these characters were bitter about the grotesque transformations their bodies had undergone and hated being superheroes. The first issue refers to them as "victims of a cruel and fantastic fate."

These were not the typical, bright, "shiny teeth" (as Neal Adams called them) DC heroes. They were flawed freaks. "I decided I want a superhero for the nerds of the world," Drake would say of the Chief.

My Greatest Adventure #80 hit racks in April 1963. *The X-Men* #1 landed that July, and the parallels were—let's say—uncanny. The chances that two comic book publishers, completely independently, would put out a new book about a team of freaks led by a genius-level, wheelchair-bound mentor within weeks of each other were on par with the chances of Aquaman investing in Seaworld stock. The similarities were far too blatant to be coincidence. At least in Drake's mind.

After *X-Men* #1 appeared, Drake walked into Weisinger's office to raise a stink. The editor simply brushed him off, telling Drake, "Don't get your bowels in an uproar. Your man-in-a-wheelchair isn't a new idea. Nero Wolfe never left his orchids to solve a murder."

But classic fictional armchair detectives like Wolfe weren't paraplegics. Professor X and the Chief were. Had Stan Lee ripped off the idea for X-Men from Drake?

Further muddying the waters was another incredible parallel. In the March 1964 issue the Doom Patrol fought a group of ne'er-do-wells called the Brotherhood of Evil. The exact same month in *X-Men* #4, Professor X and his mutants took on the Brotherhood of Evil Mutants. A single coincidence is one thing. Two is harder to explain.

But in the end it appears to have been just that: coincidence. The logistics of comic book creation make the prospect of a rip-off extremely unlikely. It would have been impossible for Marvel's editor to read *My Greatest Adventure* #80 in April and then write, draw, letter, and print a copycat by July—there simply wasn't enough lead time. As unlikely as it sounds, the whole thing should be chalked up to chance—a conclusion that Drake accepted. Initially, at least.

When asked in 1984 about Marvel copying the Doom Patrol with the X-Men, Drake downplayed the possibility. "Not unless someone was looking over my shoulder while I was writing," he said. "*X-Men* came out almost at the same time—just a little bit later."

But toward the end of his life, he'd reconsidered the charges, claiming Stan Lee had "knowingly" stolen the idea of the X-Men from him.

"I [initially] reasoned that there wasn't enough lead time for it to have been a rip-off. But back then I didn't know that many DC artists were already working for Stan," Drake said in 2003. "In short, from the day I dropped my first Doom Patrol script on Boltinoff's desk, news could have leaked to Marvel about 'a team of anti-super-heroes led by a scientific genius in a wheelchair.' So the plagiarism issue remains open. And unless someone steps up to say, 'Yes, one day, I told Stan about that,' it will never close."

When it came to the Brotherhood of Evil coincidence, it's possible that both Lee and Drake could have drawn inspiration by simply opening the newspaper. A September 24, 1963, article about organized crime that was syndicated to newspapers across the country had a headline reading, "Brotherhood of Evil." It's possible that both men spotted the story as they were preparing the issues of their respective comic books that would arrive four months later and liked the ring of the phrase.

For his part Lee is clear on the issue. He has stated on record that he had no idea DC had produced a book featuring a team leader in a wheelchair, otherwise he'd have never done the X-Men. "The last thing in the world I wanted to do was anything that was like DC," he said in 2003.

In 2005, two years before he died, Drake received an honorary award at the San Diego Comic-Con. He accepted his accolade in front of a packed house of comic book professionals, and before he left the stage he couldn't resist taking one final dig at Lee. Drake ended his speech by breaking into an a capella song he'd written that included the line, "I hears somebody said it / that Stan Lee would take credit / for Spider-Man to the King James testament." Many in attendance gasped.

The tragedy for Drake is that few people outside comic fandom are likely to know the Doom Patrol (volume 1 was canceled in 1968), a concept and series that was arguably as groundbreaking and original as the X-Men. But like so many of the head-to-head duels between the two companies, Marvel would somehow come out on top.

Stan Lee was certainly winning the PR battle. Through his magazines' letters pages and his Soapbox column, Lee spoke directly to readers in a casual tone that helped Marvel establish the fun, rollicking brand personality it retains to this day. Lee made readers feel like they were part of a special club for those smart and selective enough to be reading Marvel books. While DC's editors came off in print as what they were—middle-aged, uptight, management types—Stan brought goofy wit and a friendly personality.

"I don't know if their stuff has deteriorated or whether you have improved that much, but the competition now seems like ecch!"

—Paul Gambaccini, from a letter printed in December 1963's *The Amazing Spider-Man* #7

"There is, however, one company which puts out comics which I am not at all hesitant to call utter trash. The company has the nerve to refer to you as 'Brand-Ech' while they sit back and put out the worst comics in history."

—Robert Wilczynski, from a letter printed in May 1966's *The Flash* #161

Part of his persona was taking good-natured digs at DC in print. He referred to them as "Brand Echh," a play on "Brand X," a common euphemism in advertising used to refer to a competing product that one didn't want to name. Lee lamented the "panicky pussycats" desperately trying to imitate Marvel and offered to sell them scripts.

DC responded to the ribbing by defensively referring to Marvel in its letters pages as "Brand I," for imitator, or "Brand Ego." Robert Kanigher used the cryptic "CC Comics," presumably for "copycat" or "carbon copy." *Brave and Bold* #74 (November 1967) opened with Batman acrobatically twirling around a flag pole, boasting, "Here's one I did before anybody, including a certain web-spinning Peter-come-lately!" The Spider-Man insult aggravated some Marvel fans.

While Marvel was unleashing the "Marvel age" of comics, DC generally kept its head in the sand. Marvel, since 1961, had grown enough to make it worthy of parodying and sniping at in DC's letters pages, but to those who ran the esteemed publisher, it still did not represent a major threat from a business perspective.

"It seems that the editors at DC were so institutionalized, coming off all these wonderful accomplishments, taking credit for the invention of the superhero and maintaining it, and acting like no one else could do a superhero as well as they did," DC editor Joe Orlando said in 1998. "They were getting their asses kicked in by Marvel at the newsstands, and they were not reading the Marvel books, never analyzing or trying to figure out what the competition was doing. They treated their competitor with total contempt."

One theory put forth by DC publisher Irwin Donenfeld about Marvel's success was that it was simply an accident. Kids were getting confused at the newsstand and mistakenly buying Marvel books instead of DC, which they actually wanted. In early 1966 Donenfeld sought to remedy the perceived problem, and the result was one of the most ridiculed ideas in the history of the industry.

Beginning with titles cover dated April 1966 Donenfeld attempted to give the DC line a unified look by adding a checkboard-patterned stripe banner at the top of the cover. "Don't hesitate," house ads at the time ordered, "Choose the mags with the go-go checks!"

"In those days comics were on the newsstands with vertical slots for the magazines," Donenfeld said in 1998. "I wanted to have something that showed DC Comics were different than anything else. . . . So wherever these magazines were displayed, you could always see a DC comic from way back. It was to distinguish us from anybody else."

The go-go checks did their jobs. They did distinguish DC's books from others on the stand. Only that may not have been such a great thing.

"It was the stupidest idea we ever heard," DC's Infantino would say of the checks, "because the books were bad in those days, and that just showed people right off what not to buy."

Around the time the go-go checks were being rolled out, Arnold Drake was taking another stab at trying to get DC's management to take seriously the challenge Marvel presented. On February 3, 1966, Drake typed a blistering, seven-page memo to Donenfeld laying out the reasons he believed Marvel was ascendant and the changes he recommended DC make to keep up.

"[Marvel] succeeded for two reasons primarily," Drake wrote in the memo. "First, they were more with what was happening in the country than we were. And perhaps more important, they aimed their stuff at an age level that had never read comics before in any impressive number—the college level (let's say ages 16 to 19 or 20)."

Drake suggested developing tiers of books aimed at different age groups. The entry-level books, such as Weisinger's juvenile *Superman*, would target the youngest readers. The next step up would be Julie Schwartz's superhero books, such as *The Flash* and *Justice League of America*. Those would be for the preteen reader. Finally, titles such as Drake's *Doom Patrol* would be aimed at the oldest demographic and would contain "adult concepts, adult language, a little cheesecake, a little idol-breaking, a little 'think' stuff now and then."

Donenfeld's response to the memo was similar to his response back in 1962 when Drake and Haney had first sounded the alarm.

"You're as full of shit as a Christmas turkey," the executive fumed to Drake. "We outsell Marvel three to one."

DC's upper management may have been oblivious when it came to the evolving marketplace, but DC did show some signs of change through the decade. Arguably the most lasting tweak was the attempt to create a more coherent DC universe, as Marvel was busy doing. Starting in 1963, some two years after the modern Marvel universe had been born, DC took steps to streamline all its characters into a single world and to tighten the continuity among its titles.

DC's heroes had appeared in one another's books prior to 1963: Batman paid a visit to Superman's Fortress of Solitude in 1958's *Action Comics* #241, for instance, and the Flash guest starred in 1962's *Green Lantern* #13. But the universe didn't feel particularly coherent, and DC's grouchy, territorial editors were often not so keen on allowing their heroes to cross into other titles.

That resistance began easing with the publication of *Brave and Bold* #50 (November 1963). The series had previously been a proving ground for new concepts, similar to *Showcase*. With #50 it became strictly about teaming two superheroes together. The inaugural story starred Martian Manhunter and Green Arrow—not exactly a blockbuster duo, though subsequent pairings were to be selected by fan vote, an ad at the time promised. Soon the Metal Men were joining forces with the Atom, and Batman was fighting alongside Green Lantern.

In the mother of all team-ups, the company's two super squads—the Justice League of America and the Justice Society of America—crossed paths in *Justice League of America* #21 (August 1963). The story called "Crisis on Earth One" proved so popular with buyers—if not artist Mike Sekowsky, whose hands were probably stricken with carpal tunnel from drawing all those different characters—that it became an annual tradition. It also installed the word "Crisis" as the publisher's go-to brand for gigantic events involving numerous heroes.

DC was beginning to cobble together a universe. Unlike Marvel, whose universe had mostly been created during a few years and had been controlled by one editor, DC had to contend with decades of (often contradictory) story lines created by dozens of writers, editors, and artists. The result was a jumbled timeline into which not everything they published fit squarely.

The continuity problem would be something DC would wrestle with for years to come and still does in the present day, but the company did begin to try to address glaring errors that would irritate hardcore readers who increasingly cared about that kind of minutia.

Mystery in Space #75 (May 1962) was the first to retroactively correct a past error in order to make it jibe with continuity, a practice that would become a virtual cottage industry in later years. May 1961's *Justice League of America* #4 had included a scene in which new members are nominated for inclusion in the group. The Flash suggests Adam Strange because "he's achieved an excellent record."

Strange, a sci-fi hero, had first appeared in 1958. He was an ordinary earthbound archeologist who one day suddenly finds himself transported to an alien world called Rann. There he befriends a beautiful woman and joins in Rann's fight against alien invaders.

As a reader pointed out in the letters column to *Justice League of America* #6, however, the JLA couldn't have known about Adam Strange because they'd never been shown meeting.

Schwartz solved the discrepancy by writing a story for *Mystery in Space* set in the time between *JLA* #3 and #4, detailing a meeting between Strange and the marquee superheroes.

Around that time DC also began freshening up some of its characters, most notably Batman. The hero is a multibillion-dollar franchise these days, but back in the early 1960s Batman was on the verge of cancellation and risked fading into oblivion like other characters from the pulp era, such as the Phantom. Imagine no Christopher Nolan movies, no Saturday morning cartoons, no Batman sweetened corn cereal.

Donenfeld tasked Julie Schwartz and artist Carmine Infantino with creating a "new look" for the character, and sales improved.

Modern storytelling approaches also touched other DC heroes. Green Lantern's alter ego, Hal Jordan, proposed to girlfriend, Carol Ferris, in 1966. When she says no, he's crushed and goes wandering across America in a multipart storyline. In one issue he's working as an insurance adjuster in Washington State—one of the most powerful beings in the universe reduced to investigating fender benders.

One writer who introduced a Marvel sensibility to DC was Jim Shooter, a Pittsburgh native who sold his first story to DC in 1965 at the ripe old age of thirteen.

Shooter had grown up reading DC comics but abandoned them after he felt he'd outgrown them. A few years later, during a hospital stay when he was twelve, he discovered a pile of comics in his room. He flipped through *Superman* to find it hadn't changed much since he was a little boy. He tossed it aside, bored. Then he picked up a stack of Marvel comics, and his young mind was blown. Inside he witnessed a whole new way of telling stories, a more mature way of handling superheroes.

"The [Marvel characters] seemed more real, more like people," Shooter says. "Then I'd open a Superman comic, and Superman would be cutting a ribbon on a bridge opening or something."

The budding writer began formulating a plan to earn money for his struggling family. He thought he could help elevate DC's inferior stories by sending the publisher new ones written in the style of Stan Lee.

He crafted a tale of the Legion of Super-Heroes, a group of young do-gooders from the thirtieth century, because he felt that was the magazine that "needed the most help." He then sent it, unsolicited, to Mort Weisinger. The editor liked it, and soon Shooter was penning Superman stories as well as the Legion's adventures.

Shooter set about injecting his DC tales with some of the same elements that had attracted him to Marvel. He introduced memorable villains, including Parasite, and tried to amp up the characterization to be more in line with Marvel's unique style. On his watch the members of the Legion of Super-Heroes began to have their own distinct personalities. Ferro Lad, a riff on Iron Man in which the hero transforms himself into metal, was killed off in a shocking twist that brought a little Marvel-style angst.

Shooter soon became known around DC as the "Marvel writer"—and that was not meant as a compliment. Weisinger colleagues often criticized him for using someone who wrote like Stan Lee.

"Mort forbade me to read Marvel comics because he thought they were a bad influence," Shooter says. "I ignored that."

When Marvel launched a fan club in 1964, Shooter happily joined. Later, when Lee promised to print the name of every member in the pages of Marvel comics, Shooter lived in terror for months, fearing Weisinger would spot his name and fire him. It never happened, and Shooter kept writing.

For all of Weisinger's animosity and the dismissive attitude among the rest of DC's higher-ups toward Marvel, they were clearly concerned about the rival company and made attempts to copy it.

"There was this odd dichotomy," Shooter says. "People at DC ridiculed Marvel Comics, but they also hated the fact that they were selling. They couldn't grasp it. They thought it was like the hula hoop, that it was a fad and it would go away, even while struggling to imitate it."

"I think DC was concerned about staying relevant at a time when what defined relevance for comics had been shifted to someone else," says former DC editor Brian Augustyn. "DC started to try to ape some of Marvel's trappings, the superficial elements, that they could grab. But at this point it was forty-five-year-old men trying to understand what college students wanted."

One of Marvel's trademark elements that DC tried to copy was the Bullpen Bulletins, Marvel's chatty news page. In March 1966 the company introduced its own coming attractions column called Direct Currents. The column stands as an enlightening demonstration of how much difficulty DC had in copying Marvel's success. Again and again the publisher would latch onto elements from its rival and attempt to emulate them in a misguided or wrongheaded way.

Direct Currents tried its best to ape Lee's freewheeling, slang-filled voice, but it ended up sounding like it had been spit out of a computer called the Alliterator 3000.

"Read this page of powerful predictions of popular publications produced by DC!" read the June 1967 entry. "Find out what fabulous fiction, fraught with fascinating features, will be awaiting you at your neighborhood newsstand!"

You can practically hear the writer desperately screaming across the DC offices, "Can anyone think of another word that begins with F?!"

Direct Currents offered none of the fun of Bullpen Bulletins. It didn't offer a peek into the world of DC comics, dish on the goings-on at the office, or turn the company's artists and writers into relatable personalities. It didn't create a special bond with readers. It. Was. Just. There.

"DC tried to reach out and say, 'Hey, I'm with you. I'm one of you,' but they never really succeeded," says Scott Edelman, a Marvel editor in the 1970s. "So they'd do things that would eventually get mocked. It was like when you watch old episodes of *The Brady Bunch* or *The Partridge Family*, and there would always be an old guy wearing a Nehru jacket with an ankh symbol and growing his hair a little long and trying to connect with kids."

Part of DC's lack of fraternity with the reader came down to philosophy. The company didn't want to introduce readers to its staff because it would prefer that those picking up its books didn't know who was creating them. To DC the characters were the star. "I don't want anybody to know who *you* are, I want them to care about Superman," Mort Weisinger once told one of his writers.

Comics was anonymous work for many years. The writer, penciler, inker, colorist, letterer, and other hands that produced them rarely received credit for their work in the magazines' pages. The artist could occasionally sneak a signature onto a splash page or hide it within a background, like on a car's license plate. (Though DC would often white out those before the pages saw print.) Official credits were not the normal part of doing business.

Until Stan Lee came along.

His and Jack Kirby's names are scribbled on the upper right corner of the first page of *Fantastic Four* #1, and with issue #9 the book began including a proper credits box, giving a tip of the cape to those who worked on the issue.

"I put everybody's name. I even put the letterer's name down," Lee says. "I wanted it to seem a bit like a movie. I wanted the readers to get to know who we were and to become fans. I wanted to personalize things and not just, 'These are books. You buy them or you don't buy them. You don't know who did them and you don't care.' I wanted to give it a friendly feeling, as though we're all part of one group of fans and we enjoy what we're doing and we know each other."

DC was slow to follow suit. Julie Schwartz had printed credits for writer Gardner Fox and artist Joe Kubert in a 1961 Hawkman story that ran in *Brave and Bold*, and he did the same in other stories. But credit for DC's talent remained scattershot throughout the sixties.

"DC did not like that Marvel put credits in the front of its books," says Peter David, a longtime comics writer who has worked for DC and Marvel since the 1980s. "They considered Stan to be a boastful son of a bitch, putting his name in the comics with the artist and the inker. That was just not done."

DC held out until the talent forced its hand.

"They wound up following Marvel's lead when various creators were going, 'Wait a minute—how come Marvel does that and you don't?'" David says.

About the only ones who weren't getting proper credit at Marvel were those whom the publisher had lured over from DC. As the upstart publisher started to catch fire, several DC artists began quietly freelancing for Marvel. Very quietly. Many of them hoped to continue collecting a paycheck from DC, so to avoid the wrath of DC's editors, the artists needed to use fake names.

"I heard many freelancers say it was like the Berlin Wall," former Marvel editor David Anthony Kraft says. "You worked for Marvel or you worked for DC. You did not work for both. I think DC had that really rigid policy: you're a traitor if you do anything for Marvel."

The first to cross the wall were inkers Frank Giacoia, a competent draftsman who'd been working on the *Flash* and some romance titles, and *Wonder Woman* artist Mike Esposito. Beginning in 1965 Giacoia's Marvel work appeared credited as "Frankie Ray" and Esposito's as "Mickey Demeo." Superman specialist Jack Abel started inking Iron Man under the name "Gary Michaels," and Gil Kane, the cocreator of the 1960s Green Lantern, took the name "Scott Edward" to draw a Hulk story.

Lee reveled in the thefts and would chuckle about how many great artists DC had buried on their romance books. Marvel gave these guys a chance to really shine, but defecting could be dangerous: the artists ran the risk of losing their paycheck from DC, which at the time was a far more stable bet than Marvel.

One problem with the pseudonym strategy was that artists often drew with a distinct style, and recognizing their work wasn't all that difficult, no matter what name was signed to it.

Gene Colan, another of DC's underutilized artists, began freelancing for Marvel under the name "Adam Austin" in 1965.

"Everybody's favorite guessing game these days is trying to figure out the real identity of the Sub-Mariner's powerful penciller, Adam Austin!" Lee wrote in the December 1965 Bullpen Bulletins.

Colan drew with a delicate pencil style full of lush shading, and it didn't take long for the artist to be outed. Soon after his Marvel work began appearing, Colan got a call from a fan saying, "Don't bother trying to fool me with that Adam Austin bit. I'd know your work anywhere."

The death knell came later when Colan was at the DC offices delivering some work. As he headed toward the elevator to leave, the doors opened, and out walked Marvel honcho Martin Goodman. "Hi, Gene," Goodman said, and with that, all of Colan's plans of continuing to work surreptitiously for both companies disappeared.

The next day Lee offered him full-time work, and he went on to become a Marvel mainstay, drawing *Daredevil*, *Captain America*, and *Doctor Strange*, among many others.

Writer defections were less common then, in part because Lee was able to handle all the titles he was allowed to release under Independent News's constricting contract. As Marvel was allowed to release more material, additional hands were needed. Lee's savior would come from DC.

Roy Thomas was a Missouri-based high school teacher who was among the most prominent fans in the industry. He'd been publishing the fanzine *Alter Ego* since 1964, and his letters often appeared in publications for both DC and Marvel.

Thomas, through fandom, had developed numerous contacts in the comic book industry, and in 1965 he left Missouri and moved to New York to take a job at DC as Mort Weisinger's assistant. He'd finally realized his dream of being in the industry.

That dream soon turned to a nightmare working under the monstrous Weisinger. After work Thomas would return home to his dirty hotel room and feel tears welling in his eyes. Out of desperation he decided to write Stan Lee a letter, just telling the Marvel editor he was a fan of his work.

Lee soon phoned Thomas, offering him a writer's test. Thomas passed and was offered a job over a lunch, just eight days into his DC tenure.

He returned from lunch to the DC offices to give notice, and Weisinger threw him out of the office immediately, accusing him of being a spy for Marvel.

The hire would ultimately prove transformational for Marvel, and Thomas would become a major figure in the company's development through the 1960s and 1970s, as the publisher's sales roared ahead.

Marvel's growth was so strong, so unprecedented, that its editor would soon declare victory over DC. The April 1968 Soapbox had Lee proclaiming Marvel "the undisputed leaders of the comics industry."

The bluster was typical of Lee's boastful style. Marvel still wasn't quite number one—that milestone would take a few more years—but it had grown a remarkable amount.

Marvel's titles had been selling so well that in 1967 Goodman was able to twist Independent News's arm into allowing him to release even more. Suddenly the characters who had previously been forced to share the so-called split books got their own stand-alone titles. *The Incredible Hulk, Sub-Mariner, The Invincible Iron Man, Nick Fury: Agent of S.H.I.E.L.D.*, and *Captain America* appeared on newsstands, substantially increasing Marvel's presence in 1968.

The expansion was not just about sating readers' desire for more Marvel; Goodman had an ulterior motive for pumping up the company's output—namely, he was laying the groundwork for Marvel to be sold. After decades in the business, churning out pulps, men's magazines as well as comics, Goodman had grown tired and desired to spend more time with his family.

"Coming into 1968 Goodman had been publishing for forty years," says Robert Beerbohm, a historian and retailer who opened one of the country's first comic book stores in Berkeley, California, in 1972. "Goodman doubled or tripled the output. You get *Iron Man* #1, *Captain America* [in his own title]. All of a sudden there's a small flood of romance and war comics. Reprints crank up. What that did is gave the perception of higher circulation numbers so he got more money than he should have gotten when he sold Marvel."

Goodman unloaded Marvel in 1968 for around $15 million to Perfect Film and Chemical Corporation, a hodgepodge conglomerate with a name so bland that it sounded like a corporate front for a James Bond villain. Perfect Film included a range of interests, from paperback books to *The Graduate*–approved "plastics." The sale would move Marvel from a modest, family-owned business to a corporate concern and mark a significant step on the publisher's long, slow road from niche children's publisher to corporate licensing and IP factory.

Marvel's new owners didn't have any particular fondness for superheroes. The publisher was just another notch on Perfect Film's corporate belt.

"They were terrible owners. They stunk," says Mike Hobson, Marvel's publisher from 1981 to 1996. "They didn't give a damn about things at all. They just tried to buy everything."

Perfect Film did have one asset that would soon prove valuable to Marvel: Curtis Circulation, a magazine distributor.

Goodman's deal with Independent News was set to expire, and he and those at Marvel felt that having your competitor control your access to newsstands was a major disadvantage—that Independent didn't work as hard to sell their books as DC's. Lee likened it to Ford having hired General Motors to sell its cars.

Independent's salespeople have claimed that their loyalty was first and foremost to what sold and that they didn't show any particular favoritism to their sister company. That might have been the case. DC's Infantino recalled a visit to a newsstand near DC's office and was enraged to find his company's titles taking a back seat to Marvel's.

"I was . . . watching these jerks promoting Marvel over us—and they were working for us!" Infantino said in 2010. "Marvel got better slots on the newsstands, which made no sense to me."

Whether or not working with Independent was actually hurting Marvel's sales, the company cut ties with its longtime distributor and moved to Curtis. Starting with the comics cover dated September 1969, Marvel had a new distributor.

More important, the company had cut financial ties with DC. Marvel's rival no longer benefited from every Marvel comic sold, and suddenly Marvel's success became a much bigger threat.

DC Desperately
Chases Marvel

"Change had to come or we were going to get killed.
We couldn't stay still."

—DC's Carmine Infantino

*T*he sixties were a simpler time, a time when a six-pack of beer cost 99 cents, the TV dial offered just three networks, and a couple of shady guys who ran parking lots could buy out America's top comic book company.

Parking lots. Future multibillion-dollar properties Batman and Superman were then on the same level as a chunk of asphalt in Manhattan.

Marvel wasn't the only one with new owners heading into the end of the sixties. DC had also been bought out in 1967. Beginning in the early 1960s DC head Jack Liebowitz, then approaching retirement age, had begun looking for a potential buyer for the company. He hired an investment banker to assist in the search, and in 1967 he began negotiating with Kinney National Service, a haphazard collection of businesses that had been formed after a New York parking company merged with a Jewish funeral parlor chain, a cleaning contractor, and other seemingly unrelated businesses.

Kinney was rumored to have nefarious connections, but Liebowitz didn't seem to care.

"They were hamisha [comfortable] people. Jewish, Jewish-oriented," he wrote in his memoir.

With DC riding high from the publicity and profits generated by the 1966 *Batman* TV series, Liebowitz knew he would be selling at an advantageous time. Kinney agreed in July 1967 to acquire DC for $60 million in stock. (Two years later Kinney, in its seemingly never-ending bid to gobble up other companies, bought movie studio Warner Bros. DC would later become a division of Warner Communications.)

The Kinney merger shook up DC mightily and led to the first major personnel changes in years. Liebowitz remained on the board of directors, but Irwin Donenfeld, the son of DC's cofounder Harry, was forced out.

"They made me all kinds of promises of what I would be in this new company," he would later say. "And none of those promises came to be."

Donenfeld exited so abruptly that he left behind his own personal copies of *Action Comics* #1, *Superman* #1, and other vintage comic books that today would be worth millions.

Editorial was also in flux, with no clear leader. Mort Weisinger and Jack Schiff were considered most senior, but Liebowitz didn't want to appoint one as editor-in-chief for fear that the other would quit, according to Arnold Drake. Bringing in a publishing executive from outside the company was also discussed, but Liebowitz ultimately concluded that none of them would get near the low-prestige comic book business.

So Liebowitz made a completely out-of-the-box choice.

"I went into Jack Liebowitz's office one day and asked, 'Jack, who do I answer to now? Who's in charge?'" Carmine Infantino recalled in 2010. "He said, 'You are.' Pow, that was it. How do you like that one between the eyes? I was stunned. Everybody was stunned."

Stunned is right. Infantino was well regarded as an artist—he'd drawn the revamped Flash in the fifties—but he had zero executive experience, and his promotion didn't exactly inspire confidence among the troops. Artist Gil Kane nearly fell on the floor laughing when he heard the news.

Dig a little deeper, and the pick wasn't all that laughable. At that juncture in DC's history a safe choice just wouldn't cut it. The market was changing, and DC was getting left behind. Handing the keys to an entrenched member of the old guard wasn't going to do much to help DC catch up.

"Marvel was kicking the hell out of DC," Infantino wrote in 2003. "DC was stuck in a time warp, very comfortable with what it was doing until

Marvel came along with very clean, new, sharp material and chopped them up. DC needed a kick in the rump. And they brought me on board to do it."

Infantino also proved a logical choice because he excelled in the one area of publishing his bosses cared most about: cover design. Before his promotion to editorial director Infantino had been put in charge of all of DC's covers. Irwin Donenfeld, who analyzed sales via cover images like a gambler studying a racing form, had discovered that Infantino's covers sold better than those drawn by other artists. So Infantino stopped penciling *The Flash* with November 1967's #174 and concentrated almost exclusively on the publishing house's covers.

The move drew the attention of Stan Lee, who soon reached out to Infantino to offer him a job at Marvel for $3,000 more than the $20,000 Infantino was currently making at DC. Money talks, and Infantino decided to take the offer. He even went as far as to tell his editor, Julie Schwartz, he was quitting.

Then Liebowitz called, asking to take Infantino out to lunch. Over the meal at a nearby French restaurant the DC president slyly challenged Infantino's fighting spirit. He told the artist, "I like you a lot. But I never thought you were afraid of a challenge." The line hit Infantino "between the eyes," and he vowed to return to DC the next day.

With a raise, of course. Thanks to the offer from Lee, DC upped Infantino's pay to $30,000 a year. It was money well spent. DC's covers soon improved.

"It was a very seismic shift because the DC covers had been writer-driven," says Mark Evanier. "They were about an interesting situation, which you could figure out if you read the word balloons. Most of the *Superman* covers for a long time had Superman and Lois Lane just standing around reacting to some plot point. And then after Carmine took over cover design, the covers more and more were depicting interesting visual scenes."

At the time Marvel's covers were leaping off the newsstands. They were about energy and dynamism and often captured the split-second before cataclysmic violence erupted, complete with cocked fists and gritted teeth. A streaking Silver Surfer is about to smash into a coiled Thor, or the Thing and the Hulk are set to unload punches to each others' faces. (It was rumored that DC's artists were discouraged from depicting violent conflict on the covers.)

"Marie Severin, who oversaw every cover coming out of Marvel, gave me a tutorial one day," says Steve Englehart, a future star writer who began at Marvel in 1971. "She said the whole secret of Marvel is: you can stand across a room and look at a Marvel cover and know what's going on. That's not the case with DC's covers. She said our covers are easier to understand."

Severin really believed in the superiority of Marvel's covers—not just for their ability to sell product but from a philosophical standpoint as well. Pinned to her office wall was a blow-up of the cover to *Flash* #198 (1970). The soppy image showed the hero on his knees, hands clasped in prayer, gazing heavenward with a tear streaming down his face, pleading, "Please make it come true, God." When asked why she decorated her wall with that image, Severin replied, "Because they're a bunch of spoongroins over at DC."

Improving DC's covers was a step in the right direction, but to quote an adage from DC editor Jack Schiff, "The cover sells that month's issue. But the insides sell next month's." DC's problem in 1968 under its new owners was that the insides of its books hadn't changed all that much.

But Infantino, now in charge of editorial, set out to chart a new course.

"Infantino was certainly under a lot of pressure," says Friedrich, who began writing for DC in 1967. "DC has corporate owners. Marvel is now releasing tons of titles and threatening DC's space on the newsstands. DC was getting their hat handed to them, and they knew they had to do something different."

The company's new editorial director began trying to let some "fresh air" in by hiring new people. DC had been virtually a closed shop, with the same men in editorial working with the same batch of writers and artists for years. New talent wouldn't even bother applying because they knew they had little chance of breaking in.

One of the only new faces who had been able to break through was Neal Adams. In the early sixties Adams had been doing advertising work and drawing a syndicated comic strip. When that was canceled, he went looking for work. He phoned DC, and to his surprise he was given a meeting with DC's war books editor Bob Kanigher. The editors had shut him out previously, but now with Marvel's surge, DC was in panic mode and needed new blood.

"I was the only one that they hired who came in out of the sky from their point of view, and they wouldn't hire anyone else. I was the only one

"Have you noticed the sorry mess of Marvel IMITATIONS making the scene lately? Imitation may be the sincerest form of flattery and all that jazz, but we wanna make darn sure no dyed-in-the-wool Marvel madman gets stuck with one of those inferior 'Brand Echh' versions of the real thing."

—Stan Lee on the competition in October 1965

"That's why everyone calls his magazines Brand I. I is for imitator and I for 'I'm great.' Actually, we feel this hambo will be remembered when Shakespeare and Scott are forgotten—not before!"

—Superman editor Mort Weisinger on Stan Lee in March 1966

since 1953," Adams says. "They had built up the habits of a decades—let's keep all the other people out, give work to the people that you have, protect them, and that's it. Don't change. I was able to penetrate the insanity."

Adams was assigned short stories at DC, beginning in 1967. As it turns out, he might have ended up at Marvel instead.

"When [Adams's newspaper strip] *Ben Casey* was canceled, I rushed into Stan's office to get him to call Neal to sign him up," says John Romita Sr., a former Marvel artist and art director. "But he'd already signed with DC."

It would be a missed opportunity. Adams would go on to create some of the most iconic images in DC's—and comic book—history, and his art would become closely associated with the publisher during that formative time period.

DC gradually gave its new artist more substantial work, including the debut of Deadman, introduced in the October 1967 issue of *Strange Adventures*. Deadman was the ghost of a murdered acrobat who had the power to possess living things. The strip, written initially by Arnold Drake, was among DC's more sophisticated offerings and would go down as an important step in the maturation of the art form.

Adams's art was certainly a leap forward. Detailed and nearly photo-realistic, without a trace of cartoony-ness, it was something new for DC.

Adams also shook up his pages with creative panel layouts beyond the usual grid pattern. The look was so jarring that it took some time for DC's readers to get acclimated.

"Neal Adams' artwork was just terrible," a letter writer griped in *Spectre* #4 (June 1968), another superhero strip Adams was drawing. Today original covers and pages of that same "terrible" artwork would go for tens of thousands of dollars at auction.

In 1968 Infantino began airing out DC's musty editorial ranks. He felt that the editors had too much of a "literary" bent (the pipes and elbow patches didn't help), and he attempted to emphasize the art side of the business for a change. Comic books are, after all, a visual medium. Infantino helped bring in four new editors, all of whom were artists. The move was a risky one and represented a major break from tradition. Editors were typically writers, not artists. Did artists know enough about story and dialogue to oversee comic book production?

The first two hired were Joe Orlando and Dick Giordano. Orlando was an Italian immigrant who'd drawn for *Mad* and a horror magazine called *Creepy*. Giordano, considered one of the medium's all-time best inkers, had been working at Charlton, a second-tier publisher in Connecticut that produced superhero, war, and horror comics.

"When I went to DC, they wanted me to respond to Marvel," the late Giordano said in 1998. "They were looking for new editors because they had been comfortably sitting on their oars and Marvel sailed right past DC as the industry leader. So DC was looking for ways to get back into the business."

Joe Kubert was also brought on staff. Kubert, a professional artist since the 1940s, was best known for his work on DC's war titles and for cocreating the Silver Age Hawkman. In the seventies he would open a New Jersey school for cartoonists bearing his name.

"Wear a tie," Infantino told Kubert. "We're editors now."

The last of the new batch of editorial hires was Mike Sekowsky, a tall, pale artist whose head was gashed by a big scar left over from a childhood accident. Sekowsky had worked for Marvel before embarking on a long run of DC's *Justice League of America*.

Longtime editors Julie Schwartz and Murray Boltinoff were kept on for "balance," in Infantino's words, but those considered a drag on DC's bold, new direction were let go, including George Kashdan, who'd been handling *Aquaman* and *Metamorpho*. Jack Schiff, who'd overseen Batman in the late fifties and early sixties, retired.

To Orlando and the others, coming into DC's entrenched culture in 1968 was an intimidating experience.

"It was like walking into a bank and asking for a loan without any collateral," Orlando said in 1975. "The analogy being that I didn't have any collateral as an editor and here I was sitting behind a desk making decisions. I'd hear whispered things like, 'This won't last.'"

With the new editors came an influx of new talent—young new writers and artists, the likes of which DC hadn't seen for years. The migration caused a bit of a culture clash.

One day in 1969 the DC executives were bitching to the editors that two delivery boys were being allowed to sit in an outer office all day. "Those aren't delivery boys," Giordano told them. "Those are our writers."

The "delivery boys" were Steve Skeates and Denny O'Neil, both in their twenties. Skeates had previously worked at Marvel and had written Charlton's Judomaster, a martial arts hero. O'Neil was a former journalist and a counterculture rebel. When he'd graduated high school, the principal told his mother, "We don't ever, under any circumstances, want to see Dennis here again." O'Neil had been attracted to comics by their outsider status.

"Comic books were disreputable, and that was fine by me," O'Neil says.

Like Skeates, O'Neil had also worked for Marvel and with Giordano at Charlton and was lured to DC with the promise of more money. (During their early days at DC the two were forbidden from walking by the president's office, lest the old man have a heart attack from their unkempt appearance.)

Mike Friedrich was another fresh face. He'd become acquainted with DC's editors by writing fan letters, and he sold his first professional script in 1967 while still just a teenager. Desperate to shake up the aging company, DC was suddenly hellbent on working with people who were born after the horse-and-buggy era. New editor Orlando swore he wouldn't hire a writer over the age of thirty-five.

"I wrote a couple of scripts for them my freshman year, and they rolled out the red carpet for me in the summer of 1968 and treated me like the second coming," Friedrich says. "I was the guy who was going to deliver the young perspective."

Marv Wolfman and Len Wein, longtime fans then in their early twenties, also began getting work. New blood began filtering in on the art side as well. Editors were pressured to modernize the look of their books, and the solution was often to bring in new pencilers and inkers.

"When Carmine rose to power he began throwing out a lot of old free-lancers," Evanier says. "There were a lot of guys who had been working for DC since the forties, and Carmine decided that their work was stale, which perhaps it was."

Many of the artists who'd been handling the art chores on the Superman titles for years were cut loose, including Wayne Boring, Jim Mooney, and George Papp.

"Before Carmine was put in as the editorial director, there was a strict house style, and if you couldn't draw that style, you couldn't get work," former production manager Bob Rozakis says.

Infantino continued to try to make DC a friendlier place to outsiders. He set aside a break room where freelancers and writers—but no editors—could sit around and talk shop. Adams, who often worked in the office, also began inviting artist friends to stop by and hang out. It ultimately proved to be a backdoor way into the company.

"When a problem came up, Joe Orlando or someone would come down and go, 'I got a new story to assign. Want to do it?'" Adams says. "I'd say, 'I have to finish some stuff. You want to try someone else? Bernie Wrightson is right over there.'"

In that way Wrightson, a horror specialist who'd go on to cocreate DC's enduring monster character Swamp Thing in 1971, got in the door. So did Howard Chaykin, Alan Weiss, and others who would become industry mainstays. When DC editors needed an artist, Adams probably had one hiding in his room.

The writer ranks experienced their own culling after Arnold Drake, *Superman* writer Otto Binder, *Batman* scribe Bill Finger, and others approached DC publisher Liebowitz and asked for benefits, such as higher pay, medical insurance, and a retirement plan. Liebowitz, never one to be particularly generous with the checkbook, shrewdly—and cynically—used the industry's two-party system to his advantage. He told the writers to speak to Marvel, and if the brass over there agreed to go along with the group's demands, so would he. You can probably see where this is going.

Drake called up Marvel and was told Marvel would grant the benefits if DC would. And round and round they went until DC ultimately eased out the veterans.

"There were always pleas of impoverishment [from management]: 'We can't give you royalties, we can't give you health insurance,'" O'Neil says. "Yet the guy who was saying that arrived to work in a chauffeur-driven German limousine."

The writers' purge ultimately left more work for the young bucks. The upheaval marked a generational transition at DC, as the old-timers who had helped create the superheroes in the thirties and forties were giving way to fans who'd grown up reading their work. The shift also marked the arrival of Marvel's sensibility at DC.

"We younger writers were loving the Marvel books," says Wolfman, who in the late 1960s was writing stories for DC's mystery anthology. "But I believe the longtime [DC] editors felt as long as DC had Superman they'd never be beaten. But as a huge Superman fan then—and now—I didn't agree. Marvel was doing really great books, and DC at the time was still aiming at little kids."

Gerry Conway, another future star who started working for DC in the late 1960s as a teenager, recalls a meeting with the young staff to figure out which of Marvel's strengths DC might be able to adopt.

"Their actual attitude was very defensive," Conway says. "[Production manager] Sol Harrison started the meeting saying, 'We want to talk about what it is about Marvel that's so good. It can't be the art, because the art is terrible, and it can't be the writing, because everyone wants to write and draw for DC. So what do you think it is?'"

Conway raised his hand and politely offered that not everyone wanted to write and draw for DC. Most of the young staffers longed to be at Marvel. The DC executives' jaws dropped.

"They thought they were the premier shop," Conway says. "They couldn't understand why people were leaving DC and going over to Marvel—people like Frank Giacoia and Gene Colan, John Romita. They were like, 'Why are you leaving?'"

Some of the higher-ups may not have understood Marvel's appeal, but Marvel's success forced DC and Infantino to begin making aggressive moves to modernize its line.

Several new titles hit stands in 1968, handled by DC's crop of new editors. The Creeper, an offbeat, demonic superhero with a wild orange mane, got his own series, courtesy of writer Denny O'Neil and artist Steve Ditko, the idiosyncratic cocreator of Spider-Man who'd left Marvel in a huff a couple of years earlier.

The Secret Six was about a team of skilled operatives who were brought together by a mysterious masked leader to battle a crazed villain. It was intended as a grittier—by DC's standards, at least—real-world book.

The Hawk and the Dove, by Skeates and Ditko, featured two brothers who are granted superpowers and soon find themselves divided on how to use them, with Hawk arguing for aggressive action and Dove favoring nonviolence. The concept was a not-too-subtle take on the political climate of the day, when the Civil Rights Movement and the Vietnam War were dividing America.

Without a doubt the strangest new title was *Brother Power the Geek*, a name that elicits bemused laughter to this day. Brother Power was Frankenstein by way of Haight-Ashbury. A mannequin owned by a group of hippies is struck by lightning and suddenly comes to life, inspiring wonder in some and fear in others. The series was written and drawn by another recent DC hire, Joe Simon, the cocreator of Marvel's Captain America with Jack Kirby. To some the move smacked of desperation.

"You've got Jack Kirby doing all this new stuff over at Marvel," Neal Adams says. "So what do you do over at DC? You hire Joe Simon, his ex-partner. That's pretty fucking desperate."

DC's established superhero titles continued to be tweaked as the editors attempted to increase the hip quotient and get its line more in step with contemporary tastes. Or at least what they thought were contemporary tastes. DC had long coasted on the success of its founding heroes, Batman, Superman, and Wonder Woman, but now some three decades after their creation and with the industry evolving, due in part to Marvel, a new tack was required.

"What happened with DC was they ran out of successful things to duplicate, so that when their Superman and Batman started to fail, they didn't have anything to imitate," artist Gil Kane said in 1978. "Instead, they had to go to the only other style that was making any money and of course that was Stan Lee's style."

Back in his 1966 memo Arnold Drake had warned DC management that the company needed to evolve on its own terms, and if it didn't, it would run the risk of being forced to ape Marvel to survive.

Which is basically what happened.

What came in the years following Kinney's acquisition of DC was—in the words of comic book writer Grant Morrison—a series of "weak and ill at ease impressions of the narrative style that came naturally to Lee."

"There was a period there where a lot of the writers were told that Marvel Comics were better written on some level, and what they learned was, 'Oh, we'll put a lot of jokes in the dialogue' or 'we'll put little funny asides in the footnotes,'" Evanier says. "We'll talk to the reader in a joking manner. There are a number of issues of *The Atom* late in the run when Gardner Fox was writing what looked like somebody doing a really bad Stan Lee imitation."

"You've got fifty-year-old men responding to the sense that we have to hip up. Horribly misguided things start happening at DC," says former DC editor Brian Augustyn. "It was this absurd weirdness that arrives from people under the gun to try to make things cooler."

One of the most bizarre stories would come in *Superman's Girlfriend Lois Lane* #106 (November 1970). The tale, written by Robert Kanigher, was entitled "I Am Curious (Black)!" and involved Lane using Superman's transformation machine to turn herself into a black woman for a day so she can investigate a story in Metropolis's "Little Africa" neighborhood. Can you dig it? Us neither.

That story was only slightly more embarrassing than the slang that began creeping into DC books.

Batman showed up in a 1967 issue of *Blackhawk* and told the team of World War II soldiers, "The Blackhawks are washed-up has-beens, out-of-date antiques. . . . To put it bluntly, they just don't swing!"

The most face-palming examples of retrofitted hipness was to be found in the *Teen Titans*. The group of heroes consisting of the younger side-kicks to DC's marquee superheroes—Robin, Aqualad, Kid Flash, and Wonder Girl—had debuted in a 1964 try-out story and later graduated to their own ongoing title. In the DC tradition the kids were clean, agreeable, and well mannered, and they rarely seemed to experience the kind of adolescent angst that real people go through.

About the only thing that marked them as teenagers was their language. In the late sixties writer Bob Haney filled the characters' speech bubbles with cringeworthy slang that felt like a middle-aged man's idea of how teenagers talked. Haney claimed he picked up words and phrases from his Woodstock, New York, barber—an aging hippie—but it's unclear if anyone on planet Earth ever talked like this.

"I like to swing, but these cats are too much," Aqualad says in one issue.

"I love Bob Haney and I love his work, but Bob had a certain style," former DC writer Paul Kupperberg says. "When Bob writes the *Teen Titans*, he's actually writing Maynard G. Krebs [a beatnik character from 1959 TV sitcom *The Many Loves of Dobie Gillis*] dialogue for the teenagers and hippies of 1968. So it's like, 'Cool, daddy-o.' No one said 'daddy-o' in 1968 except the Teen Titans."

Wonder Woman was also dragged kicking and screaming into the modern world. Sales of the title had been in free fall throughout the 1960s, from 230,000 copies per month in 1961 to 166,365 in 1968. Beginning with issue #178 (October 1968), the heroine got a dramatic makeover courtesy of writer O'Neil and artists Sekowsky and Giordano. For starters, Wonder Woman lost her powers, which was an easy and increasingly common trick to bring DC's godlike heroes closer to Marvel's more street-level characters. Instead of Wonder Woman, she became plain old Diana Prince, opened a clothing boutique, and began dressing in mod fashions—hip miniskirts, groovy A-line dresses, and skin-tight jumpsuits straight out of TV's *The Avengers*.

Also notable is that Prince, like Marvel's heroes, began operating out of New York City, not one of the fictional metropolises in which DC's stories were typically set.

"That revamp was absolutely a reaction to Marvel's success," says Tim Hanley, author of *Wonder Woman Unbound: The Curious History of the World's Most Famous Heroine*. "She was made a normal woman in New York City with a day job and all of that, just like a Marvel character, and the book became more mature. There was more death, more anguish."

The new direction goosed sales—for a little while, at least. Sell-through of the rebooted issues jumped "like crazy," hitting 60 to 65 percent, according to Infantino.

"The new Wonder Woman was given a chance—(a last chance for the book)—and it worked!" Sekowsky wrote in #189, two years after the revamp. "I can honestly say that I am quite pleased to have taken a sow's ear and turned it into a silk purse. . . . I personally feel that too many of DC's stories are still being written and plotted for the year 1940 instead of 1970."

One of the books that was still stuck in 1940 was *Batman*. The Caped Crusader's sister title, *Detective*, had undergone a much-heralded reboot back in 1964, but, due to contractual obligations, Bob Kane and his studio were still handling *Batman*. When Kane got word of DC's proposed sale to Kinney, he threatened to scotch the deal, so Liebowitz paid him to go away. Kane walked with a million bucks, paid in yearly $50,000 installments for twenty years. DC was now free to begin using artists who brought a more contemporary look to the character.

"Everybody was happy that Bob Kane was gone," Infantino would say.

DC's stories also began to show a little of Marvel's patented characterization. The days when all the heroes were so homogenous that you could swap speech bubbles among them were fading. O'Neil took over the *Justice League of America* in the fall of 1968, and suddenly the heroes are bickering like something straight out of the *Fantastic Four*.

"We're trying to conduct a meeting. Save your gab-fest for later," an irritated Superman tells Batman, Green Arrow, and the Atom in issue #66 (November 1968). "Par-don us, Superman!" the Atom fires back sarcastically. "We didn't mean to offend you."

"The stories were beginning to be influenced by Stan Lee," O'Neil says. "That characterization came from Stan. We're not talking subtle, nineteenth-century novel characterization here. But you could tell one character from another."

In the end Infantino's new titles and revamps proved to be bolder in direction than in sales. Many of the recent additions to the line were quickly axed. *Brother Power the Geek* didn't even geek its way to #3. The series was unceremoniously snuffed out in its infancy after uptight editor Weisinger got ahold of a copy and stormed into Liebowitz's office.

"Don't you know what you got here?" Weisinger said. "This is all about the drug culture, hippies, drugs and street people. We can't publish stuff like this."

Liebowitz capitulated, and *Brother Power* died after just two flower-powered issues.

The Hawk and the Dove was canceled with #6 and *The Secret Six* with #7. The books hadn't been around long enough to attract an audience. Before 1968 DC had generally shown more patience, giving books a year or two to find their footing. That changed under Infantino, and now titles were being killed quickly, almost with a bloodlust.

"Carmine had no business training, he had no real sense of the changing marketplace," former DC editor Bob Greenberger says. "Carmine was very mercurial and was approving and canceling books almost on whim.

Carmine wouldn't let books breathe. At the first hint he would cancel it, and then management would come and say, 'You need five more percentage points on the newsstand,' and Carmine would approve books on a whim without stopping to figure out, 'All right, is this the right book at the right time?'"

The erratic schedule frustrated readers. Future DC writer Evanier was president of a local comic book club in the late sixties. Each week he'd stand in front of the members and deliver a news report on the industry. And every week he'd announce that another DC title had been canceled. It became a running joke.

"We had a piano in the clubhouse where we met," Evanier says. "There was another member who played the piano really well, and I would get up and say, 'And now it's time for—,' and the guy on the on the piano would play a little fanfare, and then we'd go to the DC cancellation of the week. I'd announce that they were canceling *The Secret Six*, and everyone would laugh and go, 'Well, there goes that.' That is not a healthy atmosphere for your company."

"DC experimented, but without a direction," Neal Adams says, "they had no overall plan. It was like shooting guns in the dark. They didn't know what they were doing."

One time DC's flailing executives tried to develop a strategy by talking to focus groups of children. Adams was invited to one in the late sixties at DC's offices.

"It was held in the fucking board room, and one of the executives says, 'Okay, we're here to rap about comic books,'" Adams recalls. "Ugh, really? That started it off great. Board room and guy saying let's rap about comics."

The kids were asked, If you could create your own superhero, what would it be? One young boy says his hero would be like Batman, only bigger and stronger. One girl says her hero would be like Wonder Woman only smarter and more beautiful. And so it went.

"We go out of the meeting, and the executives ask, 'We don't understand this. What did that mean?'" Adams says. "I said, 'What it means is that they don't want to create characters. They like the characters that we have. They just want us to do them better and to surprise them.'"

Simply doing better comics may not have been enough. One problem DC faced at the end of the 1960s was that the market for comics—and print media in general—was shrinking. Fewer outlets carried their wares, as newsstands and mom-and-pop candy stores began to disappear. The country was becoming more of a car culture, as the exodus from cities had shifted most of America's population from the denser urban areas to the suburbs. TV also began to consume more leisure time.

A 1969 price hike didn't help matters, dealing a crippling blow to a struggling market. Early that year DC was forced to boost its cover price from 12 cents to 15 cents. Marvel followed suit a couple of months later. The 20 percent increase clearly broke young budgets. Readers scurried for the exits, and sales of some DC titles were battered with 20 percent drops in circulation. The declines were less steep at Marvel, and for the first time the publisher was able to crack the top ten. *The Amazing Spider-Man* averaged a circulation of 372,352 for 1969, making it the seventh-best-selling title of the year.

The market was so dire that DC's new corporate master nearly took drastic—and permanent—action.

"I remember Denny [O'Neil] came down the hall in 1969 and said that the Kinney board had a vote to shut down DC," writer Mike Friedrich recalls. "And they voted not to shut it down because of the ancillary revenue, which was already enough by 1969 to make it worth keeping going a publishing entity that was in the red."

One of the few bright spots, besides the money generated from superhero merchandise, came with Giordano's upset victory for best editor at the 1969 Alley Award—a title Stan Lee had taken home every year since 1963. The news ignited a celebration at the DC offices.

But not all the talent was walking through the door at DC in the late 1960s. Some was walking out. Neal Adams, intrigued by how much control Marvel's artists had over the stories and layout, went to see Stan Lee about doing some work. Adams, a fast-rising star in the business, was already familiar to Lee.

"Stan said, 'I'll be honest with you. The only DC book the guys at Marvel are reading is Deadman,'" Adams says.

The artist was offered any title in the Marvel stable. Literally any title. Instead of opting for *Spider-Man* or the *Fantastic Four*, Adams asked what the worst-selling title was. The answer: *The X-Men*.

"Lee said, 'We're going to cancel it,'" Adams recalls. "I said, 'Great, I'll take it. You won't pay much attention to me.'"

Lee agreed, but then demanded that if Adams was going to work for Marvel, he'd have to leave DC behind. Adams said no and got up to leave.

Before he hit the door Lee was chasing him. "Wait, hang on. It's no problem."

Adams's first Marvel work appeared in *X-Men* #56 (May 1969). The title had started strong in 1963 but had long ago lost its juice, as its founding team of Lee and Kirby had moved on. Since then a succession of artists and writers (including Arnold Drake whose Doom Patrol had been so similar to X-Men) had produced it, with few sparks.

Adams, along with writer Roy Thomas, brought a little sizzle to the once-moribund title. Adams broke the page into unusual shapes and drew figures bursting from the confines of the panel borders. He peppered his stories at key moments with awe-inspiring full-page splashes that practically smacked the reader across the face with drama.

"It was electric," says Chris Claremont, then a Marvel assistant. "Neal's stuff would come in, and I'd look at it and say, 'This is magnificent.'"

The most shocking thing about that debut issue didn't come in the story pages; it came in the credit box. Following the names of Lee, Thomas, inker Tom Palmer, and letterer Herb Cooper, a line trumpeted, "And introducing the penciling wizardry of Neal Adams." No pseudonym. No nom de plume created by combining the names of his children. Adams, one of DC's top artists, was using his real name in a Marvel comic. And with that, the whole fake name game collapsed. Freelancers were now able to work for both companies without having to act like a spy sneaking into East Berlin.

"If people believe something is true, by believing it, they make it true," Adams says. "By showing them it's not true, that it's just something some idiot made up, it falls apart."

Adams informed Infantino that he was doing work for Marvel and assured the boss that it wouldn't affect his DC work. Infantino was annoyed but, in the end, chose not to put up a fight.

"Carmine didn't say anything," Adams says. "He'd have to have shoveled an awful lot of balls into his pants that morning to say something."

Another DC name who wandered over to Marvel was Jim Shooter. The boy wonder had been making a name for himself writing the Legion of Super-Heroes since 1966, but he was growing increasingly unhappy from the abuse his editor, Mort Weisinger, heaped on him.

"I lived in Pittsburgh, and Mort and I had a regularly scheduled phone call Thursday nights after the *Batman* TV show," Shooter says. "He'd call to go over what I sent in, and all of a sudden the guy's on the phone, 'You fucking idiot! You moron! You fool! Can't you spell?' I'm fourteen, and this big important guy from New York is calling up and calling me a moron."

Fed up, Shooter phoned Stan Lee in search of a new job.

"I'm a comic book writer, and I need a place to work," Shooter told Lee.

"Where do you work?" Lee asked. When Shooter told him, Lee snapped, "We hate DC stuff. If you're a DC writer, you can't work for us."

Shooter insisted he was different.

"My nickname at DC is 'the Marvel writer,'" Shooter told him. And with that, a meeting was arranged. Shooter turned up at the Marvel offices, and he and Lee clicked, talking comics for some three hours. He walked out with a job offer.

When Shooter told Weisinger he was leaving for Marvel, the editor was incensed. "Now you stabbed me in the back, you weasel," he yelled.

It was one of the last insults the cranky misanthrope would hurl while at DC. Weisinger had been threatening to retire for years, and each time Liebowitz would give him more money to stay. It was a great scheme—until it finally backfired.

In 1970 Weisinger told Infantino, once again, he was thinking about retiring, and Infantino, who'd had enough of the editor's ploys, replied, "Well, OK. We'll miss you. Bye." Weisinger was shocked. Two weeks later he even returned to the office, telling Infantino he'd reconsidered and didn't want to actually retire. He appreciated the changes that DC had been making, and he'd like to stay, thankyouverymuch. Infantino stood firm, telling the Superman editor that his career at DC was over.

After three decades Mort Weisinger, the man who once compared writers to oranges—"You squeeze them until there's no juice left then you throw them away"—the man who most embodied DC's conservative mindset, the man who was disliked by so many, was gone. His final issues were *Action Comics* #393 (October 1970) and *Superman* #232 (January 1971).

That same year would bring an even bigger news story. DC was set to pull off perhaps the greatest coup ever in the rivalry's history, a brazen act of gamesmanship that could potentially shift the industry's balance of power. In its increasingly desperate bid to compete with Marvel comics, half-measures were no longer good enough. Instead, why not go straight to the source and steal the man who was arguably most responsible for Marvel's success?

In 1969 DC set out to do just that.

The "Devilish Competition"
Pulls Off a Headline-Worthy Heist

"Carmine was trying to beat Marvel by getting Jack
Kirby, their co-creator. He thought we could get there
faster by having Kirby on our side."

—DC editor Dick Giordano

"**P**ossibly the biggest news story in Marvel history," fan magazine
Marvelmania breathlessly proclaimed at the time. Another fanzine,
Newfangles, rushed an "extra" edition to press to cover the momentous
event.

Jack Kirby was coming to DC.

The bombshell defection had been brewing for some time. Kirby and
DC's Carmine Infantino, two industry dinosaurs, had known each other
for years, and Infantino's brother, Jimmy, had worked with Kirby briefly
back in the 1950s. When Infantino was put in charge of DC in 1967, Kirby
phoned his old acquaintance to offer friendly congratulations.

"Carmine told Jack that if he ever wanted to leave Marvel, he could
come to DC," says Steve Sherman, who worked as Kirby's assistant beginning in the late 1960s.

Toward the end of 1969 Infantino found himself in California working on DC's upcoming *Super Friends* cartoon. He phoned Kirby, who had

relocated from New York to California earlier in the year, to have dinner. The two talked business, and Kirby showed Infantino three covers for a line of interconnected comic series: *Forever People*, *New Gods*, and *Mister Miracle*.

"They're sensational. When is Marvel putting them out?" Infantino asked.

"They're my creations, and I don't want to do them at Marvel," Kirby said. "Would you make me an offer?"

No one had to ask Infantino twice. He had a contract quickly drawn up that would pay Kirby more than he was earning at Marvel. It required the writer-artist to produce fifteen pages a week—a crippling amount for most people, though not for the speedy Kirby.

"It was that simple," Infantino later wrote.

Kirby sat on the news for a bit before finally phoning his longtime collaborator Stan Lee in March 1970 and dropping the atom bomb that he was going over to the "Devilish Competition," as *Marvelmania* termed it. Lee was hurt and confused.

"I used to wonder why he left," Lee said in 1993. "I said to myself that he was just sick of the credits always saying, 'By Stan Lee and Jack Kirby,' with me as the editor. I think he wanted to prove how good he was without me, but I have no way of knowing if that's right."

Kirby had been growing increasingly unhappy at Marvel and was especially dissatisfied with the new contract he was being offered. He was also becoming estranged from Lee, a man who had once been his errand boy but was now his boss. Kirby felt Lee was hogging all the credit for Marvel's success, and Kirby also despaired that the company was distancing him from his creations. When a *Silver Surfer* solo comic had been launched in 1968, it was John Buscema who's been tapped to pencil it, not Kirby, the character's creator.

"At DC, I'm given the privilege of being associated with my own ideas," Kirby said in 1971. "If I did come up with an idea at Marvel, they'd take it away from me and I lost all association with it. I was never given credit for the writing which I did. Most of the writing at Marvel is done by the artist from the script."

Lee announced the shocking resignation in the September 1970 edition of Bullpen Bulletins, downplaying the importance. "That's where we're at—under-staffed, under-manned, and under-fed—but as bushy-tailed and bewildered as ever!" he wrote. "So watch for the fireworks, friend."

"At Marvel they put on a brave face, but they were clearly upset and not quite sure what would happen," Mike Friedrich says.

The idea of Marvel Comics without Kirby seemed almost inconceivable. "Jolly Jack" had had a major hand in creating so many of Marvel's now-iconic characters—Fantastic Four, Thor, Iron Man, the X-Men, Doctor Doom. Stan Lee may have been the public face of Marvel, but Kirby was the heart. At that point in 1970 he was virtually synonymous with the publisher. And now DC had him.

Kirby's reception was somewhat chilly.

"The problem was that not everyone at DC was happy to have Jack there," says Kirby's then-assistant Mark Evanier. "They worked for the company for years and years, and all of a sudden now they're kissing the ass of the guy who was doing those books [at Marvel] that were supposedly inferior."

Whatever animosity may have existed didn't dampen DC's full-court marketing press. "The Great One is coming!" shouted an ad from the spring of 1970. "People! Places! Things! So powerful in concept, it's almost terrifying!"

Despite the hype, the announcement of Kirby landed with a bit of a thud.

According to Kirby, Infantino had initially asked him to "save" DC's flagship title, *Superman*. The possibility is difficult for our puny brains to conceive. Marvel's biggest, most recognizable artist on the world's most recognizable superhero. Kirby was reluctant to take the job, fearing that someone else would lose work to make way for him.

In Infantino's telling, however, Kirby lobbied to take over *Superman*, but the editorial director was hesitant to give him such a high-profile job and wanted to slowly ease him into the DC pool.

Either way the result is the same: Jack Kirby, the greatest living comic book artist, got put on . . . *Superman's Pal Jimmy Olsen*.

Say what, now?

The title starred the Man of Steel's freckle-faced photographer sidekick and often featured goofy adventures, like the time Olsen collected Superman's tears and ended up mistakenly building a bomb with them, or the time he was transformed into a superhero called Ultra-Olsen.

Kirby took over with #133 (October 1970) and immediately changed everything. He introduced far-out concepts and story lines that bore little resemblance to the inoffensive juvenile tripe that had come just an issue before. Straight out of the gate Kirby ran afoul of the DC corporate powers-that-be. His rougher, boxier style didn't necessarily mesh with his new company's smooth, polished look.

"There were also just some people at DC who didn't like the way he drew," Evanier recalls.

One who took exception was Sol Harrison, DC's intimidating production manager and a member of the old guard who, now that Mort Weisinger had retired, most represented the conservative, immovable DC.

"When I first met Harrison in 1970, almost the first thing he said was, 'Can you tell Jack to stop drawing square fingers? He should draw more like [DC's favored Superman artist] Curt Swan,'" Evanier recalls. "But I thought to myself: Who do you think you just got? You guys just landed the top artist in the business, and you want him to draw like everything you've been publishing for twenty years?"

Kirby soon ran into trouble with his depiction of Superman. The character was a lucrative license for DC, appearing on lunch boxes and T-shirts, and the publisher insisted that the character always appear on-model in the comics; deviation or experimentation was not tolerated. But Kirby drew the Man of Steel in his own distinctive Kirby style—a bit less handsome, a bit more angular. After Kirby turned in his art pages DC ordered other artists, whose work was closer to DC's preferred look, to redraw Superman's face. For all of DC's lip service about moving in a new direction, the company still couldn't be nudged out of its comfort zone.

"We didn't enjoy changing an artist's work," Infantino wrote in his autobiography. "It takes time and costs money, but sometimes it is necessary."

The changes were potentially about more than just licensing. The higher-ups at DC hated the Marvel style so much that they simply couldn't cope with a "Marvelized" version of their flagship character, according to Evanier. DC editor Mike Sekowsky once told Kirby's assistant that, to Infantino, having Kirby's Superman redrawn was about scoring a victory over Marvel. It was proof that Marvel's star artist still wasn't good enough to cut it at DC. (Infantino denied the accusation.)

Kirby was apparently unhappy about the touch-ups but didn't protest all that much. After all, he hadn't come to DC to draw Superman; he wanted to be free to unleash his own wild, original concepts that would harness his imagination and push the medium forward.

Late in 1970 the first of Kirby's brand-new comics hit the racks. The so-called Fourth World was an ambitious cosmic saga made up of three connected titles set in the same world with overlapping characters. It began with *Forever People* and the *New Gods*, released December 1970, and it continued a few months later with *Mister Miracle*.

The family of titles involved a battle between godlike beings inhabiting twin planets created from the destruction of a larger world. New Genesis, a fertile, Utopian planet, represented good, while Apokolips, a fiery, barren dystopian world, represented evil.

"New Genesis and that demon's pit, Apokolips, one drifting forever in the shadow of the other," one character says in *New Gods* #1, describing an eternally binary relationship that, come to think of it, nicely encapsulates the state of superhero comic book publishing.

The series introduced a host of new characters, many of whom would become DC universe mainstays. Darkseid was the angular-headed ruler of Apokolips and one of the great comic book baddies. His son, Orion, was raised on New Genesis and grows to oppose his father. The Fourth World was a potent stew of myth, symbolism, and family angst. and it came loaded with a steady stream of concepts so heady that they were likely to induce 1960s acid flashbacks. Boom tubes? Whiz wagons? Mother boxes? So much crazy stuff was packed onto every page that, for the readers of regular superhero comics in 1971, it must have been bit like trying to drink out of a fire hose.

Once at DC Kirby's animosity toward his former employer began manifesting in his work. In *Mister Miracle* #6, released in late 1971, the hero runs across a shyster named Funky Flashman, who is a dead ringer for Stan Lee, right down to the beard, toupee, and snappy banter. The character was originally conceived as a satire of a man who ran a Marvel fan club and ripped off its members, but once Kirby started drawing the story, Flashman morphed into Lee.

"In the shadow world between success and failure, there lives the driven little man who dreams of having it all!!!" read a caption describing Flashman. "The opportunistic spoiler without character or values, who preys on all things like a cannibal!!!—including you!!!"

(Kirby must have been getting paid by the exclamation mark.)

"I remember when he showed me the pages," says Kirby's former assistant Sherman. "He was laughing. We all were."

Flashman runs the Mockingbird Estates, a slave plantation, and gets paid for admittedly doing nothing. As the story opens, Flashman is seen literally taking money out of the mouth of a bust that looks suspiciously like Jack Kirby. Flashman is joined by his obsequious sidekick, Houseroy, who is clearly meant to represent Lee's then number two at Marvel, Roy Thomas. The two set out to scam Mister Miracle using Flashman's slick verbal skills.

"I felt Funky Flashman was a nasty business," Roy Thomas says. "I think Stan was a bit hurt by it, to see that nastiness coming out of Jack. In 1974, when I had a meeting with Jack when I was still editor-in-chief and Jack was thinking about coming back to Marvel, I told him that the Funky Flashman thing had hurt Stan's feelings, but he wouldn't hold it against Jack. Jack just laughed and said it had all been in fun, but I knew he was lying. And I guess he knew I knew. Nowadays I often call myself 'Houseroy,' but that doesn't mean I don't think it was a low point in Jack's personal career."

Although Kirby was a virtual one-man production facility—he wrote, penciled, and edited his comics out of his home in California—he still required an inker. The one DC assigned would prove to be a disaster and lead to yet another strange chapter in the Marvel-DC rivalry.

Vinnie Colletta was a Sicilian-born artist that the word "colorful" doesn't even begin to describe. He was a *Godfather* type straight out of central casting, with a salesman's charm and a Hollywood demeanor. His prematurely graying hair was immaculately styled at all times, and he dressed flashily, often with multiple gold chains. He once turned up at a convention wearing a white suit, white shoes, and a black shirt, unbuttoned nearly to his navel.

"Vinnie told me he thought comic book people were the dullest people in the world," says veteran inker Joe Rubinstein, who began working for DC in the 1970s. "Whether he was or wasn't, he tried to come across as a mini-mafioso, and a loan shark and tough and that he knew people, and all that stuff."

Colletta had been working steadily since the 1950s on both DC and Marvel books and had recently inked Kirby on *Thor*. His reputation was less as a great artist than as a fast one.

"Vinnie took great pride in the fact that he solved everyone's problem by inking a job in three days that should have taken ten days," Rubinstein says. "He was a hero because he got the job done. One of the ways he did it was to erase backgrounds and black out figures. It's like [artist] Gil Kane said: 'Vinnie is the best inker in the business except for everyone else.'"

DC assigned Colletta to work on the high-profile "Fourth World" books in part because Colletta was cheap and the company was paying Kirby so much that it was forced to cut corners elsewhere. It may also have been a way to soften Kirby's art and bring it more in line with DC's house style.

Kirby worked quickly, and with the *New Gods* at least, the first issue was completed about six months before it went to press—a rarity in the frantic world of periodical comics. Working so far ahead is great for deadlines. On the downside it was not ideal for security. The Fourth World was Kirby's splashy new original work for DC, and Kirby had major concerns that the pages would be leaked to his former employer.

"Jack was always either paranoid or cautious—whatever word you want to use," Kirby's former assistant Evanier says. "Jack didn't want to have Marvel rush out imitations of [his DC work], which he thought was possible, so they were under lock and key."

Even the other editors at DC were not allowed a peek at Kirby's new titles before they were published. When Evanier visited the offices in 1970, Julie Schwartz—a fairly senior honcho at the company—begged him to tell what he knew about the *New Gods*.

Kirby's paranoia might not have been unfounded.

"There were a number of cases where Marvel did stuff around that time that Jack was convinced were stolen from him, like covers and a couple of ideas for comics," Evanier says.

In one case Kirby had drawn two pages of a proposed strip called *Galaxy Green* about warrior women in outer space. It was meant for an underground-style DC magazine that ultimately never saw the light of day. Marvel later did a tale similar in theme and style.

The May 1971 edition of Marvel's *Savage Tales* magazine contained a strip called the Femizons, by Stan Lee and John Romita, about a race of futuristic Amazon-like women. Whether or not it was just a coincidence, Kirby believed his idea had been pilfered.

Kirby may have been paranoid, but the fact was that spying between the two companies was absolutely a concern at the time.

In 1971, when Kirby's Fourth World was rolling out, DC discovered that it had a real-life supervillain in its midst. Late at night, after most everyone had gone home, a certain freelance employee was ransacking the company's offices, rifling through desks and looking for corporate intel to leak to fan publications or, worse, to Marvel.

To catch the spy, DC's senior staff launched a clever disinformation campaign that, like all proper top-secret operations, even had its own code name: Blockbuster. Infantino drew up a phony corporate memo to his editors announcing that DC was going to raise prices and start putting out five-hundred-page comic books costing $1.

"They put the memo under some papers in the 'out' tray of someone in the production department because that's where [the spy] was working and basically just waited to see what would happen," recalls former DC production manager Bob Rozakis.

The trap worked. Word of the new Blockbuster books mysteriously found its way to various fanzines and, of course, over to Marvel's Manhattan offices. The next thing anyone knew, Marvel editor Stan Lee was talking about doing a five-hundred-page book for a dollar.

Neither company ever ended up producing the Blockbuster issues. As for the spy, he was soon caught after accidentally outing himself.

"He tipped his own hand by bringing up Blockbuster in a conversation with someone at DC," Rozakis says. The freelancer was henceforth no longer allowed in the DC office after hours.

Around the same time Larry Lieber applied to DC Comics. On paper Lieber was a strong candidate. He was a seasoned writer with years of experience on high-profile titles, including *Iron Man*. He did have one major ding against him, though: he was Stan Lee's brother.

"I sent the work over to DC, and I never got any word," Lieber says.

Then one day he ran into DC's Carmine Infantino at a Manhattan watering hole. "I reminded him that I sent over some work and never heard anything," Lieber says. "He looked at me and said, 'You mean, that was on the level?!' They thought that Marvel was sending me over to spy to get their wonderful secrets."

But Jack Kirby would soon become the victim of actual espionage involving his Fourth World books. One day while Evanier was visiting New York, Kirby's assistant went over to the Marvel offices to hang out, where he discovered something shocking. There he spotted photocopies of as-yet-unpublished pages from Kirby's *New Gods* #1 tacked to the wall. He was aghast. The pages that had been kept under lock and key had somehow found their way over to the competition.

"[Marvel art director] Marie Severin asked me for Jack's address in Los Angeles, and I gave it to her," Evanier recalls. "When I got back to LA I called Jack and I said, 'You're not going to like this, but *New Gods* #1 is up at the Marvel office. They've read it,' and Jack says, 'I know. I just got a fan letter from Marie.'"

The leak enraged Kirby, and they soon identified a culprit: Vinnie Colletta, perhaps the only man who had access to the work and could have given it to Marvel. The news came as little surprise to Kirby, who had suspected Colletta of being a Marvel spy.

It was also no huge shock to DC's editorial director, Carmine Infantino. Colletta had once come to him with a peculiar offer. "I know Stan Lee, I know you well," Colletta had said. "I can carry stories back and forth to you guys, whatever you want." Infantino refused.

"[Colletta] tried to make himself something he wasn't: important," Infantino said in 2010.

Leaking the Kirby pages might have been about just that.

"In Vinnie's case he was just trying to curry favor," says Gerry Conway, who was working for Marvel at the time. "He was always trying to do that. It was not appropriate, but I don't think it was part of a master plan at Marvel."

For the breach Colletta was fired from the Fourth World books, and Mike Royer took over with *New Gods* #5, *Mister Miracle* #5, and *Forever People* #6. The change may have improved the finished art, but Kirby's new DC books were unfortunately not long for this world.

The titles had sold decently enough in the beginning, with the excitement of Marvel's biggest star's defection stoking interest. The issue in which he took over *Superman's Pal Jimmy Olsen* represented the biggest sales jump in DC history from one issue to the next of an established title. Hardcore comic book readers, whose numbers were growing in the seventies, seemed to be especially smitten with Kirby.

"We just followed him," says Rick Newton, a comic book fan since the 1960s who preferred DC to Marvel but grew to love Kirby. "My Marvel friends would have followed him even if I hadn't. They knew long before I did that he was what most artists and writers were trying to be in that medium."

To many readers, however, Kirby was great with grand ideas and trippy concepts, but he needed a writer to dialogue his stories and an editor to focus his work. As much as it might have pained him, he could have used someone like Stan Lee. Without him Kirby seemed adrift.

"I remember pitching an idea to Julie [Schwartz] that would involve some of Jack's characters, and Julie was highly resistant to it," says writer Mike Friedrich. "There was a lot of reluctance to touch Jack's stuff because they didn't understand it. And who did? Most of it was incomprehensible."

"To my ear he couldn't write," says Steve Englehart, a Marvel writer at the time. "I've said for a long time: I wish that DC would republish the Fourth World in English."

Infantino finally swallowed his pride, accepted defeat, and did what needed to be done. *New Gods* and *Forever People* were discontinued with their eleventh issues. *Mister Miracle* lasted to #18, and Kirby was moved to other projects within DC.

"When they stole Kirby away from Marvel in 1970, Carmine told Kirby he could do whatever he wanted," says former DC production manager Rozakis. "And he did for a while until they started getting the sales reports, and then they thought, 'Maybe this isn't such a good idea.'"

Kirby's acquisition may not have worked out as well as DC had hoped, but DC was hardly cowed. The company also attempted to poach someone more synonymous with Marvel than its star artist: Stan Lee.

Sometime in the early seventies the bosses at DC's parent company contacted Lee about becoming their new editor-in-chief. If Kirby's defection had rocked the industry like an atom bomb, this news would have been like a supernova.

Lee had been growing increasingly restless at Marvel as founder Martin Goodman ceded more power to his son, Chip.

"Stan was intimidated a little by Martin because it was his uncle by marriage and Martin was the publisher, but Chip was just this young kid who got a job because he was the son," Roy Thomas says. "Stan didn't want to work for Chip, so he was thinking about leaving and leveraging himself a good deal at DC."

Lee had at least one meeting with DC about switching teams. It may simply have been a negotiating tactic with Marvel. Some months later in 1972 he was elevated to publisher, and his right-hand man, Roy Thomas, became editor-in-chief and largely responsible for the day-to-day operation of Marvel.

Who knows how different the industry might have been had Lee decided to leave. DC could have used the help. Marvel was on the verge of doing what seemed unthinkable a few years earlier. The little upstart company that had grown from a basically one-man company was closing in on DC in sales, and the impetus that finally put them ahead would involve a double cross so wicked that it was nearly Shakespearean in its grandeur.

Both Marvel and DC used the same Illinois-based printer back then, and the printer informed the companies that prices for paper and printing were going up. To keep up, both companies would have to jack up the price of a standard comic book from 15 cents.

Instead of a small, incremental increase of a few cents, as it had done previously, DC—driven by the boss at its distributor Independent News—decided to go for a more radical change. Beginning with the August 1971 cover date, the publisher increased its page count from thirty-two pages to forty-eight pages and jacked the price to 25 cents—a whopping 67 percent increase. The new package contained an original story as well as reprints of old stories from DC's archive.

Three months later Marvel did the exact same thing, converting its line to the larger 25-cent package. How did Marvel know what changes DC was going to make? That's the $64,000 question.

It's possible the printer told them. Infantino has said that the printer's rep would keep DC abreast of the changes its competitors were planning.

There is another more interesting possibility, however: the two companies got together and mutually agreed to raise the price and page count. In short, collusion, which would most likely have been illegal though perhaps not out of the question in such a small and insular industry.

"I don't know what kind of collusion there was, but I can't imagine there was this amazing coincidence when they both changed the price at the same time," Roy Thomas says.

Legend has it that Marvel's publisher, Martin Goodman, agreed to the price change with DC, but then after just a single month at the higher price, he suddenly dropped his line back down to a thirty-two-page comic for 20 cents. The new cover price was 5 cents higher than it had been two months previously, but compared to DC's 25 cents, it looked like a bargain.

A price war was what Goodman wanted, and a price war is what he got. The Marvel boss confided to Thomas that DC was about to "take a bath" if it didn't immediately follow Marvel's lead and lower its price to 20 cents.

"Carmine thought he had a deal with Goodman, and Goodman just couldn't wait to stick it to him," says historian Robert Beerbohm. "That's when Marvel really started stomping on DC, because you could get five Marvels for a buck to four DCs."

Marvel applied the killing blow by increasing its discount to distributors from 40 to 50 percent. The change made Marvel's wares a far better value and put DC at a severe disadvantage, rendering their comics suddenly as attractive as syphilis to the people whose job it was to get them to market.

"[The distributors] were throwing our books back in our face!" Infantino recalled in 1998. "They were pushing Marvel's books, so it really became a slaughter."

"There are indications that DC is in serious trouble," the fanzine *Newfangles* wrote at the time. "Dealers are not too keen on the 25 cent comic book, sales are skyrocketing for Marvel. . . . DC's titles are also reported to be dying in droves on the stands, if they get that far—wholesalers prefer to handle the 20 cents books, apparently."

It's possible that the sudden price change wasn't an intentional double cross by Goodman. The impetus for switching back to the smaller, lower-priced comics after just one month might have been driven by Marvel's lack of material that could be reprinted on the extra pages that were suddenly available in the new 25-cent format. DC had a massive library of back matter, going back decades, all meticulously preserved on film. Marvel did not.

"Marvel was always gearing up to fill those extra pages, and they somehow discovered in the midst of that first issue that they couldn't do it," says writer Englehart. "Or they got an immediate negative backlash. I think Martin Goodman probably backed out of an agreement that was there, but I don't know that it was premeditated."

As Marvel sales soared, Lee began taunting DC with cover bursts touting Marvel's lack of musty reprint material. "All new, all great!" advertised a colorful box on *Fantastic Four* #118 (January 1972).

In late spring 1972 DC was finally able to follow suit to decrease its page count and lower its price to 20 cents. But the damage had already been done.

That year it finally happened. Up became down, east became west, the poles in the comics world reversed, and suddenly the former underdog became the top dog.

Marvel passed DC in sales.

It had taken just eleven years from the launch *Fantastic Four* #1.

"There was definitely a sense that we were becoming the big boys on the block," says Marvel writer Conway. "The cachet of working for Marvel was no longer just about doing interesting work; it was about being the bigger company—the company that was growing faster, the company that was taking more chances, that was expanding rapidly."

To celebrate the victory Goodman gathered up the entire Marvel office and treated them to dinner. And his choice of eatery could not have been more laden with meaning: he took the Marvel staff to Friar Tuck's, located just across the street, from DC's offices, then located on Third Avenue at 55th Street and DC staffers' favorite watering hole.

"We all went there, and a fine time was had by all," says Englehart. "I'm sure from Martin Goodman's standpoint, overtaking the monolith on the block was quite satisfactory to him. I'm sure going to DC's favorite restaurant was a personal thing. He wanted to stick his finger in their eye. We were in competition with them, and we won, so we're going to their restaurant, and that's it."

Over at DC the news of Marvel's ascension was met with the usual dismissals.

"I was in an editorial meeting the first month that Marvel sales overtook DC's, and some of the old-timers were saying this was a temporary thing and we'd be back on top in a month or two," says Denny O'Neil. "Well, that was fifty years ago, and DC has never been back on top, except for an isolated month here and there."

Marvel could smell blood, and the company increased its output, deploying another tried-and-true publishing tactic designed to push a competitor off the stands. From 1971 to 1973 Marvel's releases exploded, going from 270 issues a year to 513. New titles and reprints soon abounded. Spider-Man got a second title with *Marvel Team-Up*. Doctor Strange, the Hulk, and the Sub-Mariner were joined into a team known as *The Defenders*. With so many magazines there would literally be no room for DC Comics on the newsstand racks. The company was in danger of being squeezed into oblivion.

DC's Carmine Infantino wasn't having any of it. "Screw them," he groused, vowing to match Marvel "book for book." He upped DC's output by reviving *Doom Patrol* and *Metal Men* as reprint titles and launched new series, such as *Sword of Sorcery*.

No one seemed to welcome the glut, from readers to dealers to the publishers themselves. At one particular meeting of the Comics Code

Authority—one of the few times reps from Marvel and DC were together in an official business capacity—the printer's representative complained that there were too many comics. Infantino offered a bold compromise. Marvel and DC would cut back their titles to just twenty each and see who would come out on top. The proposal seemed agreeable to the printer and the others in attendance. Everyone, that is, except Stan Lee.

"My books sell, so I'm not pulling back," he said.

Many of the new offerings failed to connect, however, and were quickly canceled. (*Champion Sports* and *Black Magic*, anyone?) One of the few books with a lasting impact to come out of the flood was DC's *Swamp Thing*. The scientist-turned-tortured-muck-monster would become one of the company's mainstays and eventually star in movies and a TV show. The character was part of a horror boom kicking off in 1972, and it provides one of the most bizarre intersections between Marvel and DC since the X-Men–Doom Patrol conspiracy back in 1963. That was weird enough, but Swamp Thing's unintentional ties to Marvel might be even weirder. It all started with an issue of *The Amazing Spider-Man*.

In 1970 the US Department of Health, Education, and Welfare wrote Stan Lee, asking if he might put out an antidrug comic book. Lee agreed and wrote a story destined for *The Amazing Spider-Man* #96 (May 1971) with a subplot involving a teenager hopped up on pills who walks off a roof before being saved by Spidey. Subsequent issues revealed that Peter Parker's roommate, Harry Osborn, was struggling with drug addiction.

By today's standards it's all unremarkable soap-opera stuff. Back in 1971, however, the comics code forbade any depiction of drugs, even with a message as heavy-handed as the one found in *Amazing Spider-Man*. When submitted for approval, the Code Authority rejected the antidrug issues of Marvel's top title. But instead of making changes or yanking the stories, Stan Lee forged ahead, publishing issues #96, #97, and #98 without Code approval. The move was a first for Marvel and any mainstream comic book—sort of like Disney releasing an NC-17 movie—and proved controversial. To Marvel's crosstown rivals, at least. DC was aghast at what they viewed as a breach of decency.

"You know that I will not in any shape or form put out a comic magazine without the proper authorities scrutinizing it so that it does not do any harm, not only to the industry but also to the children who read it," Infantino said at the time.

After the issues were published, Lee claims to have received congratulations from ministers, teachers, and government agencies, and the decision helped cement Marvel's rep as a purveyor of mature, cutting-edge material. Perhaps annoyingly for DC, it could have gotten there first.

A few months before the *Amazing Spider-Man* drug controversy, Neal Adams had penciled a cover for *Green Lantern/Green Arrow* with a shockingly realistic depiction of Green Arrow's young sidekick, Speedy, shooting up heroin like he's the fifth member of the Doors. Adams and writer Denny O'Neil had taken over the struggling series in 1970 and were trying to boost sales by steeping their superhero tales in real-world social issues such as racism and pollution.

Adams brought the heroin cover to Julie Schwartz, who at first "dropped it like a hot potato." It was too much of a stretch for the old-school editor. A few weeks later Schwartz softened, and DC staffers began debating whether to run the cover. And that's when Marvel's Spider-Man drug issue appeared.

The controversy forced the Code Authority to reexamine its rules, and in a February 1971 meeting the censorship body voted to loosen restrictions on comics, including allowing the depiction of drug use. That summer the heroin issue of *Green Lantern/Green Arrow* was finally published. The irony was not lost on its creators that it had taken Stan Lee to get it printed.

One byproduct of the Code's revision was that they also lifted the longtime prohibition on monsters. Publishers were now free to release books about werewolves, vampires, and other creatures that made their homes under small children's beds, and they took advantage.

Which brings us back to Swamp Thing.

Writer Len Wein, who had been tasked to come up with concepts for DC's mystery books, dreamed up the idea for the monster. Swamp Thing popped into his head while riding the subway to work one day. The creature made his first appearance in *House of Secrets* #92 (July 1971), just a few months after the Comics Code was altered. Bernie Wrightson drew him as a walking clump of green draped in vines and vegetation—a plant in human form. Something about the story caught readers' fancies, and the issue was DC's best-selling of the month. Swamp Thing soon graduated into his own title, though he was hardly alone in wandering the alligator-infested bayous.

Two months earlier Marvel had offered a tale of its own swamp monster called Man-Thing in *Savage Tales* #1 (May 1971). The idea had come from Stan Lee, who'd told his assistant editor Roy Thomas to write a story about a scientist working with experimental chemicals who falls into a swamp and comes out a monster. Thomas later passed on the plot to Gerry Conway, who wrote the first appearance.

The similarities between Man-Thing and Swamp Thing were impossible to ignore. Their origins, locales, character designs, and alarming lack of pants were nearly identical. Confusing matters even more, the principal architects of both creatures—Wein and Conway—were then roommates.

"There are some really obvious correlations between the first issue of Man-Thing and the first issue of Swamp Thing," Conway says. "It happens that I had the artwork from the first issue of Man-Thing at the apartment while I was sharing with Len and while Len was plotting the first issue of *Swamp Thing*. I don't say that he stole it, but there's the influence of seeing something, it's in the back of your mind and it comes out in another way."

Neither DC nor Marvel was particularly happy with the coincidence. Lee sent Infantino a threatening letter asserting that Man-Thing had predated Swamp Thing by a few months and if DC didn't drop the character, Marvel would sue. Infantino countered by pointing out that both characters were derivative of the Heap, a muck monster that first appeared in 1942. And, he asserted, a case could be made that so was Marvel's Incredible Hulk. He no longer heard any complaints about Swamp Thing from Lee.

Conway recalls the saber rattling being the other way around.

"DC was threatening a lawsuit," Conway says. "Marvel countered with the fact that, 'You do know that Gerry and Len were roommates?' And the lawsuit went away. Because what are you going to do?"

"Len and Bernie made Swamp Thing into a better comic than Man-Thing in many ways," Thomas says. "In the end they were different enough. Once we got past it, an origin is just an origin. This is not the thing of which good lawsuits are made."

Swamp Thing wasn't DC's only legally problematic expansion title in the early 1970s.

Fawcett Comics introduced Captain Marvel in 1940 during the initial superhero boom, and the title was once just as popular as *Superman*. Like the Man of Steel, Captain Marvel sold millions of copies, and the character headlined his own popular radio show.

He was Billy Batson, a child who transforms himself into an all-powerful caped hero by uttering his magic word, "Shazam!" The premise sounds like it has little in common with Superman, but the unforgiving eyes of DC's legal team saw enough similarities between the two characters to sue for copyright infringement. The suit dragged on for years until Fawcett agreed to settle, assenting to cease publication of Captain Marvel. In 1953 the hero disappeared from newsstands.

His popularity among die-hard fans remained strong, however, and in 1972 DC worked out a deal with Fawcett to publish a new series. The company that had cruelly snuffed out Captain Marvel decades earlier was bringing him back—and at a time when sales of its own marquee hero, Superman, were flagging. Even after a much-ballyhooed 1971 revamp that recast rumpled newspaper hack Clark Kent as a natty TV reporter, the title was down to around three hundred thousand copies by 1972—fewer than half of what it had been a decade before. Infantino crowed at the time that the Captain Marvel acquisition would create a "resurgence of the comics industry."

Maybe a resurgence in a lawyer's billable hours. Marvel would by no means just sit back and allow DC to publish a title called Captain Marvel.

After Fawcett had stopped printing Captain Marvel back in 1953 the trademark was eventually abandoned. In 1966 a schlocky comics company called M. F. Enterprises attempted to squat on the Captain Marvel name by rushing out a quickie title called Captain Marvel but not starring the Fawcett character. (This one's alter ego was Billy Baxton, not Billy Batson.)

Marvel was understandably none too pleased with the idea of another publisher using its company name in a competing title. Legal wrangling followed, and the upstart publisher was made to go away for $4,500.

To solidify its right to Captain Marvel, Stan Lee—on the orders of Martin Goodman—quickly folded a new character with the same name into Marvel's quickly expanding universe. First appearing in *Marvel Super-Heroes* #12 (December 1967), this Captain Marvel was a warrior from an interplanetary race called the Kree who wore a green-and-white costume with a planet symbol on his chest. He was awarded his own series in 1968 that ran for two years.

When DC got around to licensing the Fawcett Captain Marvel in 1972, it ran into a pretty major problem: DC may have owned the rights to publish Captain Marvel, but Marvel owned the name.

"We couldn't put the words 'Captain Marvel' as a logo on the cover," says Denny O'Neil, who wrote the first issue.

The legal quandary forced DC to change the magazine's title to *Shazam!*, the magic word Billy Batson utters to change into Captain Marvel. As a cheat on the first few issues, a prominent subhead was added, reading, "The Original Captain Marvel," but even that was disallowed. It was later tweaked to "The World's Mightiest Mortal" with #15 (December 1974).

Years later, with the launch of a new Captain Marvel project, DC tried again to obtain use of the title. No dice. The 1994 graphic novel was instead called *The Power of Shazam*.

"Die-hard Captain Marvel fans were always so mad that it couldn't be 'Captain Marvel,'" says Jerry Ordway, *The Power of Shazam* writer and artist. "I still hear about it on Twitter. People are so up in arms over it."

DC would get a modicum of revenge a few months after *Shazam*'s first issue in 1972. In Marvel's *Fear* #17 (October 1973), writer Steve Gerber—a former advertising copywriter who would become known for his more oddball creations, including Howard the Duck—introduced a new character named Wundarr. Gerber intended Wundarr as an homage to Superman, but in this case the line between homage and simply borrowing everything about Superman to make your deadline was blurred.

Like Superman, Wundarr was an alien from a distant planet who, as an infant, had been blasted into space by his parents just before their planet's sun explodes. He ends up on Earth, where he develops superpowers. Wundarr even dressed in a red-and-blue unitard. Man-Thing discovers his ship buried in a swamp, and the two slug it out to a draw.

When the story hit stands, DC was understandably miffed. The company claimed plagiarism. Stan Lee agreed and was just as ticked off with Gerber as DC was—he had not read the story before it was published.

"I had seen this character before it went out and told Steve, 'It's gotta be changed.' And Steve didn't change it, or he changed it very little," Thomas says. "Stan was displeased with me, and he was ready to root Steve out of there as a sacrificial lamb, partly to mollify DC but partly because he knew that Steve knew better."

After a few angry phone calls the two sides agreed to a truce. Marvel could continue using Wundarr if his origin were altered enough to differentiate him from Superman.

The threatened lawsuits along with Kirby's defection made the early 1970s a time of friction between the two companies. Soon, however, Marvel and DC would enter into a new era of detente that would see them doing something fans never thought would happen: collaborating for the first time in the pages of the same comic book.

The Universes Collide at Last

"And if you think that's gonna be a battle, wait'll you
see Marvel and DC when we start figuring out the
royalties!"

—Stan Lee plugging the groundbreaking
Superman vs. The Amazing Spider-Man

*A*lmost from the very beginning, comic books demanded participation. They encouraged a culture of interactivity that borrowed from
the robust sci-fi fandom that existed in the early twentieth century. *Action
Comics* #1, released in 1938, contained a story printed in black and white
that readers were invited to color with crayons. A subsequent issue held a
survey asking fans to weigh in on which of the stories was their favorite.

DC launched the Junior Justice Society, a fan club for its first super
team, as well as another in the early 1940s devoted to Superman.

Readers gradually made their voices heard. They published crude fanzines. They mailed letters in the thousands to the publishers, offering story
and character ideas and points of criticism. Legions of Super-Heroes diehards were invited to vote for the team's next leader in the 1960s (a gimmick revived in 2010). They were the founding fathers and mothers of the
grassroots nerd culture that has become one of the most powerful forces
in modern-day entertainment.

"After a while, I began to feel I wasn't even an editor," Stan Lee wrote in 1974. "I was just following orders—orders which came in the mail."

Fan culture began to coalesce in the 1960s. Previously it had been disorganized and disparate, providing no easy way for the Superman zealot living in his mom's basement in Illinois to meet the Superman zealot living in his mom's basement in California.

Conventions began sprouting up in the early 1960s, first as informal, DIY gatherings, sometimes at private houses and later as larger, more organized affairs. They provided fans a nonjudgmental space to mingle with other superhero lovers and fill holes in their back-issue collection. Some took the communion with the comics to a new level by dressing as their favorite superhero.

Fans flocked to official office tours—or, in some cases, just showed up at Marvel and DC. An editorial printed in a 1964 New York comic con program urged pros to begin attending conventions in hopes of diminishing the number of out-of-town comic junkies who "disrupt the schedules of the publishing companies with their visits."

Fans got older. They began sticking with the hobby longer. Continuity became more important. They began to recognize and follow specific artists and writers. They became more serious about brand loyalty. And especially after Marvel's superheroes burst onto the scene in 1961, fandom was cleaved into two camps. It became tribal. Increasingly you were either a Marvel or a DC reader, and much like today's political campaigns, the two sides frequently found themselves at odds with one another. Arguments broke out on playgrounds and in lunch rooms. Each side championed its own team.

"In the seventies I was a DC guy, and I hung with a lot of Marvel guys," says Jonathan Hoyle, a longtime comic book fan who lives in Pittsburgh. "It's like sports fans. You're going to pick on each other."

The Marvel fans dissed DC for its squeaky-clean image and its conservative mindset. They knocked the company for being tired.

"We [DC fans] got picked on because even our house ads were kind of silly," Hoyle says.

The DC camp couldn't understand how anyone liked Marvel. It was all melodrama and overwrought emotion. And why the hell are these supposed heroes always fighting each other again?

With the increasingly balkanized nature of comics fandom, the debate would inevitably turn to the superiority of each company's characters.

"The big thing we always argued about was who was stronger: Hulk or Superman?" says John Cimino, a Massachusetts collectibles dealer and Hulk superfan. "I used to bring comic books to the playground at recess time, and I remember someone making fun of me when the [villain] Abomination beat up the Hulk. 'How do you think the Hulk can beat up Superman when he can't even beat up this guy?' I remember being devastated, like, how do I get out of this?"

"No competition. Marvel winds [*sic*] hands down."
—The "Marvel Is Better Than DC" Facebook page

"They can argue all they like, we've got Batman."
—The "DC Is Better Than Marvel" Facebook page

Who *would* win in a fight between characters? These questions bedeviled comics readers, from the small children who were just discovering superheroes, to the stoned college students sitting around a dorm room. Now the fans were beginning to demand answers.

The 1970 Comic Art Convention, an annual fan gathering at Manhattan's Statler Hilton Hotel, featured a panel with editors from both Marvel and DC. During the panel a kid in the audience stood up and asked the question that was probably on the top of so many comic book readers' minds: "Hey, why don't you guys do a comic where Superman meets Spider-Man?" the youngster asked.

The professionals laughed, responding dismissively that such a meeting would never happen—copyrights, bureaucracy, profit division, and so forth.

"It was one of those, 'Oh, you stupid fans. Don't you understand how the business works?'" says Mark Evanier, who attended the panel. "This poor kid was humiliated, basically treated like he'd asked the stupidest question in the world."

Not hardly. A few years later the ongoing cold war between the two companies would thaw long enough for them to join forces to tell that exact story the kid had asked about. It would be a groundbreaking publication as well as a massive tip of the hat to fan service in an industry disproportionately devoted to it. But getting to that historic milestone would take several baby steps.

The idea of DC and Marvel's characters crossing over wasn't just one readers contemplated. It was one that excited the young fans-turned-pros who began entering the industry in the late 1960s and early 1970s. Unlike the industry's founding fathers—some of whom were gruff jobbers who worked in shirtsleeves and chomped cigars, waiting for the day when they could do something more dignified—this new wave of talent viewed life inside the industry as a dream come true. Working in it was about so much more than just a living; it was an extension of a hobby, an obsession, a way to directly shape the universe they'd been reading about since they were children.

As the 1970s dawned, the kinds of questions preoccupying many in the biz began to shift from, "When is this check gonna clear?" to "Wouldn't it be cool if the brain waves from that character we last saw back in 1964 were implanted into this new android?"

Mike Friedrich posed one of those "what if" questions. While attending a party at Roy Thomas's Upper East Side apartment in 1969, Friedrich was chatting with Thomas, then writing Marvel's *Avengers*, and Denny O'Neil, the writer for DC's *Justice League of America*, when Friedrich got an idea.

"Why don't you do some kind of crossover," Friedrich asked.

The three loved the idea. Even more so after a few more drinks. But they knew it would have to be done under the table, feeling—perhaps rightly so—that the heads of their respective companies were unlikely to tolerate their fanboy idea. Seeing as how an official, editorially sanctioned crossover wasn't possible, the writers agreed to introduce a superteam in their own comic that resembled the superteam from the other company.

Thomas's effort appeared first in *Avengers* #69 (October 1969). There he introduced a new band of villains called the Squadron Sinister, created by a cosmic game-lover to battle the Avengers. The members were based on the Justice League, with the caped Hyperion an analog to Superman, dark avenger Nighthawk to Batman, speedster the Whizzer to the Flash, and the gem-wielding Doctor Spectrum to Green Lantern.

O'Neil ultimately bagged on introducing a DC team in the vein of the Avengers, and his Marvel homage turned out far more subtle, perhaps because he was working under controlling editor Julie Schwartz. His story, appearing in *Justice League of America* #75 (November 1969), found the Justice League being forced to battle evil versions of themselves. References to the Avengers are sprinkled throughout, but you probably had to have been in on the joke back then to spot them. In one panel Batman tosses a trash can lid in the style of Captain America's shield. In another Superman's evil twin proclaims he won't be defeated because he's "as powerful as Thor."

A few readers picked up on the JLA/Squadron Sinister connection, but it's unclear if anyone figured out the reciprocal nods in O'Neil's *Justice League of America*. The under-the-table crossover flew over heads of the editors. Thomas never told Stan Lee what he was doing because Lee was wary of antagonizing DC.

"While it got fairly well known, it never came up in any conversation [with Lee]," Thomas says. "I had, of course, feared that I might be in trouble for doing that. Luckily DC never sent an angry lawyer's letter or anything, as they did in one or two other cases."

O'Neil's boss, Julie Schwartz, remained oblivious as well.

"Nobody noticed, and nobody cared," O'Neil says. "As long as we didn't violate copyright, it didn't make any difference to them. Nothing was ever said to me about it."

The illicit team-up was continued two years later after Friedrich took over writing duties on *Justice League of America*. He and Thomas ginned up another rogue crossover. Friedrich concocted a new team called the Champions of Angor, who showed up in *Justice League of America* #87 (February 1971) and were meant to stand in for the Avengers.

Thomas responded by introducing in *Avengers* #85 (February 1971) the Squadron Supreme, a team of good guys whose origin is related to the Squadron Sinister, with the same similarities to the Justice League of America.

In the years since the secret 1969 crossover, however, JLA editor Julie Schwartz had evidently become more savvy. He confronted Friedrich about the illicit crossover, brandishing a copy of the *Avengers* #85, and demanded, "I suppose you think this is funny?"

"Yeah," Friedrich answered.

"Don't do it again," Schwartz said.

"I wasn't penalized or yelled at," Friedrich recalls. "DC people weren't reading Marvel comics at the time, so who gave Julie that Marvel comic? I'll never know."

(Marvel would bring back Squadron Supreme in a 1985 miniseries, suggesting in an ad that it would be the Justice League done right. The move prompted angry phone calls from DC.)

The successful meta-crossover soon emboldened the younger crop of writers to try something even more radical. They'd attempt to snake a single story through several Marvel and DC titles.

In 1965 Roy Thomas had met a fan named Tom Fagan at a New York comic convention. Fagan lived in Rutland, Vermont, a town of fewer than twenty thousand people that hosted a lively Halloween parade down its main street each year. The event took a superhero bent when Fagan suggested making Batman the grand marshal in 1960. Thomas attended in 1965 (dressed as Plastic Man), and the news about Rutland quickly spread within the comic book community. Soon writers and artists were trekking north every October to dress as superheroes and party in Fagan's twenty-three-room Victorian house.

Thomas set a 1970 *Avengers* story at the parade. Denny O'Neil and Neal Adams followed suit in *Batman* a year later. And the real crossover would kick off in 1973, orchestrated by DC's Len Wein and Marvel's Gerry Conway and Steve Englehart. Englehart was then relatively new to the business. He'd begun working with Neal Adams on weekends after he graduated college in 1970, hoping to be an artist. He soon switched vocations to writer.

"Len, Gerry, and I were friends, and we were sitting around, and we thought, 'Why can't we do something together?'" Englehart says. "And the answer was, because we worked for different companies. Then we said, 'Well, we can solve that problem.'"

The writers, absent of any clearance from their respective bosses, cooked up a storyline set in Rutland and involving Englehart's car getting stolen. The first installment of the multipart tale ran in Englehart's *Amazing Adventures* #16 (January 1973), the second in Wein's *Justice League of America* #103 (December 1972), and the final in Conway's *Thor* #207 (January 1973). Each story stood on its own, but when all were read together, they provided a fuller narrative.

"It was just about, 'Can we pull this off without either one of the companies getting pissed off about it?'" Englehart says. "It was known in whatever fandom existed at that time, but we didn't flaunt it or say, 'Oh, we stuck it to Marvel or DC.' Neither company was upset about it."

Writer Steve Englehart would later pull off a different type of under-the-table crossover when one of his creations would follow him to DC when he went to work there. Mantis was a green-skinned martial arts expert who debuted in *Avengers* #112 (June 1973) and eventually became a member of the Marvel team. (She had a prominent role in 2017's *Guardians of the Galaxy Vol. 2*.) But after Englehart moved to DC to write the *Justice League of America*, a fan at a convention asked him if that meant the end for Mantis. He thought about it and decided it shouldn't be.

"We'd done the Rutland thing already, so I thought I could put her in the Justice League just as long as no one got sued," Englehart says. "Of course she has a distinct skin color and a distinct pattern of speaking, as long as I call her something else—that seems to be the legal standard—I can make his happen. I don't recall any adverse reaction from either company."

These early wink-wink crossovers paved the way for the first official crossover in 1975. But the eventual cooperation would require management changes at Marvel to lessen the tension between the two rivals. Martin Goodman, who had been bought out in 1968 by Perfect Film but was kept on as the publisher, retired in 1972. His son Chip—an amateurish businessman who'd once optioned the media rights to all of Marvel's characters for a few thousand dollars—was soon forced out. Both father and son had no love for DC and were known to harbor grudges and act vindictively.

"[In the early 1970s] the companies were so antagonistic toward each other at the management level that you could have never gotten these people to sit down and talk," says Gerry Conway, then a top Marvel writer.

Which is not to say that Marvel and DC weren't communicating at all during that period. Lee and Infantino remained friendly, though their relationship had been strained when DC poached Kirby.

"Carmine Infantino was a friend of mine," Lee says. "I'd meet him every couple of weeks, and he'd bring a few guys from DC. I'd come with a few guys from Marvel, we'd have a few drinks and kid around."

Infantino had been promoted to publisher in 1972, and it's pretty clear that he and Lee would come together occasionally to discuss business issues—and not always with the most positive of outcomes. The two met for lunch one day in the summer of 1974, and their discussion would have dire consequences for Marvel.

A freelance artist named Frank Robbins, who'd been drawing *Batman*, was seeking work at Marvel, and when Marvel asked how much his page rate was, he exaggerated what DC had been paying him. Lee found out about the white lie and blew his top. He discussed the issue with Infantino over lunch, and according to Lee the two executives agreed to share rates in the future. (Infantino vehemently denied ever agreeing to share rate info with Marvel. He claimed he flatly refused to do so.)

When Lee returned to the Marvel offices he told editor-in-chief Roy Thomas what had happened at lunch, and Thomas was appalled. He dashed off a memo to Lee, calling the collusion "immoral, unethical and probably illegal." Lee asked him if he was resigning, and Thomas said yes.

"Lee didn't think he was breaking the law," Thomas says. "They'd always gotten along doing whatever they wanted to do. It was no big deal."

Thomas's resignation put the issue to rest. Marvel and DC did not end up checking freelancer pay with one another in the subsequent years. (Infantino later denied that he and Lee discussed page rates.)

The next year Lee and Infantino would stumble upon another unexpected problem between them. Marvel had been planning an adaptation of *The Wizard of Oz* when Lee learned that DC also had one in the works. Instead of risking issuing competing comics, Lee and Infantino agreed to simply coproduce the issue. *MGM's Marvelous Wizard of Oz* was released in late summer 1975, becoming the very first Marvel-DC intercompany crossover.

The book was a historic first, but it never rose beyond a curiosity to the fans and collectors. After all, this was not really a team-up of Marvel and DC; it was a team-up of their legal departments. The readership was after more than just the companies joining their names on the two-point type of a magazine's indicia; they wanted to see the rival publisher's superheroes actually meet in the same story and God willing, start smashing in one another's faces during a colossal smackdown the likes of which hadn't been seen since the days of the epic poem.

They wouldn't have to wait long.

The story would begin with David Obst, a literary agent who represented Carl Bernstein and Bob Woodward, the Watergate journalists behind *All the President's Men*. Obst had been a comic book fan as a kid, and one day in the early 1970s he cold-called Stan Lee and told the Marvel guru, "I think Marvel could be so much more than comic books."

"And, like an idiot," Obst recalls, "instead of saying 'movies,' I said 'books.'"

Obst partnered with Lee to release a series of hit hardcover books from Simon & Schuster, including 1974's *Origins of Marvel Comics* and the sequel, *Sons of Origins of Marvel Comics*.

Around the same time Obst was out one night in New York City and got to talking with Howard Kaminsky, the head of Warner Books, a sister company to DC Comics. Obst told Kaminsky he'd been working with Lee on the Marvel books and suggested, "Why don't we do a book together: Superman vs. Spider-Man?" Kaminsky loved the idea and pitched it to the folks at DC. They agreed, and Obst took it to Stan Lee.

Lee liked the concept but was a bit nervous about proceeding, wondering why he should lend a helping hand to DC, whose sales were deteriorating badly. Lee asked Thomas, who had stepped down as editor-in-chief but was still working for Marvel, what he thought. Thomas was all for it, estimating that the team-up would boost Marvel's number-one character, who at that point had been around for only thirteen years.

"I told Stan, 'It's a wonderful deal for Marvel,'" Thomas says. "It's parity. You have Superman, who at one time was one of the three best-known fictitious characters in the world—Superman, Sherlock Holmes, and Tarzan—so just to be on the same page is saying that Superman and Spider-Man are equal. You're elevating Spider-Man. It's a win-win situation."

Obst, being an outsider, was able to serve as a neutral arbiter and bridge the divide between the two companies. Both sides eventually agreed to move ahead, but working out the details of the crossover proved difficult, as both Marvel and DC jockeyed to make sure their interests were protected.

"Ecumenical conferences from the Middle Ages were not as carefully adjudicated as this was," Obst says.

One sticking point was money. DC initially wanted more than half the profits because they insisted Superman had a higher distribution. They also demanded that Superman's name come first in the title, as he was the more iconic character.

"That goes back to what I consider the Carmine kind of approach, and it wasn't just Carmine; it was all the editors and people at DC. They had a very superior attitude," says David Anthony Kraft, then a Marvel editor. "Marvel was never that stroppy. You want to have Superman's name first? Fine. Whatever."

To produce the book, the contract called for dividing the labor between Marvel and DC. Marvel would provide the penciler and the colorist, DC would deliver the writer, inker, and letterer. Even that straightforward division of labor led to friction and provided opportunities for one side to tweak the other.

When it came time to choose a writer, Infantino passed over the veterans he had in house and instead turned to Gerry Conway, whom he'd not-coincidentally just poached from Marvel. The theft wasn't nearly as high profile as that of Jack Kirby, but it had made waves in the industry.

Conway had begun writing comic books as a teen and found steady work at Marvel in the early seventies. He'd quickly risen to helm the publisher's signature books, *Fantastic Four* and the *Amazing Spider-Man*. In the latter he'd introduced gun-wielding vigilante the Punisher and killed off Peter Parker's girlfriend, Gwen Stacy, in one of the most shocking moments in comic book history.

Despite his prominence at the company, Conway left Marvel in 1975 after he was passed over for the editor-in-chief's position in the wake of Roy Thomas's resignation. The post instead went to Len Wein, who'd begun his career at DC but had become one of Marvel's go-to writers by the mid-1970s.

Conway reached out to DC and, in 1975, jumped ship. The news did not sit well with Marvel.

"Back in the seventies you really perceived yourself as playing for a team—either Marvel or DC," Conway says. "Going to DC, especially after Kirby's move in 1970, it really felt to the people at Marvel that I was betraying the company."

DC wasted no time touting its shiny new acquisition. House ads for Conway's line of books, known as Conway's Corner, began appearing. For Infantino the Conway acquisition was another step in taking down Marvel.

"We're going to show those guys at Marvel," Infantino told Conway. "We're going to eat their lunch."

At the first editorial meeting since Conway's hiring, Infantino got a rude awakening. The DC boss had always been dismissive of the company's new crop of young staffers, whom he referred to derisively as "the kids," and at this particular gathering he was touting Conway and how the new hire was going to help DC give its books more of a Marvel feel.

Suddenly Carl Gafford, a young production assistant, looked at Carmine and said, "You do realize Gerry is younger than all of us?"

"Carmine's jaw dropped," says Bob Rozakis, then a young assistant. "It was like someone had sold him the Brooklyn Bridge. He'd been convinced that he was stealing this expert editor away from Marvel. Gerry was, like, twenty-one or twenty-two at the time."

Young or not, when it came to choosing the writer for *Superman vs. Spider-Man*, Infantino tapped Conway because he'd written both characters. But the choice was also a way to rub Marvel's nose in DC's acquisition of Conway.

"Carmine was a competitive guy, and he offered me the book because he knew it would piss off Marvel," Conway says. "He wanted to put a finger in their eye."

For the artist, Conway suggested Ross Andru, the longtime penciler on *The Amazing Spider-Man*. Conway had teamed with him previously at Marvel, and like Conway, Andru was one of the few in the business who'd handled both Spider-Man and Superman. The choice had an added advantage to Infantino and DC: drawing the crossover book would require Andru to take a break from *The Amazing Spider-Man* for a couple of months. The book was then Marvel's top seller, and losing its artist might hurt sales.

"You've got this guy who's recently left your top-selling book to go work for the other company, and now he's writing this big book, and he's taking the artist on your top-selling book," Conway says. "So there's a bit of a screw you there too."

Although Len Wein was then in charge of Marvel's superhero comics, it was Marvel president Al Landau who agreed to DC's request for Andru's services. When Wein complained to Landau about temporarily losing the artist on *The Amazing Spider-Man*—a comic he also happened to be writing—Landau told him the details of the *Superman vs. Spider-Man* assignment were none of his "fucking business." Wein threw himself at the executive, determined to "rip out his throat" and had to be restrained by Marv Wolfman.

For the crossover's inker DC selected Dick Giordano. Giordano had been among the wave of new editors who arrived at DC in 1968 in an attempt to modernize the stodgy company. But after clashing with Infantino, Giordano left and formed his own art studio with Neal Adams, Continuity Associates, in 1971. He still freelanced extensively for DC and embodied the publisher's house style.

With the art team in place, work shifted to the story. In theory telling a one-off tale of two guys in long underwear should be simple, but in practice it proved thorny. One of the challenges was that Marvel and DC's heroes are cut from different cloths. They're philosophically different and don't fit easily into the same story. DC's characters are clean, well-mannered boy scouts, and Marvel's heroes are flawed and more human. Superman's power level is also far superior to Spider-Man's.

"So we sit down, and we can't get two sentences into it when both sides are already screaming at each other," Obst says. "The one quote I remember someone saying is, 'Are you fucking kidding me?! If Superman ever hit Spider-Man, he'd knock him past Jupiter.'"

"They squabbled like two old ladies," Denny O'Neil says.

Another challenge was crafting an interesting "vs." story in which the opposing sides are both good guys. Neither company, for obvious reasons, wanted its character to look at all like a villain.

"You have this problem. Comic book [heroes] live in this world of black and white," Obst says. "You can't have them be black, ever. It messes with the brand. How do you have white versus white and keep it interesting? You can't."

Conway took the challenges to heart.

"From a realistic point of view, a Superman versus Spider-Man fight would last about two seconds," he says. "I always tried to see the humor in these characters and these situations, so to me, the idea of having Spider-Man fight Superman, there are ways to fix that so that it can happen, but you can have so much fun with the absurdity of it too."

Because bad blood lingered between Conway and Marvel editors Wein and Wolfman over Conway's departure, neither side wanted to have much to do with one another. The compromise was for Marvel's Roy Thomas to serve as a "consulting editor."

Conway eventually worked up a story pitting Superman and Spider-Man against DC's Lex Luthor and Marvel's Doctor Octopus. But before the heroes took down the villains, Supes and Spidey meet and, in a now-clichéd plot device that Marvel pioneered in the 1960s, start fighting due to a misunderstanding. Spider-Man gets in one good lick. The Man of Steel then returns fire, generously deciding to pull his punch but still sends Spidey flying hundreds of feet. It was the moment fans had been anticipating for years.

The fight, of course, ended in a draw, and balance in all aspects of the special issue was critical. Superman and Spider-Man had to get equal screen time, including the same number of large, full-page images. The cover, which Infantino laid out, featured the two heroes squaring off atop the Empire State Building. It had to be revised several times to give both Superman and Spider-Man equal prominence.

Neither company's universe got a boost either. Instead of having one hero zapped into the other's realm, the decision was made to set the cross-over in a world that was home to both Superman's Metropolis and Spider-Man's New York City and one in which the heroes are aware of each other's existence but have never met. The choice meant valuable story pages wouldn't have to be devoted to explaining what credulity-straining MacGuffin would serve to teleport Superman into the Marvel universe or vice versa.

As work on the issue progressed and artwork began to trickle in, industry insiders began to get excited.

"I remember the spread coming in—the first time that Superman and Spider-Man were on the same page together," says Joe Rubinstein, who was working as an assistant to Giordano at the time and helped fill in black areas on the issue. "It's pretty humdrum now, but back then, it was really exciting. 'Oh, my God! It's Clark and Peter together!' And that was great."

Because of the back-and-forth and all the approvals needed from the two companies, the issue took seven months to complete. *Superman vs. The Amazing Spider-Man* was released the first week of January 1976 and cost a whopping $2—eight times the price of a regular Marvel comic book. The opening page held two (equally sized, of course) messages from Stan Lee and Carmine Infantino, commenting on the historic nature of the publication.

"Comics, which usually reflect history, may in this one momentous undertaking prove détente can be more than theory," Infantino wrote.

The book sold half a million copies, according to Infantino, in spite of its awkward size. The large, tabloid format meant *Superman vs. The Amazing Spider-Man* wouldn't fit in the standard comic book racks, and stores might have been confused about how and where to display it.

"They didn't make as much money as they should have," Roy Thomas says.

The project, even with its accompanying bureaucratic tensions, lessened hostilities between Marvel and DC and served as a heartening reminder of the progress that had been made in relations. Just a decade prior, freelancers had to use pen names to work for both companies, and DC's haughty editors hadn't even deigned to acknowledge Marvel. Now the two were partnering on a single high-profile comic book. The companies would collaborate more a few years later—sometimes successfully, but in one case so disastrously that the failure would kick off a new cold war that would last another decade.

Superman vs. The Amazing Spider-Man may have ushered in an era of cooperation between the two comic book titans, but it marked the end of Infantino's reign at DC. Fresh off a January 1976 promotional tour for the Marvel/DC collaboration, Infantino was in the middle of an editorial meeting when the brass summoned him upstairs. The execs were unhappy with DC's losses, which had been driven by the industry's declining sales and Infantino's decision to try to equal Marvel's voluminous output.

"You lost a million dollars last year," Jay Emmett, the powerful founder of DC's lucrative licensing arm, Licensing Corporation of America, told Infantino.

"Right," Infantino countered. "And Marvel lost two million."

The bosses weren't buying the argument, and Infantino was fired on the spot. His demise might have been down to more than just profit and losses. In addition to his lack of business acumen, Infantino was not universally liked. He admitted to drinking in the morning to deal with stress. He could be prickly and vindictive, bad-mouthing people as soon as they left the room.

"Carmine was a prick," says inker Joe Rubinstein. "Once I was at [Neal Adams's studio] Continuity Associates, and I picked up the phone. It was [DC editor] Joe Orlando, who was such a sweet, sweet guy. He asked, 'Is Neal there?' I said, 'No, he's not.' He proceeded to lay into me: 'Tell that motherfucking cocksucker, blah, blah, blah.' And then silence. And then he said, 'Sorry, I had to do that because Carmine was in the room.'"

Infantino had enemies, including inker Vinnie Colletta, whom he'd removed from Jack Kirby's heralded Fourth World books. Whispers around DC in 1976 were that Colletta had pulled strings with some of the shadier elements rumored to be connected to Warner Bros. to get Infantino ousted. The day the axe fell, Gerry Conway ran into his now ex-boss heading to the elevators. Infantino looked shaken.

"What's up? Are you okay?" Conway asked.

"There are going to be some changes around here. I can't really talk about it," Infantino replied. "Don't worry about it. I got your back, kid."

With that, Infantino walked into the elevator and was gone. Seconds later, almost on cue, the doors on the adjacent elevator opened, and out walked Colletta. He saw Conway standing there and said triumphantly, "I finally got rid of the bastard!"

"Vinnie knew about it apparently before anyone else, which gave rise to the suspicion that he had it in for Carmine," Conway says.

Infantino would again freelance for the company in the years after he was fired, but legend has it that he was so bitter about his treatment that he never set foot in the DC offices again.

His dismissal cleared way for yet another major management shake-up at DC, as the company continued to try to keep pace with the now market leader, Marvel, and stem its losses in the eroding periodicals market. Before things would turn around, DC would be hit with a major catastrophe that would threaten to end the company once and for all.

DC Reboots to Take On Marvel

"I got DC comics sent to me, and I'd show them to
Stan [Lee], and we'd sit there laughing at the stilted
dialogue and all the stupid stuff they did. Look at
Superman coming in for a landing with his toe pointed
and his leg tucked. Nobody does that."

—Former *Marvel* editor-in-chief Jim Shooter

Working at DC in the mid seventies, artist Barry Windsor-Smith
once lamented, was "a little like quitting comics."

Kirby's ambitious Fourth World had fizzled, and he'd moved on to titles that did little more than fulfill his contractual obligations. DC's line
was an uninspired mix of leftover mystery and war titles alongside DOA
new offerings like *The Stalker* and *Richard Dragon, Kung-Fu Fighter*. The
latter title, introduced in 1975, had been an attempt to capitalize on the
early seventies martial arts craze, as Marvel had successfully done with
Master of Kung Fu two years earlier.

Young writer Denny O'Neil was a fan of chop-socky films and, like
those at Marvel, had recognized their potential to translate into comic
books early on. He'd pitched a martial arts series to DC in 1973 but was
turned down.

"I went to one of DC's big dogs and made my case, and I will never forget what he said, because this was one of the most corporate things I've ever heard," O'Neil recalls. "He said, 'I don't like the numbers, chum.'"

Two years later, when DC came to its senses and finally green-lit *Richard Dragon*, the genre's popularity had cooled, leading to the standing joke at DC that by the time the company got around to following a trend, you could be sure the trend was over.

Sales were dropping on DC's marquee titles as well. Circulation of *Superman* had fallen below 300,000 in 1975, some 150,000 fewer than five years prior.

"I have next to nothing favorable to say about Dull Comics," former DC and then-Marvel-writer David Anthony Kraft told the *Comics Journal* in 1977. "There's some kind of curse that hangs over that place, an uncanny certainty that no matter what you do or how hard you work at it, it'll still somehow manage to come out looking just like every other shitty book they publish. . . . They don't publish comics, they publish ass-wipe."

A new direction was clearly needed. And new leadership. Carmine Infantino had "relinquished his post" in January, as DC's official fanzine charitably put it, and when it came to picking his replacement, the Warner executives appeared determined to go for an even bolder pick than they had made with Infantino, because they chose someone with three qualities nobody in the business was expecting.

First, the new hire had no comic book industry experience. Second, the pick was a youthful twenty-eight. And third and perhaps most surprising of all, he was not a he at all. A venerable company in a field historically populated almost exclusively by men was now going to be led by a woman. Legend has it that when DC editor Joe Orlando heard the news, he immediately went to the bathroom and puked.

Jenette Kahn had grown up in Pennsylvania, the daughter of a rabbi. She'd read comics as a child after her brother turned her on to them. She earned an art history degree at Radcliffe College but fell into publishing at age twenty-two when she and a friend raised money to publish *Kids*, a children's magazine. She later launched *Dynamite*, another publication for young people.

Her experience in children's publishing clearly made her attractive to the suits at Warner Bros. (It also suggested how they viewed comic books—as strictly kids' stuff.) Bill Sarnoff, the head of Warner Publishing, invited Kahn to lunch in 1975. As they ate and chatted, Sarnoff revealed that he thought DC should no longer publish new comics and should instead focus solely on the lucrative licensing. Kahn disagreed, explaining that she saw DC as an important ideas lab, and without new stories, the value of the characters would soon diminish.

Sarnoff must have liked what he heard. The next day he offered her the job of publisher, a choice that stunned the industry.

"When Jenette came in, it was such a relief. It wasn't another old white guy," says former DC writer Paul Kupperberg.

"We didn't know Jenette Kahn, and we worried that she did not know comics," says Irene Vartanoff, who worked in editorial, production, and the rights department at Marvel and DC in the seventies and eighties. "Did any of us think about what in her background led her to be chosen to run a very important comic book company? Not really. We simply wanted whoever it was to understand comics."

Kahn started work at DC on February 2, 1976, and soon established herself as a fresh and energetic—if somewhat eccentric—presence.

"Jenette was unbelievably creative," says Dan Raspler, a DC editor in the eighties and nineties. "She was spacey but sort of like a shark. She was oddball, a striking woman in a flamboyant dress. If you imagine a Batman villain, that's what she often looked like. Crazy outfits and a crazy office with bizarre furniture."

Kahn had two items on her to-do list straight out of the gate: make the comics better and, in an industry notorious for abusing its talent, start treating the writers and artists better. Easier said than done.

Kahn set out to learn the business of comic books, often sitting with Schwartz in his office as the editor worked up a story with a writer. She also attempted to smash the editorial fiefdoms that still existed and tighten the company continuity in what she called "centralization."

She altered the way new series were developed. DC would no longer, say, churn out five half-ass sword and sorcery imitations because *Conan* was hot. New series would be forced to climb a ladder, with approvals on every rung, beginning with a pitch, then moving on to a script and art sketches, and finally concluding with a finished comic book.

An age problem still beset DC. Its editors were, as Kahn put it, "of another generation." *Batman* and *Superman* editor Julius Schwartz was in his sixties, as was Murray Boltinoff, who handled some horror and war titles. Joe Orlando was closing in on fifty. One of the few young people they did have on staff, Gerry Conway, left a few weeks after Kahn's arrival to become editor-in-chief at Marvel, succeeding Marv Wolfman.

Kahn set out to recruit new talent and began reading Marvel comics to see who might be worth bringing over.

"She wanted to get a younger vibe to the whole thing," says Bob Rozakis, then a DC assistant editor. "She recognized that the Marvel characters had more appeal to the audience than ours did, and she wanted to get the same vibe at DC."

In the end Kahn targeted two names to poach. One was John Buscema, the penciler of *Conan* and *Fantastic Four* whose style was so representative of Marvel that he would coauthor a book on how to draw comics the Marvel way in 1978. Kahn recruited the artist and thought she'd hashed out a deal for him to defect. But Stan Lee caught wind of the change and swooped in to make Buscema an offer he couldn't refuse, and the DC deal was squashed.

The other Marvel name Kahn set her sights on was Steve Englehart. Soon after Kahn arrived at DC Englehart quit Marvel after a disagreement with newly installed editor Gerry Conway. Two days later he got a call from Kahn inviting him to lunch.

"We got together in Manhattan, and she said, 'I want you to do for the *Justice League* what you did for the *Avengers*,'" Englehart says. "'Our characters need to be rejuvenated. You had a good thing going with the *Avengers*, and we want that same thing for the *Justice League*.'"

Englehart, eager to pay back Marvel for letting him walk, agreed under the conditions that he'd work for only a year (he planned to travel around Europe) and that he would be allowed to write Batman. Kahn assented.

Englehart's stint began with trying to revamp the *Justice League of America* in early 1977, establishing a tone and feel to serve as a template for DC's other books.

"They were trying to make their books more like Marvel. That's why I was there," Englehart says. "What Marvel was doing was still mysterious to DC. Jenette told me, 'Our sales are trending downward because we're not keeping up with Marvel, and no one here understands what's going on.' DC didn't have anybody who could do what I was doing at Marvel, so they went and got me."

The writer also took over *Detective Comics* and produced a hugely influential run with penciler Marshall Rogers and inker Terry Austin that helped return Batman to his dark roots. The story, for perhaps the first time, introduced sex into the G-rated DC universe.

"The thing that's always bothered me about DC's books is that all their grown-up superheroes acted like little boys," Englehart says. "If Lana Lang or Lois Lane ever made any kind of romantic overture, all these grown men become tongued-tied and bashful. Even as a kid I thought that was stupid."

Englehart created a love interest named Silver St. Cloud for Batman's alter-ego Bruce Wayne, and in one panel Silver is shown lounging in a negligee telling Bruce that she's "suffering exhaustion" after their night together.

"I wanted to say Batman and Silver were having a mature, adult sexual relationship," Englehart says. "That was not only unheard of, it was *unthought* of."

Certainly at DC it was. The company's sexual politics had always been just this side of a nunnery. Until at least 2006 DC's official position was that Wonder Woman was a virgin, according to copublisher Dan DiDio. In the 1940s Superman editor Whit Ellsworth was tasked with "de-sexing" Lois Lane and deemphasizing Superman's jock strap. About the only action Batman ever got was in the demented mind of 1950s critic Fredric Wertham, who claimed Batman and Robin were "a wish dream of two homosexuals living together."

Marvel, as with most things, was much looser when it came to sex. A 1968 issue of *Nick Fury: Agent of S.H.I.E.L.D.* by writer-artist Jim Steranko (in)famously included a wordless, ten-panel grid of provocative images, including a phone with its receiver off the hook and a close-up of a woman's lips, suggesting an encounter between Fury and a female spy. The sticks in the mud at the Comics Code Authority objected to some of the imagery, and the last panel showing the couple locked in an embrace was hurriedly replaced with a photostat of Nick Fury's gun shoved tightly into its holster—a picture that, in hindsight, is more wonderfully suggestive than the one it replaced.

Elsewhere, Fantastic Four couple Reed Richards and Sue Storm dated and were shown marrying in 1967. They later had children, suggesting their relationship was consummated. Daredevil shacked up with his girlfriend, the Black Widow, in 1972.

"We sort of give the idea that our characters are reasonably normal human beings who won't turn the other way if a pretty girl comes by,"

Stan Lee said in a 1970 radio interview. "We don't attempt to play up the sex in any way. But if a story should call for somebody who is attracted to somebody of the opposite sex or whatever, we try to put it in so that it makes sense."

To DC's credit, they never complained about the mature themes in Englehart's *Detective Comics*.

"I think they were looking to me to give them ideas that they hadn't had," he says.

Kahn's arrival at DC split the company into two factions, with those embracing change on one side and those fearing it on the other. Kahn soon promoted allies, putting Joe Orlando in charge of the editorial department and elevating Paul Levitz to editorial coordinator. Levitz was a former "BNF"—big-name fan—who had published a popular fanzine as a teenager before landing part-time work at DC in the early 1970s. He attended New York University but dropped out to work in comics. He would continue to rise through the ranks in the decades ahead, ultimately ending up in the top spot.

To head the art department Kahn made an unusual choice.

"One thing that really didn't work out too well was her hiring of Vinnie Colletta as art director," says Jack C. Harris, a former DC editor. "Rumors said that he only got the position because he was the only comic book artist she knew at the time."

Colletta still might not have been the greatest artist in the world, but there's little doubt he brought an amazing amount of color to the staid DC offices.

"My office was down the hall near Julie Schwartz's, and anybody coming up from the elevators would have to pass my door," says DC writer Paul Kupperberg. "I could see Vinnie's door pretty clearly. He had a bookie who would come pretty regularly, and there were a variety of young ladies who would arrive, and the door would close and not open again for a half-hour. I assume it was Vinnie doing large model sketches."

Rumor had it that Colletta enjoyed a cozy relationship with the Bond girl from the latest flick. He also, inexplicably, had an interest in a fried chicken restaurant in midtown Manhattan. He'd often work out of its basement, propping his drawing board atop soda crates.

"We went there once, and we all asked, why does Vinnie have a chicken place? No one knew," Kupperberg says. "Maybe it was a front for something? Who knows?"

Colletta would leave the art director post three years later.

Another of Kahn's targets for change was DC's name itself. Although informally known as DC, the publisher's official name was National Periodical Publications. Kahn, rightly so, felt it was anachronistic and obscured that the company was in the comic book business. Kahn's objective paralleled what rival Martin Goodman had done back in the 1960s, organizing the comics published by his various shell companies (*Fantastic Four* #1 was officially released by "Canam Publishers Sales Corporation") under a single, zippy new umbrella name, Marvel Comics.

"National Periodical Publications didn't sound like fun," says Denny O'Neil. "Jenette said, 'No, we're comic books, and we should be proud of it. We're an American art form.'"

National Periodical Publications soon officially became DC Comics, and the change was reflected in the books on sale in late 1976.

"We always referred to the company as 'DC' in the first place, so we welcomed the change," Harris says. "Of course, someone pointed out that 'DC' originally stood for 'Detective Comics,' so the new name was actually 'Detective Comics Comics,' which we thought was funny."

DC's crosstown rivals were less impressed.

"When we decided to change our name, I came up with Marvel because it was a great word to use," Stan Lee says. "When they changed theirs, what did they come up with? DC. I think that's a perfect example of why we outsold them. Whoever was making the decisions there, they were just unimaginative. I'm sorry I'm saying this."

Kahn also set out to update the company's logo, which at the time was a white circle with a red "DC" in the middle, flanked by two red stars on either side. For the job Kahn hired Milton Glaser, the legendary designer behind the "I Heart New York" campaign.

Glaser worked for a few weeks and presented the DC brass with several new options. His favored look was a circle striped with bands of red, yellow, and blue with a blocky, sans-serif DC knock-out in the middle. The novelty was, the logo came in several slightly different variations that seemed to connate movement through space. Imagine a frisbee sailing through the air and how the object might look different depending on where you're standing but is still recognizable as a frisbee.

"It was like a flying object," Glaser says. "That was the first time that that's ever been done, as far as I know, where the logo would change based on your vantage point. They approved it, and I assumed that would be their logo."

It wasn't. For whatever reason DC opted for another option Glaser presented—a riff on their current logo in which the circle and stars were tilted 45 degrees.

"I have no idea why they didn't do it," the designer says. "I guess they took the most conservative position. The one they chose is risk-free. They knew they wouldn't suffer any misunderstanding."

The DC bullet, as it came to be known, debuted on titles cover dated February 1977, and the change had some staffers snickering that they could have tilted a circle for much less than the $25,000 DC was rumored to have splashed out on the overhaul.

The DC offices themselves were updated in an attempt to make the atmosphere more fun. The walls were covered in loud polka-dot wallpaper, and office nameplates were created in the shape of comic book word balloons. A statue of Superman was installed in the lobby. At a time when ads were touting the upcoming *Superman: The Movie*, Kahn had a baseball jacket made for herself that read "Superman: The Comic Book."

"They weren't earth-shaking changes, but they made you happy to be doing comic books," Denny O'Neil says. "It became more than just a way to get next week's paycheck."

DC's stiff office culture began to relax somewhat. A few of the younger staffers would sneak down the emergency stairs to the building's basement and fire up a joint. Even the company's notoriously stringent dress code began to break down. In 1977 two writers, Cary Bates and Marty Pasko, decided to test the limits by turning up at the office in sports coats and open-collar shirts—but no ties. And they were allowed inside.

"The news swept the industry," says Jim Shooter, then Marvel's associate editor. "Everyone was on the phone: 'They let them in!' It was a big deal, like they'd chopped down the Berlin Wall or something."

For a couple of years Marvel and DC had been locked in a war of escalation, as each company steadily ramped up its output in an effort to drown its competitor. Kahn launched an even more aggressive initiative, announcing that DC would push out still more new titles while dramatically increasing each comic's page count—as well as its price. In June 1978 the company's comic books were set to rise from thirty-six pages to forty-two, with an accompanying price increase from 35 cents to 50 cents.

Kahn touted the change known as the "DC Explosion" in a "publishorial" appearing in the company's comics. She promised "an explosion of new ideas, new concepts, new characters, and new formats."

To produce all this new material, DC was forced to adopt an editorial policy that writer Mike W. Barr termed the "warm body theory." If a body was warm, it could write a DC title. The company also poached several artists and writers from its rival. Gerry Conway returned after a brief stint as Marvel editor-in-chief, and *Amazing Spider-Man* artist Ross Andru took a job as editor. Len Wein, another former Marvel EIC, left the House of Ideas after DC offered him *Detective Comics* and Stan Lee refused to let him work for both companies. DC's spokesperson, Mike Gold, admitted at the time that the raid was also done in hopes of crippling Marvel so that it would no longer have enough talent to follow DC's lead in producing thicker, higher-priced comics.

DC need not have worried. At a 1978 college speaking engagement, Stan Lee was asked about the coming DC Explosion and whether he'd follow suit. He was blunt.

"Unless they do so well and the kids buy nothing but their books and we lose a fortune, then I'll do it, but I don't expect that to happen," he said. "I have a feeling that we'll sell more books than ever, and they're going to fall flat on their face."

In addition to a talent for snappy dialogue and self-promotion, it seems Lee was also a gifted soothsayer. Just three months after the DC Explosion began, it was suddenly called off, leading to one of the biggest bloodbaths in comic book history.

DC's parent company, Warner Communications, had become increasingly concerned with the comic book division's lackluster sales, especially after a particularly brutal showing in the winter of 1977–1978. Some of the slowdown may not have been DC's fault, however.

"Just about the time the books started rolling out, the Northeast got hit with an ice storm, a blizzard, and another ice storm," says DC's Rozakis. "For three weeks trucks were just not able to get out on the road and make deliveries. You had a whole load of comics that got printed, shipped to warehouses, then three weeks later, they got sent back. So the Warner people looked at the numbers and said, 'No, this whole thing is a failure.'"

In the minds of the Warner execs drastic action was required. And that's what DC got. Nearly half of DC's entire line was killed off in a single day. Gone were newcomers, including *Firestorm* and *Steel*, as well as planned titles that never even saw a first issue, such as *Vixen*. Of the fifty titles launched by DC in the previous three years, only six were spared in 1978. In order to better compete with Marvel, the format of DC's remaining titles was brought back in line with its competitor's. The page count was reduced to thirty-two and the price was lowered to 40 cents. Staff was fired. The purge became known as the "DC Implosion"—a darkly humorous take-off of the DC Explosion—though the employees were careful not to utter the phrase around the office in front of executives.

"The Implosion was a huge shockwave," says artist Steve Bissette, then a student at New Jersey's Kubert School, where classes were taught by professionals, including some from DC. "Teachers would show up to work, and their eyes would be red from crying on the train."

The cuts were painful, but the economics may have made sense in the long run, as the Implosion allowed DC to kill off its marginal titles and focus on its marquee heroes, who brought in the rich merchandising money. After the distributor took its cut and production costs were accounted for, a middle-tier title might have earned DC only about $400 in profit per issue—hardly even worth getting out of bed for. Once again there was genuine fear around the DC offices that the company, in its present form, might just go away. Editorial would be shut down, and production of original material scrapped in favor of reprints.

The reduction in titles threw numerous freelancers out of work. DC suddenly had many fewer pages to fill, and dibs went to the talent whose contract guaranteed them a certain amount of work each month. The day after the Implosion out-of-work freelancers lined up at the Marvel offices as early as 6:30 in the morning, hoping to land work.

DC's troubles naturally benefited Marvel, and some staffers reacted callously to DC's plight. "More market share for us" was the sentiment among some.

But Marvel was facing its own challenges. Stan Lee's day-to-day involvement with publishing was diminishing each year, and he was focusing more of his efforts on landing TV and movie deals. "Comics are sort of beneath him," an unnamed writer would complain to the *New York Times* in 1979. Lee's abdication of the top spot in 1972 had given way to a tumultuous six years that saw a game of editorial musical chairs, with a procession of five different editors-in-chief.

Each of the new bosses had difficulty keeping up, as the company went from producing about twelve titles a month to forty or fifty in the mid-1970s.

Marvel's increased production schedule sowed chaos. Mistakes were rampant. Deadlines were missed, forcing last-minute replacement with reprint material. Writers operated under little editorial oversight.

"Stan's attitude was, you have three responsibilities," Marvel writer Chris Claremont says. "Get the book in on time, write good stories, don't be a pain in the ass. You can choose two, but he'd prefer all three. So basically you'd get a book and be on your own."

"We would plot a story and do the best we could there, but we didn't know what the issue after that was going to be," Marvel's David Anthony Kraft says. "That was the job for the next plot. We were making the shit up as we went along, and that's the only way you ever get a Howard the Duck."

Even Jack Kirby's return didn't provide much of a boost. After DC failed to offer Kirby a contract renewal he was happy with, the artist returned to Marvel in 1975. Although some staffers weren't so keen to see him return after his defection.

"There are a couple people there who were telling me, 'Well, he left. We don't want him back,'" recalls Roy Thomas. "I thought they were idiots. He was still identified with Marvel. He was the best superhero artist. And it's better that you have him than DC, because even though his stuff hasn't done that well at DC, sooner or later he might hit it."

Kirby took over his cocreation, *Captain America*, and soon launched new titles *Devil Dinosaur* and cosmic saga *The Eternals*.

"He came back, he got to do his Captain America, and he was feeling that the Marvel universe had gone on without him," says previous *Captain America* writer Steve Englehart. "Stan was able to make it work without him. I think he was pissed off at the world, he was divorced from the Marvel universe, and he thought he'd just do his Kirby stuff because that was the Marvel universe."

The toll of working for so long in an industry that had taken advantage of and undervalued him was evident. Kirby, nearing age sixty, seemed burnt out and disinterested.

"I was editing [Marvel newsletter] *FOOM*, and I was talking to Jack on the phone, trying to promote *Devil Dinosaur*," says Kraft. "I said, 'Is there anything you can give me to help me push this book?' He paused and he said, 'Yeah, Devil Dinosaur. He's red.' That's what I got."

Kirby's work polarized readers, and many wrote critical letters printed in the comics' letters columns. With his powers and his stature among fans diminished, he would leave Marvel for the last time in 1978. He later found work in animation.

"Kirby had come from really crappy treatment from Marvel on his return there, and animation was like night and day to him," says animator Darrell McNeil. "He got to work with young guys like me who loved and revered his work, and the pay and health benefits he received were so much more to his liking, he became a much happier person."

Back at Marvel, into the chaotic scene came yet another editor-in-chief. Jim Shooter, the man who'd gotten his start writing for DC at age thirteen, took over early in 1978 and immediately brought a harsh discipline that the freewheeling Marvel had been lacking. He imposed new rules and new protocols, and he hired new staff, including a traffic manager and a production expert, to help alleviate the strain on the overworked editors. He demanded clearer storytelling and supervised books more closely. He canceled underperforming titles.

In a way it was like DC's more regimented system had come to Marvel.

"This was wild and crazy Marvel," says Kraft. "People would be having water pistol fights and doing pretty much whatever we wanted. And here comes Shooter out of the DC world. He set up a system where each editor has a family of books, and they have an assistant editor. He instituted that system I really despised over there."

Whether or not the staff liked the new order, it led to increased sales. Marvel's slim lead in market share would soon balloon to double digits.

Much of Marvel's rise would come on the back of one particular book, the *Uncanny X-Men*. The story of the mutant outcasts had ceased publishing original stories and turned to reprints in 1970. The title was revived in 1975 with a whole new set of characters, and it would soon rise to become Marvel's best-selling title and a force in the industry. And strangely, much like *Fantastic Four*, it owes its existence, in part, to DC.

The idea for a revival came in the early 1970s from Marvel's then president, who recognized the importance of overseas licensing and suggested creating a team composed of international heroes. Writer Mike Friedrich, editor-in-chief Roy Thomas, and a freelance artist named Dave Cockrum went to lunch in midtown Manhattan to hash out a concept. Thomas pictured the book as a mutant spin on DC's Blackhawks, a team of soldiers from various countries.

Cockrum, who was then illustrating the Legion of Super-Heroes for DC, had been angling to draw something for Marvel and showed Thomas sketches for a group of characters he had developed for DC in 1972. One was a fanged killer with big hair and sideburns whom Cockrum called Wolverine. Another was a demonic blue creature with three fingers and a tail called Balshazaar. A third was called Typhoon and could control weather.

Cockrum's DC editor at the time, Murray Boltinoff, rejected the characters because he "was very conservative and didn't want to do anything to offend his readers."

DC's loss was Marvel's gain. Many of the characters were ultimately adapted for the revamped X-Men.

The new series relaunched with 1975's *Giant-Size X-Men* #1, and the team included Wolverine (now Canadian with sharp claws that popped from his hands), German teleporter Nightcrawler (adapted from Balshazaar), Colossus (a metallic, Russian strongman), and Storm (a weather-controlling African whose powers were borrowed from Cockrum's Typhoon and her look from another of his characters called Black Cat).

It's fun to speculate how comics history might have been different had DC accepted Cockrum's characters for the Legion of Super-Heroes.

"Those characters probably would have disappeared," says Mike Friedrich. "They wouldn't have been gigantic hits. It was about the relative positions in the market, and X-Men had a bigger brand name relative to the Legion of Super-Heroes."

The title's new writer was Chris Claremont, a Marvel associate editor who'd landed the gig after offering story suggestions to Cockrum and editor-in-chief Len Wein. Claremont, a part-time actor, brought a knack for drama to the title.

"Chris had this operatic thing that Jack Kirby might have done the best, plus a level of soap opera, plus having strong female characters, plus this basic idea of misfits hanging together, hounded and hunted by the rest of the world," says Ann Nocenti, the *Uncanny X-Men* editor in the 1980s. "It was a combination of things that worked beautifully."

John Byrne, a Canadian fan-turned-artist, began drawing the book in 1977 after Cockrum's departure, and *X-Men* soon exploded, unleashing many now-classic stories.

"When comics went up to 35 cents in 1976, that's when the readership really dropped off. We had hundreds of readers who just stopped reading comics," says California dealer Robert Beerbohm. "What brought them back was the John Byrne *X-Men*. I started ordering more heavily. By [1978's] #114, I was up to ten thousand an issue."

The *X-Men* creative team would soon become superstars (Marvel sent them on a European tour in the eighties), and the franchise's success would help reinvigorate the comic biz and become Marvel's prime driver for years to come as the publisher continued to outpace DC.

The June 1979 sales chart published in the *Comic Reader* showed Marvel completely dominating. The first DC book, fantasy series *Warlord*, came in at number twenty-one.

"[Circulation director] Ed Shukin and I were talking one time," says Jim Shooter, "and he said, 'DC has better production than we do. They outspend us on advertising twenty to one. Everything about their books is better, except we beat them between the covers.'"

Even in the 1980s DC continued to struggle to understand what made Marvel's books sell and to launch a Marvel-style hit of its own. That would soon change. And it would take grabbing some talent from Marvel to do it.

DC's task would become easier after Jim Shooter was put in charge of Marvel in 1978. Shooter's new order and blunt manner rubbed some veteran staffers the wrong way and sent a few scurrying over to DC.

"I remember somebody at DC saying Jim Shooter's the best recruiter we've got," says Denny O'Neil. "There were only two companies. If you couldn't stand Marvel anymore, DC was where you could go. And DC got some good talent that way. I remember Jenette mentioning that."

One of the main points of contention was Marvel's allowance to let some writers serve as their own editors, a system partially driven by the huge amount of titles the company was releasing. Shooter set out to end the practice.

One of the aggrieved was Roy Thomas. DC had been making overtures to the writer-editor since the mid seventies, but Thomas had always resisted, not eager to write DC's superhero titles. But following a bitter contract dispute with Marvel in 1980, he finally bolted for the competition. His fifteen years at Marvel were over, and someone who was perhaps second only to Stan Lee in being so closely associated with Marvel was going to DC.

"There's only two or three people up at Marvel that I'd even care to be in the same county with," an angry Thomas said at the time.

One of the reasons DC coveted Thomas was because of his success writing *Conan the Barbarian*, the licensed, swords-and-sandals title launched by Marvel in 1970 that had become a phenomenon and spawned a slew of imitators. DC asked Thomas to create something similar, and he responded in 1981 with *Arak, Son of Thunder*.

Gene Colan, a penciler on Marvel's hit *Tomb of Dracula*, bolted Marvel in 1981 after he became frustrated with Shooter forcing him to make corrections. Shooter says Colan was "hacking" and his work had gotten lazy. Colan was soon put on the prestigious *Batman*.

"If Gene Colan is being positioned as having been rejected from Marvel Comics, we can only say we dearly hope Marvel will continue to reject all their talents of comparable stature," DC's Paul Levitz told *The Comics Journal* at the time.

Arguably the most significant defection was Marv Wolfman, Marvel's former editor-in-chief who'd been writing *Fantastic Four* and *Amazing Spider-Man*, among others. Wolfman became disgruntled when he was no longer allowed to be a writer-editor and after his long-running art team on his well-received *Tomb of Dracula* was broken up against his will. He phoned DC's Paul Levitz and soon hammered out a contract that began on the first day of 1980.

"I don't really begrudge DC Marv," Shooter told the press at the time. "I think they really need some top quality people there, and it's healthy for us if they do have some top-quality people."

Marvel didn't appear particularly worried about the talent drain. The company believed not only in the strength of its remaining talent but in the inherent superiority of its characters and storytelling technique—that mystical formula that Jack Kirby and Stan Lee had conjured back in the 1960s. It wouldn't matter who its competitor stole, they believed. Marvel would always have the edge, no matter what DC did.

Shooter once got some troubling news when an in-house tattletale informed him that one of Marvel's staff colorists had been on the phone with recent DC defectors Len Wein and Marv Wolfman "letting everyone at DC know what we're doing."

"You know what?" Shooter responded. "Let's invite [the DC people] over. Let them come to our meetings. They can listen to every damn word

I say. I don't give a damn what they know. We can do it, they can't. We are better than them, and we will win."

But in 1980 DC would produce a bona fide Marvel-esque book—arguably its first since *Doom Patrol* in 1963.

When Wolfman had committed to DC, one of his requests was that he wouldn't be put on team books. He didn't like them. That prohibition soon went out the window, and thank God for DC that it did. The writer had been developing ideas for a new book with Len Wein, a DC editor and Wolfman's good friend. The two began batting around a modern spin on the *Teen Titans*, a book about teenage heroes that had debuted in 1966 and had sputtered along before being canned in 1978.

Wein and Wolfman assembled a team of new and preexisting characters and pitched the idea to Jenette Kahn. DC's publisher wasn't wild on the idea, having loathed the previous incarnation of *Teen Titans*—one of the only books in the company's history that was canceled not because it was unprofitable but because it was judged embarrassingly bad by those in house.

Kahn became more open to the idea after Wolfman recruited artist George Perez. Perez was a Bronx-born comic book fan who, in his early years, had worked as bank teller across the street from DC's offices. There he would geek out when the various DC editors would come in to make deposits, and Perez would dream about one day drawing superheroes professionally. In the mid-1970s he got a job as an artist's assistant and soon began landing regular work from Marvel. That eventually led to a star-making run on the *Avengers*.

DC was so enthusiastic about the *New Teen Titans* that a sixteen-page preview was inserted free of charge in *DC Comics Presents* #26, costing the company a considerable amount. That sneak peek was followed by issue #1, released August 1980, and from the first few issues it was clear that the adventure of these college-age heroes were to be more sophisticated than previous incarnations. (The creative team had hoped to drop the "Teen" from the title but couldn't due to copyright concerns.) The *New Teen Titans* was a similar mix of superhero action, soap-opera characterization, and dangling subplots that had made Marvel's *X-Men* so successful.

"George and I always called it DC's first Marvel book," Wolfman says. No surprise considering that the three responsible for the *Titans* were "three refugees from Shooter-land," as one magazine put it.

"That was basically our version of the *X-Men*," says former production manager Bob Rozakis. "It was definitely about trying to do the same kinds of things that was making *X-Men* sell."

Almost immediately fandom began referring to the book as "DC's X-Men," although the truth was that Wolfman had actually been attempting to do a riff on the *Fantastic Four*—a family book. The Titans weren't related, but they shared rooms in a tower and had a dynamic similar to a family, with all the joy, angst, strain, and camaraderie. Robin, the leader, was like the responsible, stern father; Wonder Girl, a young Amazonian, was the mother; Starfire, a skimpily attired alien princess, was the hormone-fueled daughter; Kid Flash was the studious older brother; and shapeshifter Changeling was the mischievous little brother. Half-man-half-machine Cyborg was the angry teen sulking in a corner. And Raven, a mysterious witch from another dimension, was like the weird cousin that ruins Thanksgiving.

New Teen Titans quickly earned buzz and became a major success for DC, surprising many. Perez visited a local comics shop after the first issue was released, only to find the store hadn't ordered many copies, convinced the book would soon be canceled—after all, DC hadn't had a hit in years.

The fact that the *New Teen Titans* was well written and beautifully illustrated didn't hurt. It may have even been one of the first DC books to crack the Marvel Zombies—those fans who slavishly bought everything Marvel put out. And only Marvel.

"As Marvel expanded, that Marvel Zombie collector was facing a tough financial decision where they couldn't collect them all anymore," says Bill Schanes, who, with his brother, founded distributor Pacific Comics in 1971. "By the time the eighties rolled around, a lot of those collectors became more title specific. Prices were going up, and the competition had more compelling items, such as *New Teen Titans*."

"It was a fun book," *X-Men* writer Chris Claremont says. "I enjoyed reading it because Marv is a really good writer and George is a kick-ass artist, but I thought, honestly, the X-Men characters were better. If you look at Teen Titans—Robin, Kid Flash, Wonder Girl—they were all derivative of other characters [Batman, Flash, and Wonder Woman]. Cyborg and Changeling were the only nonderivative characters."

"After the *Titans* became a hit, Marvel did try to lure me back to them," Wolfman says. "But I was really happy with the freedom I had at DC to do the kinds of comics I loved."

New Teen Titans may have been a massive sales success, but in the early 1980s it remained one of the lone bright spots in DC's lineup. The comic book publisher continued to sputter, and Marvel widened its lead, doubling its rival's circulation by June 1984.

"We were concerned about DC's sales numbers, to be honest," says writer Peter David, then working in Marvel's sales department. "Whether there's rivalry or not, let's face it, the comic book industry can't really survive if DC goes away. We always felt our mutual survival depended on each other."

DC had introduced a new marketing slogan in 1983 proclaiming, "There's no stopping us now!" Someone pinned up one of the ads in Marvel's office, and Claremont once walked by and cracked, "Yeah, there's no stopping us now because we're heading straight downhill."

The widening sales gap rekindled the rivalry between the companies.

"There was no enmity for a long time between Marvel and DC until after the Implosion and when we really started taking over," Shooter says. "That changed the landscape a bit. We kept winning and winning and winning. They started getting pissed off."

After a New York City comic shop owner told a newspaper that Marvel's lead came down to Shooter's willingness to "play hardball," the Marvel editor-in-chief promptly had a plaque made with the phrase to proudly hang on his door.

Another factor adding to the rising hostility was Marvel's 1982 move to new offices some thirty blocks south. Before the move DC and Marvel's offices had been within walking distance of one another and also close to Central Park, so employees from both companies would regularly meet there to hang out and play volleyball.

"Now, we were too far downtown," Shooter says. "We didn't play volleyball together anymore. They didn't come over and hang out anymore. It started being them and us, and they just really seemed to hate us."

(Wolfman told a British fanzine at the time that Shooter "systematically kept people away from a DC/Marvel friendship like we used to have.")

Once-straightforward business matters, such as price increases, suddenly became a source of intercompany sniping. After DC announced a raise from 40 to 50 cents in 1980, Marvel scoffed, vowing not to follow its rival's lead.

"That doesn't really impress me. I don't think it impresses the people upstairs either," Shooter told the *Comics Journal* at the time.

Two months later, though, Marvel announced an identical price increase to take effect the same month as DC's. Copies of previous news stories wound up pinned to DC's communal bulletin board, with all the quotes denigrating DC's increase gleefully highlighted.

Even the regular softball games between the two companies became heated, with the casual matches in Central Park taking on an increased significance. Shooter, who played first base, says he suspected that DC might have been bending the rules to get the coveted W. At one game Shooter noticed a particularly athletic and strapping guy on DC's team whom he didn't recognize, despite the industry being small at the time.

"What do you do for DC?" Shooter asked the stranger.

"Uh, I do production," the man said.

"Oh, do you use rubber cement one coat, or how do you work?" the Marvel editor-in-chief inquired.

The man paused and said, "Uh, I do production."

A 1979 deal for Marvel and DC to cooperate on a new batch of crossover books didn't help relations. In fact, it made things worse. Much worse.

The one-and-only superhero team-up between Marvel and DC, 1976's *Superman vs. The Amazing Spider-Man*, had been a decent hit, and Jenette Kahn was eager to do more. She invited Shooter to lunch near DC's Rockefeller Center offices in 1979. The two hashed out an agreement to produce at least three more crossovers in the coming years, a slate that tentatively including a meeting between Hulk and Wonder Woman and another with Batman and Captain America.

The two sides agreed to switch off production duties, potentially avoiding the political maneuvering that had bedeviled the 1976 cooperation. Each company would have approval rights, and the profits would be split right down the middle.

The first entry was to be an encore meeting between A-list characters Superman and Spider-Man, a book that alone would add some $300,000 to Marvel's coffers. For a creative team Shooter chose Marv Wolfman to write it, John Buscema to pencil, and veteran artist Joe Sinnott as inker, but after Wolfman defected to DC, Shooter opted to write it himself, reasoning he was one of the few who had written both Superman and Spidey.

He drafted a plot, using some of Wolfman's ideas, and sent it over to DC for approval. According to Shooter, DC took four months to get back to him, putting the project dangerously behind schedule.

Buscema began drawing and made quick work of the story that pitted Superman and Spider-Man against Doctor Doom and Parasite, a DC villain that could absorb the powers of anyone he touches. Shooter had hurriedly begun to add dialogue to the finished pages when word came from DC that Warner Books was publishing a second, smaller, paperback-sized version of the comic, pushing the deadline back four months, ostensibly giving more time for the harried project.

"I thought we were saved," Shooter says. "But the contract still had the original due date. There was no amendment. I didn't think it needed it."

A few days later Shooter joined in a regular Friday night poker game for comic pros at Paul Levitz's Village apartment.

"When are we going to get this story? It's technically overdue," Levitz asked.

"Warner Books moved it back four months," Shooter replied.

"Technically it's due," Levitz said.

The next Thursday Shooter got a call from Levitz saying if DC didn't receive the finished book by Monday, they were canceling the project. Shooter was scheduled to fly to England for a comic convention but nonetheless headed over to DC to meet with Kahn, Levitz, and Joe Orlando, DC's designated project editor.

"I kept explaining, 'I have a convention. I'll get it to you the following Monday,'" Shooter says.

While Kahn was sympathetic, Levitz insisted that, according to the contract, the story was past due and must be delivered. No exceptions, despite the four-month Warner Books reprieve.

"I was steaming. It just didn't seem right," Shooter says. "I was like, 'What's the matter with you, you little worm?' If Paul was half my size, I would have thrown him out the window."

Shooter skipped the convention and finished the book over the weekend. *Superman and Spider-Man* (the "and" as opposed to the "vs." on the 1976 effort perhaps signaling a level of détente between the company that didn't exist) was released in spring 1981. It was followed by *Batman vs. The Incredible Hulk* later that year and, in 1982, *The Uncanny X-Men and the New Teen Titans*, a pairing that was supposed to feature the Legion of Super-Heroes until *Titans* sales took off.

Those team-ups came with some hiccups here and there but were relatively friction-free. Not so with the next proposed crossover—a project so fraught with difficulties and rancor that it killed cooperation between the companies for more than a decade.

Readers had already gotten to see characters from both companies meet and, in some cases, fight, during the three previous crossovers. The ones released so far had been like the ultimate in fan fiction, providing stories some readers never dreamed they'd see. But there was still one giant itch left to scratch. The companies' two trademark super-teams had still never gone head to head.

The Avengers were going to have to battle the Justice League.

On paper the project made all the sense in the world and was just another in an increasingly long line of joint efforts between Marvel and DC. In execution it turned out to be an earth-scorching disaster that left both sides longing for the relative civility of *Superman vs. The Amazing Spider-Man.*

JLA/Avengers had been announced as far back as 1980 for a potential 1981 release, and a contract was finally signed in 1982. DC's executive editor, Dick Giordano, who had returned to the company in 1980 after a decade of freelance, assigned Gerry Conway to write it. George Perez, the red-hot artist behind *New Teen Titans*, was set to draw it.

Conway's plot involved time-traveling villains, Marvel's Kang, and DC's Lord of Time, using a powerful gem to manipulate the DC and Marvel heroes into fighting each other in various historical eras.

Shooter found the plot nonsensical and gave it to Marvel staffers to review and attempt to fix.

"There were all these plot holes," says Tom DeFalco, then a Marvel editor. "One scene stays in my mind. At some point Hawkeye and Green Arrow are facing off, and they fire arrows at each other, and their arrows collide head first, which is really cool. The arrows hit each other, and then for some reason both arrows turn at a 95-degree angle and fly into some disc that causes time to reverse itself. Flying off at a 95-degree angle? I remember [editor] Mark [Gruenwald] and I laughing about that."

Marvel demanded rewrites, touching off months of back-and-forth between the two companies.

"On a personal level I was really pissed that Shooter trashed me in the process of criticizing it," Conway says. "I'm as much a professional as anyone, and I gave that book 150 percent of my attention and effort, and I think Jim is very good at a lot of things, but he is not one of the best comic book writers in the world. And to have him, especially after the work he did on his [*Superman and Spider-Man*] crossover, criticize my work as being unprofessional or hackwork was just really offensive, and I took great offense."

(Shooter and Conway have since made up and are friendly.)

By late August Marvel had still not given its approval, and Perez angrily walked off the project, vowing never to work for Marvel as long as Shooter was in charge.

JLA/Avengers was quickly earning a bad reputation in the comic book press as an increasingly deflated fanbase followed the squabbling and waited for word on when the long-delayed project might actually see print.

In October 1983 DC's Paul Levitz and Marvel's publisher, Mike Hobson, met for lunch in a last-ditch attempt to save JLA/Avengers. They agreed to issue a joint press release (that Hobson would write) saying JLA/Avengers was back on track, but none ever came. Levitz phoned Marvel about it numerous times but never got a response. The plug was soon pulled.

"On a practical business level it was like, okay, the creative guys can't play nice and make this happen," Levitz says. "We like our creative guy [Giordano] and trust what he says. If he says he can't make this work, end of story."

The companies later fired one last volley at each other in the form of dueling editorials published in their respective comic books. The shockingly transparent essays attempted to explain what went wrong with the "dream" project and to point the finger at the other side for the demise.

"In my view," Giordano wrote in his Meanwhile column, "the JLA/Avengers team-up book will not be published because somebody, or several somebodies, at Marvel simply doesn't want it to be published." A four-page postmortem published in a 1984 issue of Marvel's official fanzine, *Marvel Age*, called that allegation "unfounded and foolish."

"There was a dislike between Jenette and Paul and Shooter," says former DC production manager Bob Rozakis. "It was more of a one-upmanship on an individual basis. I think it was more on Shooter's side, his personality. He had to be number one. It was like, 'I'm in charge of the number-one company, so I should have the final say on everything.'"

The bad blood generated by the failed JLA/Avengers team-up soured relations between the company even further and put an end to the inter-company crossovers for years to come. DC officially gave up on the aborted project and returned the unused artwork to Perez in 1994. He promptly sold it.

The scrapping of JLA/Avengers killed a potential million-dollar windfall, but in hindsight that would be pennies compared to a new outlet that the industry was just beginning to exploit.

Motion pictures.

You Will Believe a Man Can Fly

"In a way, we were the laboratory experiment. Because
we succeeded, the others came on, from Batman to
Dick Tracy to even The Flintstones."

—*Superman* star Christopher Reeve

*D*uring the darkest days of the DC Implosion the staff held onto one
glimmer of hope on the horizon. Their salvation might come not in
the form of a new comic book or the zillionth update of Batman but in an
entirely different medium altogether. The cinematic version of Superman
was set to arrive six months later in December 1978 and, with it, a chance
to rekindle interest in DC and its preeminent hero.

"It began to be generally assumed by the staff that the fate of DC Comics was conjoined with the fate of the movie," Mike W. Barr, then a DC
proofreader, said.

Staffers pored over magazines and newspapers for any factoids and
traded gossip in the hallways, desperate to get a read on the film's direction and potential for success.

The prospect that your employer's and, by extension, your survival
might depend on a superhero film must have been a particularly terrifying
prospect in 1978. Superheroes had been adapted for the big and small
screen virtually since the birth of the genre, but the results had been de-
cidedly mixed.

DC had wisely set out to exploit its marquee characters, almost from the moment of their creation. By 1940, just two years after Superman's first appearance, DC flew a balloon in the annual Macy's Thanksgiving Day Parade and hired an actor to play Superman at the New York World's Fair. (It can't hurt to point out that while DC's founders grew fabulously wealthy, Superman's creators, Siegel and Shuster, spent much of their lives destitute, fighting for a fair share of the character's riches.)

DC's first leaps into another medium came with Superman's popular 1940 radio show, followed by a series of animated shorts by Max and Dave Fleischer. The cartoons were beautifully rendered and gloriously art directed. And they reportedly cost a fortune to make, with studio Paramount dropping $50,000 on the first ten-minute episode alone.

DC's first live-action adaptation starred not Superman but its other popular hero, Batman. The Caped Crusader burst onto movie screens in a low-budget 1943 serial from Columbia that starred doughy unknown Lewis Wilson in the title role. Superman got his own live-action serial in 1948.

The Batman serial is generally considered schlock, whereas the Superman one is regarded more favorably, but what is unusual is how much control DC exerted over its properties, even at a time when many people viewed comic books as trash probably not worth protecting. But DC saw the value in them and demanded a say in nearly every facet of an adaptation, from the costume to the casting to the distribution. DC execs went so far as to demand one Superman prospect take off his pants so they could get a look at his legs before approving his casting.

DC and its licensing partners also understood the importance of reinforcing and protecting the image of these heroes. The Superman serial opened with an image of a DC comic—a savvy plug for the source material that millions would see. In another famous bit of marketing the producer of the Superman serial, Sam Katzman, held a preproduction press conference to announce that he had been unable to find an actor capable of playing the Man of Steel, so Superman himself would have to appear. In the serial's credits the role of Superman was listed as "Superman," even though he was played by Kirk Alyn.

While DC's serials were made for Columbia Pictures, Marvel's first effort came from Republic Pictures, an independent B-movie house that earned the nickname "Repulsive Pictures."

The fifteen-episode *Captain America*, released in 1943, is the kind of bastardized, unfaithful effort that, until the 2000s, was more commonplace with comic book adaptations. Republic's contract reportedly included no stipulation to adhere to the source material, and the character on screen bore little resemblance to the one in print. Instead of Steve Rogers, a skinny World War II soldier who was given an experimental serum that turned him into a superhero, audiences got actor Dick Purcell as Grant Gardner, a district attorney who dons a mask and takes the law into his own hands. Little separated this Captain America from many other generic pulp and comic book crime fighters from the thirties and forties. Marvel wouldn't have another adaptation until the 1960s.

DC, meanwhile, was riding high. The hit *Adventures of Superman* TV series that ran throughout much of the fifties exploded the character's popularity and reinforced DC's family-friendly image—despite star George Reeves being allegedly murdered over a lover triangle gone wrong. The 1966 *Batman* TV show, though campy, was a pop-culture smash and helped fill DC's coffers at a time when comic book sales were on the wane. The company collected $1,000 plus 20 percent of the profits from each episode that aired.

As in the comic book world, DC for a long time was the gold standard in the adaptation biz. Marvel, even after its 1961 superhero revolution, was left pulling up the rear.

"We have people now working on television shows of our scripts," Stan Lee told a crowd at Princeton in 1966. "When they go to a sponsor of the networks and say, 'We're representing Marvel Comics and we have a pilot film,' or whatever it is, and the sponsor of the network will say, 'What's Marvel Comics?' We're so in that we haven't reached the general public yet."

Martin Goodman did manage to cut a deal for an animated series called *The Marvel Super Heroes*. It debuted in 1966 and featured crude animation with limited motion. The images were swiped directly from the comic book panels, and the show ended up looking more like a story board than a finished TV show.

The next year Marvel teamed up with the same low-budget, soon-to-be-bankrupt animator to produce a Spider-Man cartoon. The show stunk. The animation was so shoddy that it looked like it had been created by unskilled prisoner labor in some far-flung Asian backwater. The animators couldn't even be bothered to draw the web pattern on much of Spidey's costume, no doubt finding it too time consuming.

When John Romita Sr., the great artist on *The Amazing Spider-Man* comic book at the time, expressed reservations about the cut-rate production values and urged Stan Lee not to air it, Lee rebuffed him, telling Romita that even a less-than-perfect product was infinitely better than nothing.

"Getting this on television is the first mountain to climb," Lee said.

But none of Marvel's early efforts was able to capture what made their comics so special. The shows existed simply to sell "breakfast food" to "four, five, and six-year-olds," as Lee admitted in 1974.

Throughout the seventies the prevailing attitude at Marvel was that the characters weren't worth much. Martin Goodman's son Chip made a terrible deal to option the entirety of Marvel for just $2,500. A few years later, in 1976, Marvel sold the rights to twelve characters to Universal. The price: just $12,500.

"Marvel in particular had so little understanding or belief in their characters outside the comic book world," says former Marvel editor-in-chief Gerry Conway.

CBS tried out a live-action Spider-Man TV series in 1977 that is best forgotten. Beneath a waka-waka disco soundtrack straight out of a vintage porno, Nicholas Hammond—a grown-up Friedrich from *The Sound of Music*—donned a shoddy-looking costume and solved capers. The series dispensed with Spidey's famous rogues' gallery and failed to capture what made Peter Parker such a lovable underdog.

The Incredible Hulk, also bowing in 1977, performed more strongly and was better able to translate the appeal of the comic book character to the screen. David Banner (Bill Bixby) is tortured by his propensity to turn into a giant green monster and spends his days forlornly wandering America in search of a cure. The series lasted five seasons, but Lee was still dissatisfied with how much it diverged from the source material.

"I'd be happier if the shows hewed closer to our original comicbook story lines; and yet, I'm aware of the reasons which caused the networks and the producers to make so many changes," Lee wrote in a 1978 Soapbox column. "Basically, they were afraid the shows would seem too 'comicbooky' if they were presented exactly the way you see the stories in our own magniloquent mags."

"I could take my grandma and put her in a cape, and they'll put her in a green screen and have stunt doubles come in and do all the action. Anybody could do [Marvel movies] . . . So to me it's not authentic."

—Jason Statham in 2015

"It's Jason Statham. He's like a featherweight. He's got nothing on me! Clearly."

—Mark Ruffalo in 2015

Even with a proliferation of TV and movie properties—Wonder Woman enjoyed a popular series starting in 1975 and Dr. Strange got a 1978 TV movie—comic books remained stigmatized. William Dozier, the executive producer of the 1966 *Batman* series, once admitted that he was embarrassed to read Batman comics in public as research. "I felt like an idiot," he said.

A 1978 *Us* magazine article on *The Incredible Hulk* promised, "It's not a 'comic book show,' the stars insist." A starchy CBS executive was quoted assuring nervous viewers, "The Hulk is not a comic book character. We attempt to surround him with mature stories and realistic people." Bixby supposedly snickered, "Really? A comic book character?" when offered the role of Banner.

So by late 1978, when the Superman theatrical film was set to hit, the idea that it would be anything other than a passable B movie was fairly far-fetched. Superheroes were a low-prestige business, and there was no precedent for a superhero project that would be taken seriously and would appeal to all audiences, not just children.

The Superman rights had been secured in 1973 by a father-and-son producer team, Alexander and Ilya Salkind, along with partner Pierre Spengler. Poland-born Alexander had never heard of Superman before his son urged him to pursue the rights after having seen a Zorro poster on a Paris street. (The elder Salkind referred to the character as "Mr. Superman.")

Warner Bros. let them go for cheap, with the then head of production saying dismissively, "It's not a good property for a film."

As with previous Superman productions, DC was intimately involved and had a fifty-four-page contract drafted, giving the publisher control over the script, casting, and costumes. One of the writers hired to produce an early draft was Mario Puzo, the celebrated author of *The Godfather* and someone who'd once worked for Marvel's Martin Goodman writing prose adventure tales.

Puzo's 1975 script clocked in at hundreds of pages and did little to capture what made Superman magical. The plot involved an assassination attempt on the pope, and the tone veered more toward the camp of the 1966 *Batman* TV series. In one scene Superman is having dinner with Lois Lane and decides he needs a bottle of Champagne. He scans the world with his super-vision and discovers that the Queen of England is about to christen a ship. Superman rockets across the globe to swipe the bottle. In another misstep Telly Savalas from TV's *Kojak* was to make a comical cameo and deploy his catchprase, "Who loves ya, baby?" after Superman mistakes him for his bald nemesis, Lex Luthor.

"When the script for the first Superman film was presented for my approval, I couldn't believe it," DC's then-publisher Carmine Infantino wrote in his autobiography. "This was not Superman. . . . The original script would have bombed and been a terrible embarrassment to the company."

Subsequent rewrites excised the camp, and director Richard Donner, who was brought in after James Bond franchise director Guy Hamilton left the project, was intent on making a serious film—one that pushed back against the prevailing notion that superheroes were exclusively kids' stuff. "It's a movie for adults that children will go see," he said in 1977.

The director hung a banner in his office reading "verisimilitude" to serve as a constant reminder not to capitulate to the temptation that comes so easily when making a story about a man in a red-and-blue leotard. Do not devolve into parody.

The film's reported budget of $50 million—five thousand times that of an episode of 1948 Superman serial—allowed for special effects that made the character viable. Flying had always been a bugaboo with on-screen adaptations of Superman. Portraying the power in a realistic fashion was simply beyond the technology of the day. The movie serial had punted altogether, subbing in an animated Superman whenever flight was necessary. The Salkinds spent $2 million testing various methods, including dangling lead actor Christopher Reeve from a crane, until a special effects man from *2001: A Space Odyssey* came up with a solution. His process involved the actor lying stationary in front of rear-projection footage. The camera would zoom and rotate, giving the illusion of movement.

"You'll believe a man can fly," the movie's tagline promised. But audiences would have to wait until opening day to see Superman in flight. The film's marketing department made several choices it hoped would stress that this was a movie adults could enjoy. One was deliberately keeping the flying effect out of the trailers, knowing that the movie would fail if audiences did not buy it. Another was recoloring Superman's garish, bright red and yellow "S" chest emblem to a more stately, muted silver on the film's poster.

"We had a very expensive film and a very difficult problem in marketing it," Warner Bros. executive Rob Friedman said in 1981. "How did we convey to the public that it wasn't a cartoon or a quickie Saturday matinee serial? How did we appeal to an adult audience without turning off the youth audience?"

The campaign worked, and people of all ages flocked to see *Superman* when it opened on December 15, 1978. The film raked in $7 million its opening weekend, on its way to becoming the then-sixth-highest-grossing movie of all time.

The DC staff attended a screening at a Times Square theater four days before the movie opened to the general public. What they saw blew them away. The film had understood the essence of Superman, embracing it instead of rejecting it for fear that it might turn off mainstream audiences. Here, on the screen, was everything that made Superman great, and it filled the DC staff with pride for their character and the company's long history. For the first time in a while a sense of optimism and community filled DC's halls.

"We thought Superman would be the start of something," says DC writer Paul Kupperberg.

The Marvel staff also recognized the historical importance of the moment for the comic book industry. Soon after the film opened, a group of some thirty staffers walked en masse to a 10 a.m. showing in Times Square. They loved it, discussing it on the walk back to the Marvel offices and for days afterward.

The film would go on to serve as the template for future comic book movies. Donner—and his cry of "verisimilitude"—had finally earned respect for a once-contemptible genre, taking a character who had dangerous potential to veer into the cornball and treating him and the world he inhabited seriously. The filmmakers added to the legitimacy by casting respectable actors not usually associated with spandex. They'd splashed out the exorbitant sums on special effects that were required to allow the audience to suspend disbelief long enough to believe a man really could fly.

This very same formula would later be adopted to produce most every subsequent superhero film. Just not right away. Although *Superman* had been a box office sensation, a deluge of copycat films did not immediately follow, as might be expected in Hollywood's stamp-'em-out culture.

"*Superman* wasn't perceived to be replicable," says DC's Paul Levitz. "No one else thought there was room for another superhero to make a lot of money."

Strangely, the next DC character to get the big-screen treatment was Swamp Thing, the muck monster that had been created for a one-off story in a horror anthology back in 1972. The 1982 flick was directed by a young Wes Craven and starred Adrienne Barbeau and a man in a rubber suit. The movie did little to improve the image of properties adapted from comic books, as Superman had.

At the Swamp Thing DC staff screening, however, there was at least one rave.

"After the movie finished, there was stunned silence," says writer Paul Kupperberg. "Suddenly, from the front row, [Swamp Thing cocreator] Len Wein shouts, 'That was great!'"

The Superman franchise soon descended into schlock as well, completely jumping the shark with 1987's *Superman IV: The Quest for Peace*, which critics savaged and movie audiences largely ignored. The heavy-handed message movie had the hero squaring off against campy villain Nuclear Man, who, with his blond mullet and tight, sleeveless costume, looked like Hitler's masseur. An attempted spin-off, 1984's *Supergirl*, didn't fare much better. It sputtered at the box office and got terrible notices. Roger Ebert branded it "unhappy, unfunny, unexciting." It was so awful that DC's sister company, Warner Bros., declined to distribute it, and the movie was shunted over to TriStar Pictures.

"Just about any superhero movie was going to be wrong in those days," Kupperberg says. "Nobody was going to get it right. There was no interest because adults weren't going to pay to see them. *Superman* was a momentary glitch."

Audiences would have to wait until the end of the 1980s, more than a decade after the first *Superman*, for the next history-making comic book blockbuster—longer if you were a Marvel fan.

Since the late 1970s Stan Lee had been spending an increasing amount of time in Hollywood, attempting to set up movie and TV deals. In the wake of *Superman*'s success, the drive got more determined, especially because Lee felt Warner Bros. had ripped off Marvel's patented formula for its hit movie.

"The first *Superman* movie had a lot of the Marvel pacing, and yet they never had that kind of stuff in the Superman books," Stan Lee said in 1987. "I used to figure if we ever did Spider-Man the right way, the way the books have done him, people would think we were imitating *Superman*. You can imagine the way that makes me feel."

In 1980 Lee left New York and moved permanently to Los Angeles with his wife and daughter. There he worked at Marvel's animation studio and also shepherded a gaggle of potential live-action projects. But it would be years before Marvel was able to replicate DC's *Superman* success.

One confounding aspect of the Richard Donner film was that it did not lead to a boom in comic book sales, as many in the industry had expected. The 1966 *Batman* TV series had launched a feeding frenzy on nearly everything connected with the character, including comic books. Sales of the Caped Crusader's comics had jumped to near a million copies per month, and back issues suddenly became hot collectors' items. Rumor has it that in 1966, at the height of Bat-Mania, a twelve-year-old boy pulled up outside a New York City magazine store in a chauffeur-driven limousine, hopped out, and calmly dropped $25—a then-obscene amount of money—for a few *Batman* issues.

"*Superman* didn't have any effect on sales," says Marvel's then-publisher Mike Hobson. "We talked about it, but no one knew why."

For all its success, the *Superman* movie demonstrated the increasing compartmentalization of superhero characters. When Superman debuted in 1938, there was only one way for fans to commune with the character: read his comic book. Now he—and many other superheroes—had moved beyond those narrow confines and made the leap into other media, from cartoons to Atari 2600 video games to feature films. Being a Superman fan no longer required a trip to the newsstand, and some may not have primarily associated superheroes with floppy, newsprint comic books.

"After the first *Superman* movie came out, I met someone at a party, totally unrelated to comics," says DC's Bob Rozakis. "He asked what I did, and I told him I worked in comics. He said, 'They still publish those?'"

DC was loath to abandon hope that the comic book's expansion to motion pictures would salvage the business. The company did what it could to capitalize on the films, whether that meant keeping the ailing *Swamp Thing* title alive in anticipation of the movie or more stringently policing the series' content so as not to offend potential new buyers. There were cosmetic steps as well. Supergirl's costume was changed in 1983 to reflect the design that DC believed was going to be used in the upcoming film. The new outfit included a goofy red headband that everyone on the book's creative team hated. By the time the movie hit theaters the filmmakers had wised up and ditched the headband, but DC was stuck with it.

The lack of a sales boost was a blow to the ailing industry. Sales at mainstream newsstands were continuing to shrink, as many merchants began to favor more profitable items. When a copy of *Playboy* and a copy of *Superman* took up the same amount of shelf space and a sale of the comic earned a merchant just a few cents, it became a no-brainer as to how rack space should be allocated. Other retailers avoided carrying comic books at all, including larger grocery stores, for fear they'd have kids lying in the aisles reading the books for free.

Another issue was comic book distribution, which was spotty. For devoted readers, finding the latest issues often proved challenging.

"The method of producing, distributing, and selling comic books has changed so drastically in the past 30 to 40 years that it's no longer a viable method," DC's Dick Giordano said in 1980. "They [print] it on reinforced toilet paper and send it to 40 [wholesalers], 30 of which send it back to you without unpacking it. Comic books are considered fodder. . . . You've got to be lucky if you get anything on sale. . . . When you're dealing with those kinds of numbers you've got to know that you only have a few years to go."

The ailing industry was about to find its salvation in an unexpected way—not by expanding its focus but by narrowing it.

The Battle Moves to a New Arena—
the Comic Shop

"There are comic book readers who want to be sold
to in a definite manner. The reader wants a place
where the purchaser is acknowledged as a person,
and not someone who is somewhat off key. Comics
are a hobby that deserves to be catered to."

—Carol Kalish, *Marvel's* former direct sales manager

*B*y some estimates comic books were headed for extinction by 1984.
A lifeline was needed, and it came in the form of a new outlet. Why
overprint hundreds of thousands of copies in hopes of reaching newsstand readers when you can sell directly to the people who want your
books?

By most accounts the first comic book specialty store opened its doors
in San Francisco's Mission District in 1968. Owner Gary Arlington started
the San Francisco Comic Book Company less as a retail venture and more
as a place to store his massive comic book collection. More stores specializing in comics soon followed, including Roy's Memory Shop in 1969 in
Houston, Texas. Its owner was a comics fan and opened it when he was
out of work and looking for a way to turn his hobby into a career.

"There were few specialty stores, maybe twenty-five in the nation," says Bill Schanes, who launched a mail-order company at age thirteen in 1971. "They catered to a smaller, collectors' market."

These stores had a major impact on comic readers lucky enough to live near one. Entering one was like dying and going to comic book heaven—albeit in some cases a heaven with a serious dust problem, lit with fluorescent lights, and located in a strip mall on the wrong side of town. For the put-upon comic book collector these stores solved nearly all the problems the hobby presented. No longer would he be forced to search drugstore spinner racks. The specialty shops carried all the titles, new and unruffled, and often got them weeks before they'd show up on the newsstands.

As devoted as the customers might have been, the big publishers considered sales to these stores negligible. They barely qualified as a rounding error in a business whose sole focus was the newsstand market.

That would begin to change in 1973. That summer at the Comic Art Convention, a fan gathering held each summer at New York City's Statler Hilton Hotel, one savvy dealer and a well-timed gift would change the course of comics history and potentially rescue the industry from certain oblivion.

Sellers at the Comic Art Convention usually dealt in back issues. But Ed Summer, owner of a store on Manhattan's Upper East Side called Supersnipe Comics Emporium, decided to sell something different. The week before the convention Summer went to see the local newsstand wholesaler and asked if he could buy a few comic books off him—as in, every single comic book destined for New York's newsstands that week. To grease the wheels, Summer brought along an expensive case of whiskey. The wholesaler agreed, and Summer set up shop at the convention.

"This had never been done, bringing new comics to a convention that aren't on the stands yet," says comic dealer Bob Beerbohm. "He set up spinner racks and put out all these new comics, and it was like watching a piranha feeding frenzy, like a cow falling into the Amazon river."

The astonishing development caught the eye of two particular bystanders: Sol Harrison, DC's then production head, and Phil Seuling, the convention founder. Seuling was a longtime comics reader who worked as a Brooklyn English teacher and sold comics on the side. He had begun organizing New York City–area conventions in 1968.

Summer's sales gambit at the convention that day quickly opened Harrison and Seuling's eyes to the power of comic fandom. Here was a group far more enthusiastic than the casual readers who then still made up the bulk of readership. These people lived and breathed comics, savoring the mythology and hungering for each new issue. They would sometimes buy two or three copies of a single issue at a time, and instead of tossing them or lending them to a friend when they'd finished reading them, they saved them like precious collectibles.

Later that year Seuling went to DC with an offer. He would buy comic books directly from DC, cutting out the distributor middle man, and sell them to dealers and specialty stores at a deeper discount. He would be allowed to order exactly the books in the quantities he wanted—no more random bundles thrown off the back of a truck.

The catch was that, unlike sales to newsstand distributors, sales through Seuling would be nonreturnable. In this channel, whatever product retailers bought, they'd be stuck with, and the publisher would not grant credit for unsold issues.

That single provision went a long way toward mitigating one of the riskiest elements of the business for DC. Returnability meant the publisher never had a decent handle on sales numbers, and the system was rife with fraud. Wholesalers were no longer required to return torn-off covers for publisher credit and were now simply required to sign an affidavit testifying to how many copies went unsold. Instead of destroying those unsold copies, as required, some unscrupulous dealers secretly sold them out the back door.

DC was torn on Seuling's proposal. On the one hand, management liked the prospect of finding another more profitable and less corrupt means of distribution. On the other hand, it worried about ticking off the powerful wholesalers to whom it had been selling its products since the beginning.

"The newsstand market kept declining and becoming more problematic," DC's Paul Levitz says. "The thinking was, there were a few of these comic shops. They'll buy some comics. Maybe we can sell another two books."

Shortly after he cut the deal with DC, Seuling approached Marvel's circulation manager, Ed Shukin, with a similar offer. After some back-and-forth, an agreement was hammered out, and the so-called direct market was born.

The new revenue stream soon proved lucrative. Marvel rang up $300,000 in direct market sales in 1974, the initial year. That money would continue to grow, and by 1979 that $300,000 had ballooned to $6 million.

"It was pretty clear to a number of us by 1976 or 1977 that this would be a viable part of the business," says Levitz. "It wasn't clear that it was going to be *the* business until the end of the seventies or early eighties."

Comic books stores continued to spring up across the country (and distributors to serve them), numbering as many as three thousand in the early eighties. These shops provided a much-needed focal point for hobbyists.

"It gave people a place to go where they could talk about this stuff, because the newsstand guy at 7-11 doesn't care about comics," says Scott Koblish, a Marvel staffer in the 1990s and current *Deadpool* artist. "When I started liking comics in '78 or '79, it was kind of a secret thing. You didn't want to get beat up for reading comics, and back then, it felt like you could get beat up. I kept it quiet back then."

Direct sales began accounting for a larger share of both companies' output, especially at Marvel. Sales to comic specialty outlets accounted for 20 percent of the publisher's sales in 1980, compared to less than 10 percent for DC.

Marvel was initially more aggressive than DC in exploiting this new outlet. In 1980 the company hired former DC and Marvel writer Mike Friedrich to oversee its efforts in the blossoming direct market.

"Even though DC was the first one to cut the deal with Phil Seuling for direct only, it was Marvel to be the first to hire Mike Friedrich to manage it and build it," says former DC editor Bob Greenberger. "DC's efforts were always a step or two behind Marvel, and Marvel, as a result, was able to go gangbusters."

DC followed in 1981, tapping writer Paul Kupperberg to spearhead its direct-market efforts. Parent company Warner Communications also sent over a consultant to help analyze data and strategize for this new revenue stream.

Jim Shooter had noticed the direct market's impact shortly after taking over as editor-in-chief in 1978. He was scanning sales reports and saw a not-insignificant line item at the bottom marked "Seagate" that he didn't understand. He soon learned that Seagate was Phil Seuling's company and that these were the copies being sold into the direct market. This one channel accounted for some 6 percent of *Uncanny X-Men* sales.

To test the viability of the direct market, Marvel decided to release a title that could be bought only at specialty stores, not on newsstands. They quickly determined that it shouldn't be one of the company's more popular magazines. *Fantastic Four* and *X-Men* readers might send a killer Sentinel over to Marvel's office in protest if the company released an issue fans had trouble finding at the usual outlets.

In December 1980 Marvel launched a new title starring Dazzler, a musical superheroine who had been created two years earlier via a partnership with LA-based Casablanca Records (of Donna Summer fame). The first issue was offered only to comic shops.

Regardless of the unorthodox distribution plan—not to mention the inherent drawbacks of having a disco-themed superhero—*Dazzler* #1 sold an astonishing 428,000 copies.

"That surprised me, and I think it surprised everyone," *Dazzler* writer Tom DeFalco says. "It was such a giant number."

Never one to let a competitor's good idea go to waste, DC soon followed with a direct-only book of its own: *Madame Xanadu* special #1, released in April 1981. The special, at $1, was priced at double that of a regular comic and still sold some one hundred thousand copies.

The same year Marvel—encouraged by *Dazzler*'s success—converted three of its titles that were struggling on the newsstand, *Micronauts*, *Moon Knight*, and *Ka-Zar*, to direct-only books.

"At the time the focus was the newsstand. That changed gradually," says Marvel's former publisher Mike Hobson.

"When I first started editing at Marvel in 1983 most of the titles came from newsstand, two-thirds newsstand and one-third direct," says former Marvel editor Carl Potts. "In a couple years that inverted."

Both publishers soon became convinced that the direct market was the future of the business. Not only was it a fast-growing element of an industry that had been stagnant for years, but its profitability was unlike anything else in publishing. It was like printing money.

"Over here we have this [old] distribution system that throws away 70 percent of everything we send them and steals from us, compared to a distribution system that's nonreturnable and has better margins," says Milton Griepp, former head of a distribution company and now industry analyst. "The direct market was and is the most profitable system for print distribution in the United States for magazines, books, anything."

It wasn't long before the company's ledgers began to feel the effects. In 1982 the direct market accounted for 50 percent of Marvel's sales but 70 percent of the company's profits, due to the higher prices on the titles sold in comic shops and the nonreturnable nature.

The unexpected success of the direct market and its hefty profits began to change how both Marvel and DC approached not only the business of comics but also the content of the comic books themselves. Soon the tail was wagging the dog.

"By 1981 the companies were clearly focusing in on what the fans wanted," Paul Levitz says.

The growing sales and marketing departments at both publishers set out to study this new breed of buyer who differed from the casual newsstand customer. This direct-market customer was generally older. He was more devoted, sometimes buying nearly every title a publisher offered. It became increasingly clear that what sold on the newsstand wasn't necessarily going to work for comic shops.

"I know for a fact that Marvel was very committed to working closely with the retailers who were selling their books," says Marvel's former PR head Steve Saffel. "And this was an interesting problem at times because a lot of those store owners were comic book fans, and to some degree they preferred to support projects they liked—sometimes more than projects they could sell."

To better lure the direct-market customer, both companies began to tailor their output. Suddenly fannish material once deemed too niche for the broader market was possible. A 1981 Marvel house ad announcing direct-only titles spoke specifically to the growing number of comic book superfans.

"That means these titles are being designed just for you, the discriminating Marvel reader," the ad read. "For this exciting experiment to succeed we need your reactions and your ideas. Just tell us what you'd like to see in these titles—and we'll listen."

DC especially began to launch a slew of sophisticated series aimed at this more discriminating reader, tackling subjects that would have made old-school *Superman* editor Mort Weisinger choke on his pipe.

Camelot 3000, a twelve-issue limited series released to the direct market in fall 1982, was a futuristic spin on Arthurian legend that tackled heady issues such as gender identity and incest. It was written by Mike Barr and drawn by acclaimed British artist Brian Bolland. Barr had conceived of the tale of the reincarnated Knights of the Round Table after taking a literature course in college.

The Omega Men (April 1983) was another direct-only title that made waves for its adult content—in this case graphic violence and cannibalism. The comic spun out of *Green Lantern* and featured a rag-tag team of extraterrestrial mercenaries. Its extreme content unnerved some store owners and had a few industry veterans publicly calling for a ratings system to be imposed on comic books, similar to what movies had.

"Most of the complaints come from older readers who seem to cherish an image of DC comics from the 50s and early 60s like, 'You did all this great stuff back then, why do you have to do more violent comics now?'" *The Omega Men* editor, Marv Wolfman, explained in 1983. "They want the books to be harmless as they were when no one was buying them because they have these fond memories of books they don't even like."

Both companies experimented with different formats. Marvel began releasing a line of sturdy graphic novels—oversized, book-length stories with a $5.95 cover price—in 1982. The first, *The Death of Captain Marvel*, found the cosmic hero, who'd been created for copyright purposes, succumbing to cancer. The book ultimately sold some two hundred thousand copies.

The burgeoning direct market allowed both companies to begin using higher-quality printing techniques that were not affordable with newsstand returnability. Marvel switched from letterpress printing, an archaic method that offered low resolution and muddy art, to the crisper offset printing. DC followed suit in 1981.

One of the biggest breakthroughs would come later in 1983 with DC's publication of *Ronin*, a six-issue miniseries from writer-artist Frank Miller about a feudal-era samurai transported to the future. Miller was a lanky kid from Vermont who, as a teenager in 1976, had moved to New York to break into comics. He'd gotten small jobs at DC and soon became friendly with then-Marvel-editor Denny O'Neil.

"He's one of the few people I met who I could talk to about the work," O'Neil says. "We'd go to Central Park and play volleyball for a few hours, and walking out of the park to get some snacks, Frank would ask really intelligent questions about my work."

Miller was soon assigned to draw Marvel's *Daredevil* with #158 (May 1979). The book quickly became the talk of the industry and its young creator one of its biggest stars, especially within the direct-market and the

hardcore fanbase. Miller, like Jack Kirby and only a handful of others before him, became one of the few whose name on the cover was enough to
guarantee sales. The direct market had the power to make stars of its creators, and the creators were starting to realize it.

"Who the creators were on a title didn't make any difference until the
direct market got up and running," says Marvel's former publisher Mike
Hobson. "The direct market made heroes out of the creators."

The shift changed the way creators were compensated. Since the beginning comic book artists and writers had been paid shoddily. Most collected a page rate—a one-time fee for each page produced—and rarely
received any money beyond that. Even when their work was reprinted,
they got nothing. No money from movies, toys, or all the other items produced as a result of their creation. As writer Arnold Drake once said, the
comics industry was like a brothel, with the publishers acting as the madame and the talent as the girls.

"These companies won't do anything until you stick a knife in their
side and make them bleed," says Neal Adams, who's been on the front
lines of the creator-rights fight since the 1960s.

DC's new publisher, Jenette Kahn, had made it a priority to begin offering royalties soon after her arrival in early 1976, but the business—and
DC—was in such poor shape that no money was available. That changed
in a few years, in part due to the direct market. She believed it was morally
right and felt DC would get better work if creators participated in the
profits. DC hoped to get more books like *Daredevil*, which the company
considered a prime example of what happened when talent was passionate about the work. The royalty system would also, fingers crossed, serve
as an incentive for Marvel's artists and writers to jump ship to DC.

"In 1980 we figured out how to pry the money loose from our budget,"
Paul Levitz says. "We had interesting debates about who deserves more
and how to do it, since the industry had no history of doing it."

DC's royalty plan was announced in November 1981 and would pay a
creative team a percentage of sales above a one hundred thousand sales
threshold, with 2 percent going to the writer, 1.4 percent to the penciler,
and .4 percent to the inker. (The paltry inker percentage was due to the
fact that DC's editor Dick Giordano was an inker himself and didn't want
to be seen as favoring his own kind.)

The new plan meant quite a bit more money for creators—assuming
they worked on hit books, that is. DC's best-selling title that month, *The*

New Teen Titans #12, sold 217,000 copies at a 60 cents cover price. Under the new royalty plan writer Marv Wolfman would pocket an extra $1,404, penciler George Perez $982.80, and inker Romeo Tanghal $421.20. And because Wolfman and Perez had also created some of the characters, they split an additional 1 percent.

DC's plan spurred Marvel to action. "We're not going to just sit there," editor-in-chief Jim Shooter told the press at the time.

"I didn't think they wouldn't [follow]," Giordano fired back. "As a matter of fact, I welcome them to the group. I welcome the competition."

Shooter had been working on his own royalty plan, but implementing it had been held up for various reasons. Marvel's lawyers were wary of offering participation because they worried it might imply that the writers and artists owned their creations. The company also had trouble figuring out how exactly to structure the plan.

"I got mine approved first, but the Marvel bureaucracy slowed it down," Shooter says.

DC's announcement finally forced Marvel's hand. Less than a month later Marvel unveiled its own royalty system that was virtually identical to DC's.

"Marvel was crying poor," Denny O'Neil says. "They said they couldn't manage to give out royalties because so many people worked on every story. They couldn't manage the bookkeeping. When they had to do it, it's amazing how fast and easy it was."

"Jim was able to push through a matching plan in about a month, which was great for them, great for the creative people, a little frustrating for us," DC's Paul Levitz says.

One of the obstacles Marvel faced was that its titles were selling many more copies than DC, meaning it would be on the hook for higher royalty payouts than its rival. Marvel paid out $2 million its first year.

"It really cost us a fortune," Shooter said at the time, before taking a shot at DC. "We don't have Daddy Warnerbucks to fall back on."

Under Kahn DC amped up its efforts to poach Marvel's talent.

"When Archie Goodwin was [editor-in-chief in 1977], we came up with this idea, because we had all these artists coming up and showing portfolios," Shooter says. "I said, 'Let's give them a test, a five-page story and see what they do with it.' It got to the point where, if we would give a guy a five-page tryout, DC would offer them a contract. It was insane."

Soon DC got bolder in its tactics.

"Shortly after Jenette came in, they started getting aggressive and not going after beginners but going after Frank Miller and other big shots," Shooter says.

"There were funny stories of Jenette trying to take Frank Miller," says former Marvel editor and writer Ann Nocenti. "The story was, Jenette would have someone she was trying to [poach] to DC over for dinner, and she'd have cookies made with the character that they were working on. She'd have Walt Simonson over, and she'd have Thor cookies made. She actively tried to poach high-selling people away from Marvel."

Kahn, like everyone in the industry, had been particularly impressed with Miller's *Daredevil* and coveted Marvel's rising star. Kahn invited Miller to lunch at the Warner executive dining room and told the hot artist, "Tell me what it is that you would really like to do. I don't care how offbeat it is or if it's never been done before. Whatever it is, we'll try to make it happen."

Miller laid out his plan for *Ronin*, which he had contemplated doing for Marvel's new graphic novel line. He poured out to Kahn not just his vision for the story but his vision for the package in which it would be presented. Miller pictured something far removed from America's cheap, disposable monthly comics and closer to the book-like graphic novels commonplace in Europe. And most important of all, it would be creator owned.

"We were willing to do things that maybe Marvel wasn't," Paul Levitz says. "Print the book on real paper, find the paper stock that Frank liked from France, work with [painted] color, put it out at a higher price tag, put his name on the front. You had never seen that on a mainstream comic at that point."

Instead of potentially producing *Ronin* with a Marvel imprint, Miller agreed to work with DC, signing what was rumored at the time to be the richest comic book contract ever.

"When Frank Miller went over to DC to do *Ronin*, it was kind of shocking, because here's the *Daredevil* guy going over to do this weird book that no one has ever heard of," says inker Joe Rubinstein, who worked with Miller on the 1982 *Wolverine* miniseries. "I talked to Frank and was on the side of, 'Stay loyal to the company who brought you to the dance.' But I guess he did what any good creator does, and he went and did it somewhere else."

Ronin was released in a forty-eight-page, ad-free format at $2.95. It was hyped by DC's publicity machine and presented Miller's unfiltered

vision, almost entirely free of editorial interference. But the audience response was lukewarm.

"*Ronin* provoked in me not only disappointment," reviewer Kim
Thompson grumbled in 1983, "but also a sense of pessimism with regards
to Miller's future career."

"Frank had decided he could do whatever he wanted and was going
to do this experimental storytelling, and he did this chaotic story,"
Shooter says. "They sold it [to comic shops] really well, but it didn't
sell through [to customers] at all. No one wanted it. [Dealer] Bud Plant
said to me, 'Hey, you wanna buy some *Ronins*?' I said, 'What would I
do with *Ronins*?' He said, 'Firewood. I roll 'em up and sell them by the
cord.'"

Jenette Kahn considered *Ronin* to be among the most important series
DC ever put out, regardless of the relative clarity of its storytelling. It suggested what might be possible in the medium and demonstrated that DC
was willing to give creators the freedom to tell all kinds of stories, not just
those involving corporate superheroes aimed at the bobby-socks brigade.
It would be a philosophy that would serve the company well and would
help usher in what Kahn termed "an Elizabethan age" for DC.

And not a moment too soon.

Even with *Ronin* and DC mega-hit *New Teen Titans*, the company was
struggling. The brass at DC's parent company Warner Communications
was still not sold on the idea that publishing could be a profitable aspect of
its business. The worry for years had been that Warner was going to shut-
ter the underperforming DC and simply milk the characters for licensing
money.

"There were rumors of that every single week I worked at DC," says
Jack C. Harris, a DC editor in the 1970s.

The whispers often reached the rank-and-file staff of Marvel, who
would sit around imagining what they might do if given a crack at the
competitor's iconic superheroes.

In February 1984 they almost got the chance.

Jim Shooter was sitting in his office one day when, out of the blue, he
got a call from Bill Sarnoff, head of Warner Books. Sarnoff had an unexpected offer.

"Look, I've been thinking about this," Sarnoff said. "You guys make a
lot of money selling comics."

"Oh, yes, sir, we do," Shooter replied.

"We lose our shirts every year. Million and millions of dollars," Sarnoff said.

"I know. I can do the math," Shooter said.

"We, however, make a bloody fortune on licensing. You guys hardly make any money in licensing," said Sarnoff.

The Warner boss laid out a proposal in which DC would license its characters to Marvel to publish. The proposal, as incredible as it was, did not mark the first time DC had explored selling out to Marvel.

"Stan told me that some years before Sarnoff called and that a similar offer had been made by Warner Publishing to the Marvel brass," Shooter says. "Marvel made some offer. Nothing came of it."

Shooter brought this latest proposal to Marvel president Jim Galton, and Galton promised to call Sarnoff. The next day Shooter followed up with Galton and was told the deal was off.

"The characters must be no good," Galton said. "They don't sell."

"No, no, no! Those idiots are doing them. We can make them work!" Shooter fired back.

The editor-in-chief proceeded to put together a business plan.

"What's in it for Warner Com is, of course, guaranteed no-hassle money—the elimination of a huge overhead cost and the possibility of a new life for their dying properties," Shooter wrote in a 1984 memo. "What's in it for us is the money we'd make publishing those characters and the elimination of an irritation."

After all these years Marvel would finally be able to strike a killing blow to its "irritating" rival. The plan called for Marvel to begin by publishing seven DC titles: the obvious core characters—Superman, Batman, Wonder Woman, Green Lantern, and Justice League of America—along with two series that were strong performers at the time, particularly in the direct market—*New Teen Titans* and the *Legion of Super-Heroes*.

"I was conservative as possible and had us making $3.5 million in the first two years," Shooter says.

At a meeting with circulation head Ed Shukin and direct sales manager Carol Kalish, Galton asked Shukin what he made of the projections.

"Ridiculous," Shukin said, as Galton shot Shooter a withering look like, *You see?*

"We can double this," Shukin concluded.

Negotiations commenced, and the deal called for Warner to receive a royalty on every copy sold. Perhaps one of the sweetest perks for Marvel was that the company would receive a percentage of any increase in licensing that came as a result of Marvel making the DC characters more successful. Warner's powerful subsidiary, Licensing Corporation of America, might also potentially agree to help Marvel in licensing some of its properties.

Word of the negotiations leaked to Marvel's bullpen, and the excited staff was once again daydreaming about what would happen if they could have a crack at DC's characters.

But it never happened. In the spring of 1984, as the deal was being discussed, indie publisher First Comics filed a lawsuit against Marvel alleging anticompetitive practices. The Chicago-based publisher, best known for Howard Chaykin's award-winning *American Flagg*, claimed that Marvel was flooding the market with titles to try to keep smaller companies off the racks. Retailers had only a certain number of dollars to spend each month, and Marvel increasingly ate up more of the budget, leaving less money to be spent on the indie titles.

The lawsuit raised monopolistic concerns about Marvel and meant that it probably wasn't the best time for Marvel to think about absorbing its biggest competitor. The DC deal was abandoned.

"I think we would have made those characters go," Shooter says. "I worked at DC for a long time, and I knew those characters. I think we would have killed it, done tremendously."

"Then I guess we really would have been a monopoly."

DC's Big, Bold Gamble

"I remember hearing that DC was going to focus
most of their sales on the direct market. And once
I heard that, I turned to [editor] Mark Gruenwald and
said, 'We won't have to worry about them anymore.'
I thought it would be the end of DC comics."

—Former Marvel editor-in-chief Tom DeFalco

*B*y the early 1980s it became clear that Marvel was beating DC at its own game. DC had introduced the American superhero, but in decades since, Marvel had done it better and rocketed ahead. To stay relevant, DC needed a new way forward.

It would start with the creation of a momentous miniseries, one that would impose sweeping changes on the previously staid DC universe and ultimately become one of the most important publications in the company's history.

Continuity had always been a bugaboo at DC. Unlike at Marvel, whose universe was mostly created in a few years by a small handful of people, DC's world had been haphazardly assembled piecemeal over the decades without an overriding plan or a single guiding voice. As a result, its in-story history was rife with inconsistencies. Marvel's Jim Shooter once joked that it was like "a Swedish movie with no subtitles." In a single month in 1974, for example, the Atom declares in an issue of *Action Comics* that he's unable to shrink inanimate objects; over in an issue of *The Brave and the Bold*, however, he's shown minimizing a camera.

To most of us that mistake would be no big deal. We're well aware that a story about a man who can shrink to the size of a dust mite isn't exactly a documentary. But to the hardcore fans this lack of cohesive continuity was a major annoyance. As DC began catering more to the direct market, these hardcore readers who made up the bulk of it became far more important. Those inconsistencies, which once were simply confusing, now threatened to harm DC in the marketplace.

"Don't put conflicting books on the stand at the same time so the kid can . . . decide, 'I'm going to read Marvel where things make sense,'" DC writer Marty Pasko said in 1977. "And then DC loses its audience."

This lack of cohesion also gnawed at writer-editor Marv Wolfman, the man behind the hit *New Teen Titans* who'd come over to DC from Marvel in 1980. His worries grew more pronounced when, in 1981 while editing *Green Lantern*, he received a letter from a reader complaining about a particular story hole from a recent issue. An obscure sci-fi hero had failed to recognize Green Lantern even though they had been shown meeting in an issue three years earlier.

The letter got Wolfman thinking about how to clean up the DC universe. During a train journey he began plotting a far-reaching series he called *The History of the DC Universe* that was intended to take DC's jumbled continuity and create a single, clean timeline in its place. He pitched it to DC the following Monday and was given the green light. The series was mentioned at a 1981 comic convention and then briefly noted in a December 1981 issue of the *Comics Journal*.

Wolfman's twelve-part maxi-series "will propose to tie together the entire history of the DC Comics world," the blurb read.

To sort out everything that had come before, DC in 1982 hired a— very lucky or unlucky, depending on your viewpoint—researcher to sit in the company's extensive library and read through Every. Single. Comic. DC. Had. Ever. Published.

He worked for two years, compiling careful notes on character histories, travels, powers, weaknesses, deaths, births—pretty much every development that had happened in DC Comics—and handed them over to Wolfman.

Putting it all together into a series proved no easy task. The project had originally been announced for 1982. It was later bumped to spring 1983. Finally DC decided to schedule it to coincide with the company's fiftieth anniversary in 1985 and to call it *Crisis on Infinite Earths*. George Perez was tapped as penciler, and he relished the gig, believing it gave him an opportunity to strike back at Marvel.

"It was to get revenge for not being able to do the JLA-Avengers book," Perez said at the time.

Meanwhile the series' ambitions grew. It set out not only to clean up continuity but also to shake up DC's image.

"When people think of DC, they think of a very staid company that doesn't change characters, that publishes the same Superman stories that they published in 1955," Wolfman said in 1985. "I think we're publishing some of the better comics, but we have a very bad reputation for being set in our ways. The *Crisis* is an indication against that."

The series centered on a mysterious cosmic villain called the Anti-Monitor who begins destroying the vast parallel earths—and their inhabitants—that existed within DC's continuity. The Superman we know was said to live here on our earth, but there was also another, different Superman (with gray hair at his temples) from an alternate universe dubbed "Earth 2." Issue #1 hit stands January 1985, and eleven issues later, only one universe would remain. DC could essentially organize its convoluted universe by picking and choosing which events and characters from its long history to keep and which to jettison.

The scope and consequence of *Crisis* was unmatched in DC's history, and a series combining so many heroes into a single, far-reaching story might have blown minds even more—had Marvel not offered something similar a few months earlier.

Marvel Super Heroes Secret Wars had been born in 1982 when toy company Mattel had lost its bid for the DC license to rival Kenner. The company approached Marvel about producing a line of superhero action figures to compete with Kenner's. Fearing Marvel's roster was not as well known as DC's, Mattel asked Marvel to come up with a special promotion that might goose interest in the characters. Editor-in-chief Jim Shooter, drawing on the letters he got from young people almost every week, proposed a massive miniseries chockablock with more than fifty Marvel heroes and villains.

Mattel agreed, suggesting that the series be called *Secret Wars*—two words that research had discovered resonated with young boys.

The series introduced a powerful cosmic figure called the Beyonder, who later showed up in human form in a sequel series, *Secret Wars II*, dressed in a white jumpsuit like an interplanetary Siegfried and Roy. For sport he transports a passel of characters to a faraway "battleworld," where they are forced to face off like spandex-clad gladiators.

Secret Wars got the biggest print run of any Marvel comic for years, and its first issue (May 1984) sold an amazing 750,000 copies.

To some the timing of *Secret Wars* with respect to *Crisis* has always been suspicious—or if you're a Marvel supporter, the timing of *Crisis* with respect to *Secret Wars* has been. Which company could rightfully claim introducing the big, multipart superhero blowout?

Secret Wars appeared a full year before *Crisis*, with the final issue of the Marvel series appearing within days of the first issue of DC's. But many DC supporters were suspicious that Marvel had gotten wind of *Crisis* and rushed out *Secret Wars* to steal some of DC's thunder. A newspaper article at the time reported that the "cutthroat" Marvel had held up shipping the final issue to "overlap the premiere of the DC series." (Not true, but it gives you an idea of the conspiracy theories that surrounded the high-profile projects even back then.)

Jim Shooter says it was the other way around. Marvel had the idea first and DC was not planning a "big, company-wide crossover" until after they found out about *Secret Wars*, which was inevitable considering what a small community the comics biz was back then.

"The first issue of *Crisis* came out the same [month] as the twelfth issue of *Secret Wars*," Shooter says. "And yet they claim they came up with it first."

"*Crisis* got announced first," says DC's Bob Greenberger, who coplotted the series. "I definitely think Marvel was being calculating in doing *Secret Wars*. Jim knew we were going to make noise. Jim knew full well, and he was being commercial and strategic. There was a definite rivalry going on, and Jim was doing what he could to make sure Marvel remained number one."

DC did get in one shot on-page. Wolfman had included a subtle panel in *Crisis* showing the Marvel universe getting destroyed along with DC's parallel earths.

The kernel for *Crisis* might have, in fact, originated many years before it was published.

"When Jenette Kahn first became publisher, she had a party at her apartment on Central Park West [in 1978]," Shooter says. "She comes to me and says, 'You're the big comics guru. What do you think I should do with the DC universe?'"

"Kill it," Shooter replied. "Start it over."

The Marvel boss laid out a radical overhaul of the DC universe in which the company would announce the cancellation of all its titles, bring their stories to a conclusion, then the next month relaunch everything with a new #1. It would be a clean-slate start in which the essence of each character would be preserved but all the cumbersome continuity could be ejected. Writer Gerry Conway had floated something similar when he returned to DC from Marvel in 1976.

"As a joke I suggested it should all be blown up and restarted," Conway says. "I have no idea if that was the genesis of *Crisis*, but someone who was involved once told me *Crisis* was my joke come to life."

The joke would soon be on readers. Whatever their respective virtues and weaknesses, *Secret Wars* and *Crisis* ushered in the era of the comic book event—a genre whose increasing popularity would have harmful consequences for the industry in the decades to come. No longer would it be enough for Superman to defeat the villain of the month. Readers had now gotten a taste of a big important story that was perceived to matter more than the now-pedestrian yarns that filled the books month after month.

"The DC universe will never be the same," a 1984 ad for *Crisis* proclaimed. But once you've raised the stakes that high, where do you go from there?

As the comic publishers would quickly discover, anything branded an "event" sold to the comic book diehards, regardless of whether it was any good. Fans had invested so many hours in these fictional universes that the thought of simply skipping a story they were told ad nauseum held great importance was not an option. They, like any addict, had to get their fix—even if they hated themselves for it afterward.

Events also preyed on the completist mentality of many collectors. Failing to buy a series would leave a painful, gaping hole in their meticulously curated collections. One conflicted member of a Chicago comic book club told *Comics Interview* magazine in 1985 that every member of his group *bought* Marvel's *Secret Wars*—they just didn't *read* it. The reason for the purchase, he sheepishly admitted, was "stupidity."

Marvel's direct sales manager, Carol Kalish, bluntly told retailers at a 1984 summit, "Let's be honest. *Secret Wars* was crap, right? But did it sell?"

It certainly did. And so did its less well-regarded sequel, 1985's *Secret Wars II*. Though not in the obscene numbers as the original.

"Each time [Marvel] puts out a book like that, they lose the confidence of the buyer a little bit more, no matter how much money they make on it," New York comic book retailer Bruce Conklin said in a 1985 interview. "They're winning the battle but losing the war."

His were prescient words. Events soon became the staple of the industry, with both Marvel and DC launching dueling ones nearly every summer (prime time for comic reading) from 1986 to the present day. The hallmark of the series was that they would involve dozens of heroes battling some world-beating threat in a story spread across numerous titles. *Crisis* begat *Legends*, which was followed by *Millennium*, which gave way to *Invasion*. Marvel countered with "Mutant Massacre," "Fall of the Mutants," "The Evolutionary War," and on and on. In a few years events would become so frequent that they would begin to lose their cachet. After all, when everything is an event, nothing is.

But before that, DC would take advantage of the opportunity presented by *Crisis on Infinite Earths*. The company now had the chance to restructure its universe—to chuff off fifty years of baggage and modernize. And that, in a sense, meant bringing it closer to Marvel's.

Wolfman had originally pitched a radical coda to the twelve-issue series that called for DC to cancel nearly all its titles and restart them fresh with new #1s. Besides sending a clear signal to the readership and the industry's talent that DC was serious about revamping itself, the proposed relaunch would have the added benefit of coinciding with Marvel's twenty-fifth anniversary and would have, Wolfman calculated, "blown out" whatever special plans Marvel had for the milestone. (Marvel, in the end, blew out itself by launching a calamitous line of new titles it called "The New Universe.")

DC shied away from the full relaunch, instead settling for a targeted reset of its three core heroes known as the trinity: Batman, Wonder Woman, and Superman. Dick Giordano, then DC's executive editor, had talked about the need to rid DC of its "stodgy *Wall Street Journal* image," and *Crisis* had provided an opportunity to do just that. Suddenly the company would begin taking more chances and opening itself up to riskier interpretations of its material.

"A company with the resources of DC should not be a follower of the latest idea or trend, but the leader, the instigator!" a DC fan whined in a 1983 letter to the *Comics Journal*. "I implore you at the DC offices, quit being led around like sheep and start creating your own ideas and follow your instincts. . . . I want DC to become #1 in sales again so I can show those no-class Marvel fans who's boss."

Chasing the sales lead would require a drastic modernization of its line and an attempt to further appeal to the older, direct-market readers Marvel was so good at capturing.

"DC had to change. Marvel was outselling them hand over fist," says Steve Bissette, a DC artist in the 1980s. "Dick [Giordano] was always a pretty progressive guy. Paul [Levitz] was a smart business man, and Jenette [Kahn] was a free-thinking publisher, unlike any that had existed at DC. There was a window of opportunity to change."

DC's iconic titles had grown stale. Just prior to *Crisis* former publisher Carmine Infantino, who'd entered the business in the 1940s, was drawing *The Flash*, and *Superman* artist Curt Swan was nearing his fortieth anniversary of having first drawn the character.

"A lot of this stuff had not evolved all that much, and that was part of the problem," says former DC editor Brian Augustyn. "Something like Superman had just become to be seen as stodgy."

Before *Crisis* launched, DC began soliciting proposals to update its Trinity. Most important on the list was the Man of Steel.

"At Marvel there would be little jibes that I would hear, like about DC not knowing how to do Superman or DC not knowing what to do with their characters," says artist Jerry Ordway, who was inking *Fantastic Four* at the time.

One of those criticizing DC was John Byrne, a writer and artist who had been one of Marvel's top names since the 1970s, having taken the *X-Men* to the apex of the sales charts with Chris Claremont. Byrne had recently fallen out with Marvel after he drew an experimental issue of *Hulk* composed of nothing but full-page images, and it was rejected.

At a July 1985 housewarming party for Byrne's new Connecticut residence Wolfman and Giordano listened as Byrne laid out what he'd do with DC's top hero if given the chance. Months of negotiation followed, and Byrne was finally hired.

The news sent shockwaves through the industry. DC had, in the span of three years, managed to poach not only (arguably) its rival's top two creators but two names who had worked nearly their entire careers at Marvel and were closely identified with the company. The shocking migration led Marvel editor Al Milgrom to quip, "DC is Marvel and Marvel is DC."

"Spider-Woman has better hair, better costume, frank cho implants and a fucked up origin. Wonder Woman is a walking std farm!!"

—**Marvel writer Brian Michael Bendis on Twitter in 2009**

"I know this is part of the whole Marvel v. DC PR male privilege fanboy outrage machine something or other. But still. These sort of things are an insult to Bendis' dignity."

—**Blogger Smith Michaels responding in 2009**

"The reason [for hiring Byrne] obviously is to get Byrne away from Marvel, and [DC] felt that he had a large enough following that no matter what he did with the book he was gonna sell it," writer Steve Gerber said in 1985.

Byrne set out to "Marvelize" Superman—a term that was in popular use at the time. In other words, he would attempt to update the sterile, godlike Superman for a 1980s audience by borrowing the humanizing techniques Lee and Kirby had used on superheroes in the sixties. "The modern audience now wants a superhero who grunts, sweats, and goes to the bathroom," Byrne said at the time.

Byrne's *The Man of Steel* was billed as "the comics event of the century" and debuted in summer 1986. The six-issue miniseries updated Superman's origin and reset his world, creating a new status quo for the character moving forward.

Marvel just shrugged at the well-publicized makeover—publicly at least. Jim Shooter called *The Man of Steel* "no big deal" and pointed out that Superman had gotten a similar revamp back in 1971. "Nobody noticed, so they dropped it," he told the *Washington Post* in 1985.

The Man of Steel #1 became the best-selling title of 1986, moving more than 1 million copies—twice as many as the top Marvel offering. It led to a brand-new ongoing Superman series written and drawn by Byrne.

In 1987 Wonder Woman got a similar rehabilitation, courtesy of *Crisis* artist George Perez, but it would be the changes to Batman that would have the biggest impact on DC and the industry—not to mention on pop culture at large.

In the early eighties Frank Miller, along with Steve Gerber, had pitched bold new takes on Batman, Superman, and Wonder Woman. The proposal called for Miller to write and draw a Batman comic, which seemed a natural fit, given his dark, noir-ish work on *Daredevil*.

The proposal was later abandoned after Gerber walked away, but Miller kept his notes, hoping to one day put them to use. In 1985, as the artist's thirtieth birthday loomed two years in the future, Miller began thinking about Batman's age—a perpetual twenty-nine—and how unsettling it would be for Miller to one day find himself older than the hero he'd been reading since childhood. Miller began to conceive of a tale that would center on a mature, grizzled Batman of AARP membership age who would come out of retirement to tackle one last case.

Miller's hero would reflect an America that had become increasingly marred by violence, one in which those who fought back were celebrated. Vigilante Bernie Goetz, who gunned down four alleged muggers in New York's subway in 1984, was a tabloid folk hero, and the *Dirty Harry* and *Death Wish* film series were popular at the box office.

Miller, who had been repeatedly mugged in New York, asked himself what kind of world would be scary enough to compel someone to dress up in a bat suit and fight crime. And then he looked out his window.

"If he fights, it's in a way that leaves them too roughed up to talk," Miller scrawled in his notebook of his hero's interrogation tactics.

Miller's story introduced a fifty-year-old Bruce Wayne who has retired following the murder of sidekick Robin at the hands of the Joker. He's driven to don the cape and cowl again to battle a violent gang that has taken over Gotham. Later he tangles with Superman—portrayed as a Reagan-era sellout now working for the government—and the homicidal Joker.

According to Miller, his envelope-pushing take on DC's license-friendly character scared those at DC, and he had to twist arms to get it published. "They hated it," he has said.

"It was a very gutsy move," Mike Friedrich says. "Doing Batman in this very adult fashion had nothing to do with children's toys, which was, of course, where most of the revenue for Batman was coming from at the time. They were actually threatening their franchise by doing him in a different fashion."

The first part of *The Dark Knight Returns* was released in February 1986 in a new square-bound volume dubbed the "prestige format." It sold for $2.95 and offered a quality of production never before seen in American superhero comics. ("We'll probably copy every one of their formats," a Marvel editor conceded at the time.)

DC anticipated huge demand, setting the print run some 40 percent over advance orders. Still, within seventy-two hours of issue #1's release, the company was forced to go back to print to meet demand.

The Dark Knight Returns had a complex story and was peppered with sly commentary on the media as well as bizarre political allusions. If the Nazi women with swastikas covering their bare breasts didn't signal comics weren't just for kids anymore, nothing would. And this story was coming from the same company that just a few years earlier had killed a short, comedic story by writer David Anthony Kraft in which Batman orders a shot of whiskey. "Batman doesn't drink," the brass grumped. Well, now he paralyzes Joker during an unsettling love-hate fight inside a carnival's Tunnel of Love.

The next year Miller was tasked with resetting Batman for the post-*Crisis* universe. His "Year One" ran through four issues of the main Batman title and fleshed out the beginning of Bruce Wayne's career as a superhero. The revised origin doubled down on the darkness, casting the hero as a violent, outside-the-law vigilante, police detective Gordon as a world-weary adulterer, and Selina Kyle, aka Catwoman, a street-smart prostitute.

DC's new direction did not go unnoticed by the press. Both *The Dark Knight Returns* and *The Man of Steel* made national headlines—a rare time when the mainstream media deemed comics worthy of coverage. The hype had even reached the ears of Stan Lee, long since checked out of the publishing side of comics.

"I think DC, sooner or later, may start competing with us," he said in 1987. "Their 'new Batman' and 'new Superman' could create some interest. I know this Batman graphic novel is selling out. We'll see."

DC's post-*Crisis* revamp boosted sales 22 percent in one year. The company actually beat Marvel in direct-market share in August and September 1987—the first time that had ever happened.

After jousting with Marvel for decades and generally getting trounced, DC had found its new way forward. It wasn't just about making money in that particular quarter. DC was playing a longer game, attempting to champion projects that would elevate the medium and have a shelf life longer than four weeks. "Quality became the motivation," as one editor put it.

"We were firmly convinced that the direct market would be the heart of the business for a generation and that readers would be older and more sophisticated and be prepared to pay more," Paul Levitz says. "We felt we should move towards more creator-driven passion projects that pushed the limits of what we'd done before and see where we could go with it."

"I always felt that Marvel, especially in the eighties, was more competitive, more invested in a sense of its own uniqueness and superiority to the competition," says J. M. DeMatteis, a DC and Marvel writer since the seventies. "DC at the time felt more invested in the work at hand. I'm not saying they didn't want to dominate the market just as much as Marvel did, just that it wasn't expressed that way around me."

DC's gamble on creators and unique voices paid off, producing what is perhaps the most fertile period in the company's—and the industry's—history. This was the moment comics finally grew up and began to be taken seriously.

In addition to *The Dark Knight*, in 1986 DC also released *Watchmen*, writer Alan Moore's and artist Dave Gibbons's dense deconstruction of superheroes that made *Time* magazine's list of the best books of all time. Denny O'Neil and artist Denys Cowan turned an old Charlton character called the Question into a Zen-soaked martial arts master. It was perhaps the first comic book to contain a weighty list of recommended reading, including *The Tao of Peace*, at the back.

A few years earlier DC had missed out on another acclaimed Alan Moore strip from a British magazine, *Warrior*. In 1982 Moore had taken Marvelman, a British Captain Marvel rip-off from the 1950s, and put an ultra-realistic spin on him, trying to imagine what would happen if a Superman-like figure did actually exist.

Dez Skinn, the British publisher behind *Warrior*, had been interested in licensing the material to be published in the United States. He flew to New York and met with DC. The company, who was then beginning to embrace edgier work, loved Marvelman. The name, however, was going to be a problem.

"DC Comics publishing something called Marvelman, are you crazy?" DC's Dick Giordano told Skinn.

And then there was *Swamp Thing*, a monthly horror-tinged magazine that had become a cult classic after Alan Moore—then a little-known British writer—took it over in 1984. He and his art team quickly turned an overlooked title into among the most literate and sophisticated on the stands.

When the new team began, sales were in the toilet—below twenty thousand. The art team was earning DC's lowest page rate. To make matters worse, the title enjoyed little promotion from DC as the result of a bad deal the company had made with the producers behind the 1982 movie.

"Paul Levitz said to me, 'It was the worst licensing deal DC had ever cut,'" Bissette says. "DC had sold all rights to the producers for the duration of the contract. The only rights they'd retained were the comic book publishing rights. They couldn't do posters; they couldn't do action figures. As soon as I heard that, I knew why our page rates were so low—because there was nothing to exploit except the comic book."

Even without promotion, sales slowly improved. *Swamp Thing* began raking in the industry awards.

The title was definitely not Marvel's thing. In issue #40 (September 1985), Moore and company created a tale called "The Curse" about a female werewolf whose transformation is tied to her menstrual cycle.

DC's move toward more mature subject matter in *Swamp Thing* and other books rankled Marvel, where the stories remained all-ages appropriate, and adult content, such as swearing, was forbidden. At a 1985 Chicago Comicon panel several Marvel editors publicly voiced concern with the recent publication of "The Curse" and stated that comic books should be subject to stricter content control.

While Marvel found *Swamp Thing* objectionable, DC considered it a touchstone.

"Alan Moore's work on *Swamp Thing* directly led to Vertigo," says Stuart Moore, who was an editor for DC's trailblazing imprint launched in 1993.

Vertigo served as a home for more outside-the-box, adult work, removed from the regular DC superhero universe. It would include Warren Ellis's *Transmetropolitan* about a chain-smoking, acerbic gonzo journalist fighting corruption in a dystopian future, and most notably *The Sandman*, author Neil Gaiman's literate fantasy series about the magical lord of dreams. Those series, as *The Dark Knight Returns* and *Watchmen* before them, helped push the medium and attract a more diverse audience to comics.

The new direction led to the rise of the "DC Zombie," a counterpart to the evangelical Marvel fanboy who bought exclusively from one company. "Such creatures were almost nonexistent in the early '80s since few people knew DC was still publishing," fanzine *Amazing Heroes* reported in 1990. "With DC's latest comeback, Zombies have cropped up."

For Marvel, however, mainstream superheroes remained the bread and butter.

"Everything we could see about those [Vertigo] comics, both in our own experience and DC's, was that those comics didn't make any money," says Marvel's president in the 1990s, Terry Stewart. "They were interesting. They appealed to a certain segment of the buyers. But they never sold in any great quantities."

At least not upon initial publication as monthly comics. But many of these stories have remained in print ever since through the trade paperback, a book-format collection of several consecutive comic books that told a (mostly) complete story.

In 1986 DC cut a deal with sister company Warner Books to release a $12.95 mass-market paperback collection of Frank Miller's hit Batman series.

"Doing *Dark Knight* as a trade paperback, in retrospect, was one of the most important things I did in my career," says Paul Levitz. "We largely created that business. The trade paperback changed the game."

Other blockbuster collections followed, including one of *Watchmen*. Graphic novel sections are now a part of most every bookstore.

"I think DC had the vision that books were the format of the future, and Marvel didn't," says industry analyst Milton Griepp. "You look at something like *Watchmen* that was collected in 1987 and has been in print ever since. There's nothing like that on the Marvel side."

As DC blossomed, Marvel was grappling with internal issues. Jim Shooter, the editor-in-chief who had brought order to the chaotic company some ten years earlier, left the company in April 1987.

Tom DeFalco, who had been at Marvel since the 1970s, was installed as the new editor-in-chief. Marvel was still the overall leader in monthly comic sales, but the once-bright creative light was dimming somewhat. Writers grumbled that the House of Ideas had become afraid to take chances, and some readers accused the company of stagnation. "Marvel is a backward-looking corporate behemoth," critic Darcy Sullivan wrote, "paying lip service to the qualities it once embodied."

"It seems to me that Marvel is in the same place DC was in the late '60s—fat, complacent and throwing out something good once in a while," a reader wrote to fanzine *Amazing Heroes* in 1989. "They're resting on their laurels, and most fans follow like sheep."

Marvel would recover, of course, once again becoming the scrappy underdog with the out-there ideas. But it would take another decade and a flirtation with complete and utter ruin to get there.

From Humongous Boom to Hideous Bust

"We were not just selling the comics, we were merchandising them, giving the reader something special to glom onto. It was very obvious how much money we were making, and I heard rumblings that people at Warner Bros. were saying, 'Holy shit! What are those guys doing over there?!' We were attacking the market on all fronts."

—Marvel's former president Terry Stewart

Since its very beginning the comic book industry has careened through a series of booms and busts, like a blotto Vegas blackjack player on an all-night bender. A period of extraordinarily strong gains are often followed by a downturn so severe that it borders on existential.

The Golden Age of prosperity was killed by the 1950s anticomics crusade. The Marvel-led superhero revival of the 1960s gave way to plummeting sales in the 1970s. And so it went, continuously ping-ponging between elation and despair. Those looking for stability best look elsewhere.

But the mother of all booms and busts was yet to come. By the end of the 1980s the industry was about to enjoy a historic explosion that would inject a tsunami of money into the biz and change the way it operated forever.

And it all started with a movie.

Back in 1979, a year after *Superman* hit theaters, a young comic book fan named Michael Uslan and his partner Benjamin Melniker approached DC about optioning the film rights to the company's other A-plus character, Batman. Despite the fact that Uslan had never made a film, DC agreed—with the condition that the producers steer as far away from the 1966 TV series' Biffs! Pows! and Bams! as possible.

Uslan and Melniker obtained the rights to Batman in October 1979 and set out to make a "serious" Batman film the producers thought would appeal to a wide audience. Thus began a torturous ten-year journey that would involve rejections from every studio in Hollywood, multiple directors, and a small army of screenwriters.

Batman, starring Michael Keaton and directed by Tim Burton, finally arrived in June 1989, notching the biggest opening ever at the time. The flick quickly raced past $100 million on its way to becoming the highest-grossing movie of the year.

The movie was notable for many reasons, not the least of which was that it finished the mission that *Superman* had started more than ten years earlier, once and for all proving that moviegoers would line up to see straightforward superheroes movies.

But *Batman*'s most enduring legacy may not be at the box office; it would be in the realm of merchandising. *Batman* was a trailblazer in licensing and cross-promotion, as Warner Bros. set out to exploit the hell out of every possible revenue stream in an orgasmic frenzy of intracompany synergy.

Bat-fans could plunk down cash for some twelve hundred items—everything from a $5.95 Batman action figure to $35.95 Batcave playset. Hungry? Pour a bowl of Bat cereal, munch on Bat tortilla chips. Chilly? Strap on a $50 satin jacket. Warner Bros. record execs even strong-armed Burton into including—rather incongruously—their artist Prince in the film in a bid to piggyback an album.

Batman was able to tap ancillary dollars like no movie since *Star Wars*, ringing up an estimated $750 million in merchandising sales.

Everyone involved was getting filthy rich. And that included Bob Kane, Batman's cocreator. One day after the film opened, the seventy-three-year-old artist dropped by the DC offices to pick up a check for his

slice of the *Batman* spoils. On his way out he happened to ride the elevator down with a group of DC editors. The cocky Kane couldn't resist
flashing his check to the group, revealing a number with more zeroes than
Batman had utility-belt compartments.

"Well," one of the editors said dryly, "I guess lunch is on you."

The *Batman* windfall was such a shock to so many in the industry because of the nature of comic book properties previously.

"It's hard to imagine now, with the increasing success of superhero
movies, but superheroes were not a big deal in the merchandising business back then," says Marvel's former publisher Mike Hobson. "You could
not give away Spider-Man or Batman for toys or anything else."

Batman changed all that, and the movie's river of merchandising
money would open the eyes of many to the value of comic book–related
properties, including one man whose sudden interest in all things spandex would ultimately have a disastrous impact on Marvel.

Marvel's one-time owner, Cadence Industries (formerly known as
Perfect Film), had in 1986 sold the publishing company to New World
Pictures, the studio behind low-budget schlock such as *The Slumber Party
Massacre*. Just two years later Marvel was on the block again.

This time the buyer would be Ronald Perelman, a filthy-rich, bald,
cigar-smoking financier who specialized in taking over undervalued companies. Perelman paid $82.5 million in January 1989, tossing in $10.5 million of his own money. The Wall Street titan seemed an odd fit to run the
company, and plunking down the hefty sum had nothing do with love of
comic books. He claimed he didn't know how to read comics, how to follow the thread. It was a new art form to him. He was after what DC had.

"One of the reasons that Perelman wound up buying Marvel was the
success of the *Batman* movie," says Terry Stewart, who worked for Perelman and was installed as Marvel's president. "What everyone was really
shocked about was the half-billion, billion dollars' worth of merchandise
it sold. That was a big eye-opener there, because there's money in them
there hills."

Stewart was among the few in Marvel's new corporate management
ranks who was a comic book fan. He'd grown up in Arkansas, methodi-
cally hunting DC books at the limited outlets in his town. But Perelman
and the rest of his crew knew or cared little about the industry. What they
knew was money, and they set out to use Marvel to make as much of it as
possible. Suddenly Marvel was reduced to a moneymaking machine, with

the same kinds of earning demands that drove more traditional corporate enterprises. Creativity would have to take a backseat to profit.

"When Ron Perelman took over Marvel, he came into my office and said, 'I wanted to meet you. You have the highest-selling books,'" says former *Uncanny X-Men* editor Ann Nocenti.

Marvel under Perelman began to take aggressive steps to increase profits. In May 1989 Marvel jacked the cover price of standard comics from 75 cents to $1 and was pleasantly surprised when no noticeable decrease in sales followed.

The company improved the quality of its paper and printing to try to attract advertisers who previously had been wary of running their ads on the cheap, nearly transparent paper many comics were published on. An ad on the prime back or inside-front cover was soon commanding around $65,000.

Marvel's other strategy was simple: release more product. More product in stores meant more money.

"We saw that the market seemed to be calling for more titles and more books, particularly #1s," Stewart says. "How far can we push spin-offs, and how far can we push new comics?"

The company that had built its legend by releasing just eight titles a month was now set to ramp up its output to levels never before seen. Some of Marvel's more popular offerings, including *The Amazing Spider-Man* and the *Uncanny X-Men*, were released twice a month during the summer, continuing an experiment from the previous year. Second-tier characters no one had much cared about before were suddenly fronting their own titles. (Nomad, anyone?) And Marvel's most popular heroes were spun off into new titles that, at times, had all the creative necessity of *AfterMASH*. One particular spin-off—a gluttonous expansion of the *Spider-Man* line—would prove to be a sensation and would set the tone for the industry for the next few years to come.

For better or worse.

Todd McFarlane was a brash, young Canadian artist who'd broken into comics in the early 1980s before landing his first regular gig drawing DC's *Infinity Inc.* in 1985. McFarlane's unique visual style was evident, even on his earliest jobs. He hacked a boring rectangular page into experimental panel layouts and had a way of rendering capes in such a dramatic, billowing way that it made the lamest hero look plain cool. He was clearly a star on the rise.

During his time at DC McFarlane was desperate to live in America, and he asked his employer for help in obtaining papers. After the company dragged its feet with the request, McFarlane bolted from DC and began drawing *The Incredible Hulk* for Marvel. Fans enjoyed his unusual interpretation, but Marvel management was less thrilled—art director John Romita included. Romita griped to McFarlane's editor that he didn't like the way the artist drew the Hulk, and that complaint led to the break of McFarlane's life. He was then put on *The Amazing Spider-Man*, starting with issue #298 (March 1988).

His take on Spider-Man and the book's cast of characters was just as unique as that of the Hulk. McFarlane drew the hero in a stylized, exaggerated manner, giving him eyes so large that they rivaled Amanda Seyfried's. He posed Spidey in acrobatic positions impossible for a normal human and drew his webbing in a more realistic, three-dimensional way. He made Peter Parker's then wife, Mary Jane, look like something out of a Victoria's Secret catalog.

"Todd broke that lock of the Jim Shooter aesthetic, where everything looked staid and conservative," says artist Steve Bissette. "He busted that page up. I love looking at Todd's pages. They bristle with power and energy."

McFarlane breathed new life into the Marvel warhorse, then approaching its three hundredth issue, and in the process he became the hottest artist going.

After two years on *The Amazing Spider-Man*, the grueling schedule began to take its toll, and McFarlane asked to be taken off the title. He expected to be demoted to one of the company's lesser books, but to his surprise his editor asked if he was interested in launching a completely new Spider-Man title—Marvel's fourth starring the web slinger. And McFarlane would be tasked with drawing and writing it.

No comic book fan on earth would turn down that offer, McFarlane included. The first issue of the new series, simply called *Spider-Man*, was released in the summer of 1990 to massive hype driven by Marvel's marketing muscle. If you were reading comic books that year, it was inevitable you bought this comic. Resistance was futile.

Spider-Man #1 proved to be a sales success the likes of which had not been seen in the industry for a long, long time. Records from comics' early years are spotty, but Marvel researched sales data and concluded that a 1948 issue of Fawcett's *Captain Marvel* was most likely the all-time record holder, having sold 1.7 million copies. McFarlane's *Spider-Man* #1 destroyed that previous best-seller by a million.

"Todd was the hottest thing since sliced bread. Giving him his own title and turning him loose on that was the right thing to do," Stewart says. "We had the machinery oiled and greased to promote this stuff. The shops pushed it hard. It was sort of the perfect storm."

"*Spider-Man* #1 had a huge effect [on the industry]," says David Michelinie, a writer and McFarlane's collaborator on *The Amazing Spider-Man*. "It showed that a creator alone—by popularity or talent—could sell a lot of comics. Todd McFarlane changed the face of comics in America and deserves much of the credit—or blame—for the state of the industry today."

Sales were certainly strong. There was only one problem, however. In its hunger to drop this hot new title on the market, Marvel had overlooked a small but crucial detail. McFarlane had never written anything in his life, and it showed. *Spider-Man* #1 was loaded with McFarlane's unique artistic stylings, but the story, to put it charitably, was incomprehensible.

McFarlane was more of a jock than a sensitive poet, and at the time he admitted that he didn't "read nothing." Earlier in his career when it had become clear that McFarlane was intent on writing, DC had offered him a chance to learn the craft by penning a movie adaptation—a low-profile gig that wouldn't embarrass anyone even if it turned out badly. Marvel had required no such training wheels. McFarlane was handed the keys to Marvel's important franchise without even having been required to submit writing samples. Pairing him with a professional to help shape the story was rejected out of fear that McFarlane would become frustrated with the oversight.

"I mean, fuck, I didn't let some little thing like not being able to write stop me, so I didn't really see where that should actually be that much of a problem," the artist said in 1992. "I just wanted to test to see how much balls people had."

Comic books, by their nature, had always been somewhat driven by gimmicks. Shocking cover lines and images were often guilty of exaggerating the significance of the events inside, for example. But quality storytelling was still paramount. *Spider-Man* seemed to represent a cynical new low, a triumph of product and commerce over artistry.

The book naturally elicited eyerolls at DC, where quality, not market-ing, was thought of as the guiding principle, and the company had always had a feeling of superiority—deserved or not—to its rival. To DC, Marvel published cartoons, while it—being the home of *Sandman* and other adult-oriented projects—produced literature. A DC staffer came running up to *Sandman* writer Neil Gaiman with a copy of *Spider-Man* #1, laugh-ing that the contents demonstrated that the person writing it had never written anything before.

Amateurish writing or not, Marvel was on to something. The next year Marvel used almost the exact same formula to generate another monster success. The company tapped a hot newbie artist—this time twenty-three-year-old Rob Liefeld—to launch a hyped new spin-off.

Rob Liefeld, a self-described "young punk," had gotten his big break at DC drawing a 1988 *Hawk and Dove* miniseries that established the penciler, like McFarlane, as an artist with a unique and recognizable style—in this case, hyper-muscled men, pneumatic-chested women, floppy nineties hair, and faces slashed with lines, straining from effort. And also like McFarlane, Liefeld would defect to Marvel, where he would attain superstardom.

"The story goes that [Liefeld's *Hawk and Dove* editor] was a bit of a hard-ass, and he wanted certain things done with the art and to teach Rob certain things," says Gregg Schigiel, an editor and artist who got his start with Marvel in the 1990s. "And [Marvel editor] Bob Harras sort of pulled Rob over to Marvel saying, 'You're awesome, you can do whatever you want.' So Rob went over to Marvel and became Rob Liefeld."

Liefeld quickly parlayed his success into a high-profile, debut title. *X-Force*, a *New Mutants* spin-off about a superpowered strike force, was released in June 1991 and became an even bigger mover than *Spider-Man*, selling almost 4 million copies. Like *Spider-Man*, it too was not great liter-ature, but look at that really cool gun!

That sales record lasted for all of two months until *X-Men* #1 came along. The new title—another wallet-straining expansion of the popular mutant line—was conceived as a platform for yet another hot, young art-ist, Jim Lee. It blew the doors off anything that had come before, selling a staggering 8 million units and earning a Guinness World Record.

Marvel kept producing more and more, churning out a veritable mountain of material.

"The summer that I was there in '93, Marvel had 120 titles in August," says *Deadpool* artist and former Marvel staffer Scott Koblish. "It was a tremendous amount of product. Even something called *Darkhawk* was selling three hundred thousand copies."

Marvel was producing so many titles that over at DC, where employees got free copies of its rival's output, the mail room had to double its rounds to keep up with it all.

The aggressive strategy was paying off for Marvel. After just two years under Perelman's new management, the company's profits had jumped tenfold, which was especially good news, as Marvel had gone public in July 1991. Unlike DC, whose financial goings-on were largely hidden within the Time Warner mothership, Marvel had less cover. Its profits and losses were now a matter of public record, enormously ratcheting up the pressure to boost earnings.

Anyone who's taken an Economics 101 class knows that there are two ways to increase sales: sell your product to new customers or sell more of your product to the customers you already have. In the latter case, it boils down to, how can we get someone to buy two of something when they'd normally buy one?

The answer came with the variant cover.

The gimmick had been pioneered by DC in the 1980s, and the idea was to print the same issue with multiple cover versions in an attempt to get collectors to purchase multiple copies. John Byrne's 1986 miniseries *The Man of Steel* had been released with a newsstand cover as well another for the direct market.

In 1989, to coincide with the release of the Batman movie, DC launched a new series called *Legends of the Dark Knight*. It was the first new, ongoing Batman title in some fifty years, and the orders were stratospheric. DC's marketing chief worried that there was no way so many copies would sell through to the consumer, so he borrowed an idea from the book industry.

Some paperbacks at the time were printed with multiple covers in an ingenious bid to obtain multiple front-facing (as opposed to spine) placements in bookstores. Printing a book with different covers meant it occupied more shelf space and was more visible, so buyers were less likely to overlook it.

DC deployed a crude version of this strategy, printing four different versions of *Legends of the Dark Knight* #1 in which the only difference was the cover's background color. Then the company sat back and watched as OCD comics fans snapped up all four in a bid to obtain a complete set. Collect them all, or you will never feel whole!

It took Marvel and its rapacious Wall Street owners to take the concept to a crass, new level. Variant covers quickly became a reliable scheme to increase sales on a single issue exponentially and keep those precious dollars rolling in. McFarlane's *Spider-Man* #1 was released with thirteen different covers, including gold, silver, and platinum versions. One came sealed in a plastic bag, presenting fanboys with the *Sophie's Choice* of whether to read the comic or simply peer at it through plastic for all eternity.

X-Force #1 deployed a different sort of variant trick, offering poly-bagged versions with one of five different trading cards hidden inside. *X-Men* #1 also came in five variations, one complete with an accordion-like fold-out cover for the low, low price of $3.95—or quadruple the price of a normal comic book.

Marvel's increasing excesses did not escape industry notice. At the 1991 San Diego Comic-Con, DC editor Michael Eury was tapped to present an award to writer-artist Keith Giffen. During the introduction Eury joked that Giffen had "more ideas per minute than Marvel had covers of *Spider-Man* #1."

"Marvel's head of marketing, Carol Kalish, shot me a look," Eury says. "I *think* it was in jest."

DC didn't go as big as Marvel did on the variant trend, approving the gimmick covers only on books that that were guaranteed big sellers, such as the Batman family of titles. But the company was hardly innocent.

"DC was the first one to do it," says Brian Hibbs, owner of San Francisco's Comix Experience and an influential retailer. "I'm sure that employees at DC feel that they were less fucked up about it than Marvel was, but their hands were just as bloody."

A 1991 miniseries starring Batman's sidekick Robin was slapped with a hologram cover, and an issue of event comic *Eclipso: The Darkness Within* came with a cheap plastic "jewel" embedded on its front. Soon there would be no cover variation too gimmicky for either company. Comics were die-cut, embossed with foil, tinted in gold, and made to glow in the dark in a desperate bid to throw something novel onto the stands.

"There was this level of one-upsmanship," says former DC editor Frank Pittarese. "You do a foil cover, we're going to do a hologram cover. You do a hologram cover, we're doing colorforms. You always wanted to top the other guy."

"Everyone was doing well. It was like, 'Yay, our gimmicky comic book outsold their gimmicky comic book,'" says former DC production manager Bob Rozakis. "But if you put a glow-in-the-dark, silver-foil cover on a crappy comic book story, it's still a crappy comic book story."

The gimmicks quickly became the draw, immunizing subpar material against low sales. Fans were eagerly snapping up everything, no matter how good or bad it was.

"At the time we were like, ugh, this is kind of gross," says former *Uncanny X-Men* editor Ann Nocenti.

An industry that had generally been about telling entertaining stories first and foremost was quickly becoming little more than a four-color shell game. The publishers' marketing departments, which had been virtually nonexistent a few years earlier, became so powerful that they actually began to dictate content.

"You'd get into meetings with the sales people, and they'd ask, 'How can we add an enhanced cover that will raise the price $1 or $2? Or, 'How can we put out multiple covers?' 'How can we start this over with issue #1 or publish this twice as often?'" says Bob Budiansky, former editor of the *Amazing Spider-Man*. "This was coming from the very top. What can we do to get people's attention and get them to buy more books and more copies of books?"

"I would kick and scream and bite and scratch to avoid that stuff," says Dan Raspler, a former DC editor. "I would get yelled at. At one point [editor] Neal Pozner came to my office when I was editing *Lobo* and told me about a scheme where we could print a number on a cover, and every cover would be unique. It would have a different number on each one. He was like, 'Isn't that great? There will be nothing but unique covers. People will have to buy all of them.' I was like, 'That's the most terrible thing I've ever heard.' But I was a dick for standing in the way of profit."

The corporations weren't the only ones getting rich. Thanks to the royalties program instituted in the 1980s, the creators—who'd been trampled on and treated like whores for decades—were finally getting their piece of the pie.

"There was a lot of money sloshing around," says Koblish. "If you sold a million copies, you were probably earning somewhere between $40,000 and $50,000 per issue as a royalty."

Chris Claremont, the scribe behind the top-selling *Uncanny X-Men* title, went from pulling down a modest $769 a week in salary in 1982 to taking home a mint.

"I bought a plane," Claremont says. "You can either have a plane or you can have kids. It was an indulgence when I was doing the *X-Men*."

Legend has it that Marvel's Scott Lobdell got handed an X-Men title at the height of the boom because he happened to be walking by the panicked editor's office at the exact moment a replacement writer was needed. He was soon earning $85,000 a month in royalties.

"One time a check arrived at the office for [*X-Men* artist] Jim Lee, and the assistant was curious and held it up to the light, and you couldn't tell how much it was, but there were quite a few numbers in the check," says Ruben Diaz, a Marvel and DC editor in the 1990s. "Even if you factored in two numbers for cents, there had to be at least six figures in a royalty check. That was for work already performed and was probably not the first time he was getting paid for that work."

The Marvel editors also reaped rewards in the form of a bonus pool instituted under new owner, Perelman. If Marvel reached its profit goals, the staff would be handsomely rewarded.

"In my case the bonuses were bigger than my annual salary," says former Marvel editor Bob Budiansky. "Sales kept going up."

Unfortunately, DC's talent did not enjoy the same ridiculous windfalls keeping Marvel artists in yachts and private planes, in large part because DC's titles sold far fewer copies than Marvel's. There were exceptions, of course. Grant Morrison, the Scottish writer behind the hardcover 1989 Batman graphic novel *Arkham Asylum*, pocketed $150,000 on pre-orders alone. He soon moved into a 130-year-old townhouse on Glasgow's socalled millionaire's row.

The pay discrepancy between the companies would become a major attraction for Marvel—and a bit of a sore subject for DC. One night some twenty-five DC and Marvel staffers were out for a friendly dinner together when the check arrived. The DC editors grabbed for their wallets and began trying to parse the bill among several credit cards, exasperating the distressed waiter.

"I finally said, 'Screw it,' and pulled out my Amex and paid for the whole thing," says Chris Claremont. "I was doing it for obvious reasons. It was gamesmanship. I was showing off. 'I work for Marvel. I can afford it. Duh. I write the *X-Men*, dude.'"

The next day Claremont got an unpleasant phone call from DC honcho Paul Levitz.

"Under no circumstances will DC editors ever allow a Marvel freelancer to pay for their dinner," Levitz told him.

"He knew what I was doing," Claremont says. "It was like I was saying, 'Yes, I work for the cool guy. Maybe you should think about it next time your contract is up.'"

Claremont's subtle invitation was no small deal. At the time DC, despite some half-hearted attempts to capitalize on the gimmicks working so well for Marvel, still lagged far behind its rival in sales. And it continued to lose ground through the early days of the comic book boom. DC's direct-market share dropped in 1991, hovering around an anemic 20 percent—less than half of Marvel's. The situation didn't improve much through most of 1992. In August of that year DC actually fell behind Malibu, a smaller independent publisher that had been founded in 1986. It was the first time in history a third-party publisher had moved ahead of either Marvel or DC in direct-market sales, and it was an unimaginable—and humiliating—turn of events for the once-mighty publisher that would have been enough for the company's founder, Malcolm Wheeler-Nicholson, to throw himself on his cavalry sword, had he been alive.

"In the early nineties Marvel consistently had the whole top ten," says former DC editor Dan Raspler. "There was an inferiority complex that we all permanently had. Even Marvel's not-important titles would still be outselling important DC titles on a consistent basis. It was infuriating. You do all the right things, and then your sales go down because Marvel puts out a third alternate *Machine Man* cover. Marvel was just crushing us. Crushing us and crushing us."

DC staffers took to joking that the company was "number two with a bullet"—a nod to DC's circular logo, known as the "DC bullet."

"When I got to DC [in 1992] there was definitely a push to reclaim that market share. Not necessarily to beat Marvel, but to reclaim a piece of this pie," former editor Diaz says. "Marvel was like, we're beating DC every month and we're hip and cool and having fun in this frat-house environment. DC was like, yeah, we're nerds, but we're putting out really good books, and it would be cool if people liked us more, but if they don't, we're gonna be sitting in this corner doing our thing for the people that like what we do."

DC lagged because the company, with its entrenched corporate culture and aspirations of literature, was less prone to cash in on the fads. It also continued to suffer from the chronic popularity deficit, in comparison to Marvel, that had plagued it since the 1960s.

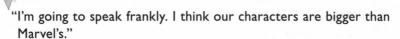

"I'm going to speak frankly. I think our characters are bigger than Marvel's."

—DC's Geoff Johns speaking in 2010

"dc sucks big hairy monkey balls.theyre just jelous"

—IGN.com commenter tony_von_terror responding in 2010

Something had to change. Enough was enough. And so in late 1992 DC set out to beat Marvel at its own game, launching a storyline so bold that it that would make national headlines and become the company's most commercial endeavor yet.

In a way it all happened by accident. The writers and editors behind the various Superman titles had been planning to marry off Lois Lane and Clark Kent. But unbeknownst to the braintrust, a TV series called *Lois & Clark: The New Adventures of Superman* was in the works at ABC, much of whose success would depend on the will-they-or-won't-they nature of the relationship between the two leads. DC's president Jenette Kahn decided that any wedding in the comics would have to coincide with a TV wedding, and so she nixed the editors' proposal.

With their carefully laid plans suddenly killed, the disgruntled group was forced to go back to the drawing board.

"Let's just kill him," longtime Superman writer-artist Jerry Ordway suggested at a planning session.

With that pronouncement was born "The Death of Superman," a multipart epic spread out over seven issues of different DC titles. The storyline was, ironically, an attempt to do something that the movie that partially adapted it, *Batman v Superman: Dawn of Justice*, was criticized for not doing—to show the horrible ramifications of a battle between two superpowered beings.

"The death actually came out of the desire to do a big Marvel-style punch fest, where there were consequences rather than just fights where cities are destroyed," Ordway says.

The climax, in which the hero is felled at the hands of a powerful villain called Doomsday, arrived in *Superman* #75 (January 1993). The death issue was of course released in multiple formats, including a special edition that came wrapped in a black bag, bearing Superman's "S" logo dripping blood and packaged with a poster and a black armband.

"We were pretty much kicking DC's butt all the way through that period, and I always felt like DC was looking at the success that Marvel was having," says Marvel's then-president Terry Stewart. "We were doing a lot of things that DC was not aggressively doing. DC was pretty much doing what it always did. There was not a lot of new direction going on there. I always felt 'The Death of Superman' was something they pretty much had to come up with—something that would bring their brand back to another level of sales success. And it was successful."

Superman's demise became a major news story and was covered on TV and in magazines and newspapers. It brought DC a much-needed dose of attention—as well as customers.

The death issue put up Marvel-like numbers, selling more than 4 million units—second behind only 1991's *X-Men* #1. It also helped DC capture the market share lead the month of its release, doubling DC's percentage from the previous month to 31 percent. In the process it also kneecapped Marvel, whose share plummeted 17 points.

At some stores customers were literally lined up by the hundreds to purchase this supposedly historic issue. The sales and media madness shocked anyone familiar with the soap-opera nature of comic books, where death was often as permanent as a pimple.

"We had no reason at the time to suspect that the world would give a shit," Paul Levitz says. "We'd killed him before."

Superman would return, of course. He was resurrected nearly a year later (sporting a sweet mullet, no less) at the conclusion of a carefully padded saga spread over multiple titles.

The success of "The Death of Superman" may have surprised many within the industry, but it reinforced the lesson that events equaled sales. If *Secret Wars* and *Crisis on Infinite Earths* had been the companies learning to crawl, "The Death of Superman" was a full sprint. Both companies doubled down on the strategy.

"I remember an editorial meeting where the sentiment was simply, 'We killed Superman and sold 4 million copies. Marvel is doing this or that, and they're selling a million copies,'" says former DC editor Brian Augustyn. "The underlying message was, 'We're not sure what it is, but these epic events are selling out and driving the market.' There was almost like a dictate that if your book is considered a comer or a mainstay, then you've got to shake it up."

Big, important stories promising massive changes for these familiar characters became the order of the day. Soon Batman had his back broken by a villain named Bane and was replaced by an apprentice. The multipart story was called "Knightfall," and it snaked through dozens of issues and lasted some two years. In 1994 Hal Jordan, who'd served as Earth's Green Lantern for thirty-five years, was replaced by a new one.

"The feeling was, there was value in events if people got excited about them," says Chris Duffy, a DC associate editor from 1993 to 1996. "The word on the street was that [editor] Kevin Dooley had gone in for his yearly review on *Green Lantern*, where you talked about what was in the works for the book. All the group editors were there and Paul [Levitz]. The success of 'The Death of Superman' and 'Knightfall' turned that meeting into, 'How can we do this for Green Lantern?' So Kevin had to throw out all his plans for *Green Lantern* because they weren't big enough, and that's when they concocted [the replacement storyline]."

The success of "The Death of Superman" led to similar mandates at Marvel.

"At an editorial meeting in 1993 or 1994 with various executives, they were noting that 'The Death of Superman' had just been mentioned on the *Today* show," says Marvel's Budiansky. "This was like DC had just dropped a nuclear bomb on us. 'They're on the *Today* show, and we're not!' Back then, to get onto a mainstream TV show was such a big deal."

Marvel began to formulate a response to DC's big event, one that might pull similarly heavyweight coverage in the process. The idea they landed on was that Peter Parker and his wife would have a Spider-baby.

"The audience of the *Today* show was considered to be a lot of women, and they'll want to grab onto something like this," Budiansky says. "This will be friendly to those kinds of shows."

The story was set in motion as part of an ongoing Spider-Man epic that reintroduced a mostly forgotten Peter Parker clone from 1975. The new story revealed that the Peter Parker, whose adventures the readers had been following since the 1970s, was not, in fact, the real Peter Parker but rather Parker's old clone, who believed himself to be the actual Parker. As one might imagine, this did not sit well with devoted readers. It was like being told you've been secretly married to your wife's twin sister for two decades.

As for the baby, the powers-that-be soon got buyer's remorse, worrying that having Peter Parker become a father would distance him from Marvel's large fan base of male, teenage readers. Mary Jane is shown miscarrying in *Amazing Spider-Man* #418 (December 1996).

"The Clone Saga" eventually dragged on for more than two years through some one hundred issues, in the process becoming one of the most torturous, muddled—and controversial—stories Marvel had ever published. Even when Marvel poached Dan Jurgens, the main artist on "The Death of Superman," to contribute, it couldn't save the storyline. Many now view it with disdain, and mentioning it in the presence of a hardcore Spidey fan might be enough to earn a swift slap.

"Here was a case where the competition between the two companies adversely affected something Marvel was doing," Budiansky says. "By trying to be a media story, Marvel came up with a story that didn't support the character in a positive way."

Events like "The Death of Superman" and "The Clone Saga" as well as the variant covers and other gimmicks propelled the industry to new heights, but what goes up must eventually come down.

"There was a ridiculous amount of money being made, a ridiculous amount of product being sold, and also ridiculous expectations during that time," former DC writer Paul Kupperberg says. "I thought, Holy God, we're headed for a fall."

Few at the time could have guessed how bad that inevitable fall would be. As it turned out, the industry's greedy practices had done little to benefit its long-term health and had instead attracted hordes of speculators who were buying up product in hopes of paying for their kids' braces down the road. Thousands of new comic book shops, who could get an account with the one of the major distributors by spending as little as $300, had cropped up across the country to deal in this newly fashionable collectible.

New faces, fueled by media hype, were showing up at comic shops across the country to buy a case of *Superman* or *X-Men* comics.

"My dad even got hoodwinked because of something he saw on TV," says comic dealer Bob Beerbohm. "He calls me up, 'Hey, kid. I've invested in comics for the first time.' He bought five copies of 'The Death of Superman.' I said, 'Pop, are you nuts? You paid $5 for these things? You're never gonna get your money back.' He didn't want to hear it. People don't want to hear the truth."

The idea that comic books were collectibles that would increase in value dated back to at least the 1960s when *Newsweek* wrote an influential article on comic fandom and noted, to the author's shock, that a copy of Superman's first appearance in *Action Comics* #1 was selling for an astronomical $100. (A copy went for $3.2 million in 2014.) Suddenly everyone had visions that the stack of Aquamans collecting dust in their garage could be worth big money.

DC editor Len Wein in the early 1980s used to keep boxes containing one hundred copies each of *The New Teen Titans* #1 and #2 under his desk, claiming they would be his retirement account. A few years later, when he left the company, he didn't bother taking the boxes.

What Wein and others were waking up to was the reality that scarcity largely drove the value of collectibles, and a comic book printed by the millions was a terrible investment. Those profit seekers who had swooped into the industry during the early 1990s soon fled the business, as did many casual readers pushed away by all the gimmicks, the increasing prices, and the flood of mediocre titles. Sales in comic shops began to taper off.

"The Death of Superman" would prove to be the high point of the era. The comic book market peaked in April 1993, then dropped the next month and continued spiraling downward.

Events that once moved millions found themselves unable to sell through. The issue in which Superman died was a pop culture sensation, but by the time he returned in *Adventures of Superman* #500 a few months later, many of the speculators who had been propping up the industry had scattered.

"I know a guy who made a throne out of unsold copies of *Adventures Superman* #500," says retailer Brian Hibbs. "A lot of people thought it would sell as many copies as when he died. And of course it didn't sell the tiniest, tiniest fraction of that."

DC editor K. C. Carlson got chewed out when he visited his local comic shop in New Jersey that had ordered big on the Superman return issue. "Why didn't you tell me not to do this?" the owner snapped.

The bubble was bursting. The comic shops that had cropped up to capitalize on the hype soon found themselves stuck with product they could not sell and were deeply in debt. They began to close their doors. By the end of the decade the number of specialty stores had dropped by 75 percent, according to some estimates.

"Certainly we overdid the number of titles," Marvel's former president Terry Stewart says. "And that's something I did. I went too far on that."

"Nobody knew when it went too far," says former publisher Mike Hobson, who left Marvel in 1996. "We had twelve years of continual growth at that time, and we thought it would go on forever, like the stock market."

The loss of a handful of Marvel's top artists, including Rob Liefeld, Todd McFarlane, and then-Spider-Man-artist Erik Larsen, compounded its growing troubles. They had quit to form an independent company in 1992 called Image. *X-Men* artist Jim Lee had at first been reluctant to join the exodus due to the ungodly amount of money he was making in royalties, but he finally acquiesced after Marvel refused to fly him and his wife first class to a convention.

Image grew quickly, gaining a double-digit market share, while Marvel's dropped. The publisher went from accounting for nearly half the direct market in 1991 to less than 32 percent in 1994.

With Image offering the first challenge to DC and Marvel in decades, the established publishers began to become more concerned about a loss of market share. And the easiest way to boost your presence was to acquire another company. In April of 1994 DC began trying to do just that. Their target was Malibu, the indie that had briefly passed them in sales in 1992. Malibu had recently launched a superhero line of its own called the Ultraverse that had garnered buzz. During a friendly meal DC's Paul Levitz floated the idea of a purchase to Malibu founder Scott Rosenberg.

"DC was concerned about market share," Rosenberg says. "They were embarrassed to be number two."

DC was also interested in Malibu's ability to create and market new characters—a rarity in an industry driven by legacy characters. Levitz told

Rosenberg that he was concerned that DC, which was better than Marvel at taking a long view, couldn't keep relaunching its core superheroes over and over forever. To survive in the future, it would need new properties.

Negotiations between the two companies carried on throughout the summer. Sample artwork was prepared, showing the companies' characters together. By the time the San Diego Comic-Con rolled around in August, the merger was close to being finalized.

"I can remember being in editorial and laughing about the rumor that DC was going to buy Malibu," says then-Marvel-editor-in-chief Tom De-Falco. "DC had [partnered with] First Comics, Comico, and a couple of other companies, and those deals never worked out. We were laughing, 'Don't these guys ever learn their lesson?'"

"Then I hear we're buying it."

Word had leaked of the intended Malibu-DC merger, and before contracts were signed, Marvel leapt into the negotiations. Terry Stewart called Rosenberg one afternoon and asked to meet the next morning. Marvel was desperate to gobble up Malibu's 5 percent market share and keep it from going to DC. The executives were terrified that DC and Malibu's combined market share could drop them into second place—a shameful turn of events that mighty Marvel simply would not tolerate. They also hoped to exploit the company's properties for film and TV projects.

"Marvel had had some interest before, but the DC negotiations completely pushed them over the edge," Rosenberg says. "It went from a normal acquisition to one that was immediate."

Perelman soon appeared at Malibu's Southern California offices for a walk-through. He showed up puffing on a cigar, in spite of the strict no-smoking rules. Marvel's lawyers were flown out from New York and put up at nearby hotel with orders not to check out until they closed a deal.

In November 1994 Marvel signed a deal to acquire Malibu, stealing the asset out from under DC's nose. The whole deal was done in less than thirty days—a lightning-fast turnaround.

"Ronald [Perelman] loved acquisitions," says Terry Stewart. "That's what his whole life has been about. Comics got so hot, and everybody was chasing these properties. Ronald thought we should do this deal, and he's the owner and the boss, so we did it."

Not everyone thought it was a good idea, though. Malibu, like the other publishers, was stumbling amidst the industry's woes. DeFalco confronted the president in the Marvel offices, asking, "Are you out of your freakin' mind?"

"Well," Stewart replied, "we can't have DC be the only aggressive buyer of properties."

Publicly the reason Marvel gave for the purchase was that Malibu had a state-of-the-art coloring system. Computer coloring was fairly new at that point, and it provided a wider array of tones and a more sophisticated look than the primitive, four-color hand separation that had been the industry standard for so many years. Computer coloring was one of the things that set Image books apart, helping the rogue publisher establish a look that would come to define the decade. But setting up a computer coloring system was expensive and difficult. DC had tried a year earlier and failed—a minor motivation for Marvel in the Malibu purchase.

"There were a lot of rumors, but none of them made any sense," DeFalco says. "If you were interested in computer coloring, all you had to do was buy up-to-date computers. They also said the Malibu stuff appealed to an older audience than we did. That was bull. Nothing they said made any sense to me."

In the end the acquisition Marvel scrambled to make never amounted to much. Marvel canceled Malibu's Ultraverse line, later relaunching a handful of titles, but all eventually faded into oblivion.

The Malibu acquisition would not turn out to be Marvel's most catastrophic of the decade, however. It wouldn't even be the most catastrophic of the year. That honor would go to the company's December 1994 purchase of Heroes World, the country's third-largest comic book distributor, located in New Jersey.

News of the takeover rocked the industry, and for good reason. The move would fundamentally change the way the comic book business worked and would have terrible implications for both Marvel and DC down the road.

Prior to the deal comic book shops could buy Marvel comics from multiple distributors. The Heroes World acquisition meant that if a retailer wanted Marvel comics—still the lifeblood of the industry, despite the publisher's recent decline—they would be forced to buy from a single distributor at whatever terms Marvel established.

The deal was a raw one for retailers, but to the Marvel brass it made all the sense in the world. During the recent industry boom the publisher had become increasingly frustrated with the lack of information available about its end consumer. Marvel knew how many copies it was selling to the various distributors, but it didn't have a clear handle on which stores were buying from them or what kind of customers were buying from the stores. Even just identifying the eight thousand or so outlets selling comics at the time proved challenging. The previous few years had led to a huge increase in the number of retail locations selling comics to try to ride the comics wave, including some nontraditional venues such as card and hobby shops. Marvel even discovered that some comic book "stores" were actually located in storage units that opened up for a day or two each week to sell comics.

"It was one of those things that if we're going to continue to grow the business, how could we control our own destiny?" Marvel's Stewart says. "And one of the things was, you can distribute your own product. This was a classic textbook, MBA kind of thing. As a proprietor, it had become impossible to get all the business information that we needed, so that's the direction we went."

Marvel's executives under Perelman came from the financial world, and to them most problems could be solved with business-school thinking. To the comic book veterans, however, the Heroes World deal raised eyebrows, just as the Malibu purchase before it. How would Heroes World, which handled a small fraction of the market, be able to scale up basically overnight to handle the exclusive Marvel load, they wondered?

"Here it is, twenty or thirty years later, and I still can't figure out why they bought it," DeFalco says.

Upon hearing the news at a convention one retailer announced he was going home, closing up his comic book shop, and opening a tobacco store.

"It made us look really, really bad—overly aggressive and predatory," says Glenn Greenberg, a Marvel writer and editor from 1992 to 1998. "The people who understood the business, the inner workings, said this is going to be a disaster and was going to have a ripple effect."

The effects did ripple. The other distributors, who had depended on Marvel and Malibu for nearly half their business, were suddenly left scrambling to cut exclusive deals with other publishers in a desperate attempt to keep their doors open.

Marvel's alliance with Heroes World shook DC's executives and marketing department, and the company was unsure how to respond. But as the second-biggest publisher, DC was suddenly in a position of power, able to field offers from distributors desperate to handle its business. In 1995 the company announced it had chosen Diamond as its exclusive dealer to the direct market. The choice essentially killed off the other distributors who could no longer survive without DC or Marvel products.

DC's contract was reported to have come with one interesting caveat: in the event of the death or retirement of Diamond's owner, or after ten years, DC had the option to buy Diamond outright.

DC's insistence on the clause looked shrewd in 1995. Two years later it looked absolutely genius. That's when Heroes World collapsed for all the reasons insiders expected, leaving Marvel without a distributor and forcing the publisher to come crawling back to the only option left: Diamond.

The DC contract has since been renegotiated, and it's unclear whether the rumored purchase option for DC remains, but if it does, and DC eventually opts to buy Diamond, it would return the industry to the days of the 1960s, when DC was distributing Marvel.

"DC wants to control that market. They want to own it," says former DC artist Steve Bissette. "DC never forgot the power they had in the late fifties, early sixties. Corporations have long memories. Even when they go through multiple iterations, there's some part of that corporate brain in the back of the cortex that wants to be back there."

If that day ever does come, DC would have Marvel over a barrel. It would assume control over certain vital aspects of Marvel's business, including depth of inventory and its position in the monthly solicitations catalog.

Whatever the future may hold, the death of Heroes World left the industry under the control of a monopoly—an arrangement that remains to this day—and it's worse off for it.

"It used to be if you wanted to buy any given book, you had twenty different choices of places to buy from," says retailer Brian Hibbs. "Then you had one. And if they didn't have it, whether from it selling out or because they just didn't give a shit, you couldn't get the book."

The mid-1990s crash wasn't all bad. It did have at least one positive effect in that it forced to the two publishers to begin cooperating again. The 1982 JLA/Avengers debacle had killed the desire to do crossovers, but after a decade tempers had cooled, personnel had changed, and both sides were potentially ready to try again.

"The early nineties were huge boom years, so Marvel and DC didn't need each other," says Ron Marz, who was writing DC's *Green Lantern* at the time. "Then the bottom dropped out and lots of shops closed. Sales went into the tank. Suddenly it was, 'Well, what can we do to boost sales for our properties but also to keep stores in business?'"

The solution was a new round of crossovers to rival *Superman vs. The Amazing Spider-Man* and the rest from the seventies and early eighties. The two sides began discussing potential projects, though Marvel's new corporate ownership was somewhat reticent to collaborate.

"The problem was, Marvel was a publicly traded company, and you're talking about taking the characters of a publicly traded company and giving some of that equity to a competitor, which is kind of crazy if you think about it," says Terry Stewart. "But I was able to convince Perelman and everybody that this is what you do in a comic book world. This is something that fans will look forward to. We'll win big. And it will engender a lot of love, the fact that the two companies have gotten together, even though we're big competitors."

One catalyst on the Marvel side involved another crossover book the company was planning: *Archie Meets the Punisher*. The one-off special, released in 1994, remains one of the most left-field books Marvel has ever published. It found the Punisher—a murderous, gun-toting vigilante created as a Spider-Man villain by Gerry Conway and John Romita Sr. back in 1974—heading to Riverdale, home of Archie, Jughead, and the rest of the kooky, clean-cut teen gang.

The oddball pairing was conceived in the early 1990s by the editor-in-chief of Archie Comics and Marvel's Punisher editor, Don Daley. They pitched the crossover to Marvel's editor-in-chief, Tom DeFalco, who was generally skeptical of crossovers.

"The Archie editor, Victor Gorelick, used to be Tom's boss [in the early 1970s], so he couldn't say no," says Greenberg. "It was the first Marvel intercompany crossover in years, and it opened the door for more. That Punisher-Archie book broke the wall down."

Archie and Marvel working together was one thing. The two entities published different kinds of comics and were in less direct competition. DC and Marvel was a completely different story. Getting the two on the same page to restart the crossovers proved difficult.

Marvel's Tom DeFalco, Terry Stewart, and Mike Hobson went to lunch one day with DC's Jenette Kahn and Paul Levitz to discuss a potential deal. The group discussed character pairings and terms as they ate and managed to hammer out a tentative agreement. But at the end of the meal Kahn suddenly dropped a bomb.

"I remember I was just getting up from the table, and everybody was congratulating ourselves because we'd somehow got past all the bullshit of the past," DeFalco says. "And Jenette suddenly says, 'This is all good, but there are two characters you can't use for any of these crossovers: Superman and Batman.' I sat back down, and I remember that Mike Hobson and Terry Stewart were both still standing."

Kahn was reticent to include Batman and Superman because both characters were involved in complicated ongoing story lines across multiple titles at the time. Freeing them for a crossover would require no small amount of coordination among editors and could turn into an in-house headache. Kahn suggested other team-ups.

"You can do things like Lobo and Wolverine," she said.

"Wait a minute," DeFalco countered. "Wolverine sells four hundred thousand copies a month. Lobo sells forty thousand. Why would we do a team-up like that? All it does is help you."

"Why not Green Arrow and Hawkeye?" Kahn suggested.

"Because it wouldn't sell," DeFalco said.

Marvel was adamant that the team-ups had to involve characters of equal stature and popularity. Without Superman and Batman—DC's best assets—the deal was off.

DC ultimately relented, and the first new wave of crossovers appeared in June 1994. It united two of the era's hottest heroes, Punisher and Batman, and had them battling Punisher villain Jigsaw. Another volume pairing the same characters, *Deadly Knights*, was released a few months later.

More crossovers followed in 1995. Cosmic heroes Green Lantern and Silver Surfer joined forces, and Spider-Man and Batman fought the Joker. Each of the universe's world-devouring villains squared off in *Darkseid vs. Galactus: The Hunger*.

The companies traded off production of the special books, with the other side getting editorial approval. (To figure out who published what, look to see which company's character comes first in the title.) The cooperation this time around was more congenial than it had been back in 1976. But some general rules still applied to ensure neither company got the upper hand.

"Everyone had to get equal time, and you couldn't have Batman beating up Spider-Man too much," says Graham Nolan, who penciled 1997's *Batman & Spider-Man: New Age Dawning.*

The need for equality led to a promotion for one Marvel staffer. Many of the crossover books contained a page listing the executive staff for DC and Marvel in two, neat, side-by-side columns.

"There was a great effort to make sure we had the same number of people they had, the same number of lines," says Shirrel Rhoades, who joined Marvel in 1996 as publisher. "I took the page to [president] David Schreff, and I said, 'Here we have Paul Levitz on DC's side. What title should I have?' Basically Schreff said, 'You can have whatever title Levitz has.'"

So Rhoades walked out of the office a new executive vice president.

This latest batch of crossovers was aimed straight at the heart of the market's increasingly insular fanbase. The recent bust had driven out many of the comic book tourists, and with newsstands becoming a less viable outlet with every passing day, the number of casual and younger readers was diminishing. The aging fanboys, who were the bread and butter of the direct market, were suddenly becoming all the industry had left. A Marvel survey in the late nineties, for example, found that the average reader was a geriatric twenty-six-year-old. The days of "Hey, kids! Comics!" were fading.

These new crossovers were not the same kind of pop-culture curiosity the original in 1976 had been. Superman meeting Spider-Man for the first time had been a mainstream news story, but the Punisher going toe-to-toe with Batman—and not the Batman that you know, by the way, but a new Batman named Jean-Paul Valley who used to be called Azrael but took up the mantle after . . . er, never mind. These books were for the hardcore hobbyists whose heads were filled with deep knowledge about every corner, character, and costume of both the Marvel and DC universes.

But for all the fan service showered on the readership over the years, there was still one project that hadn't yet happened—one that fans had been begging for, mailing letters about, and beseeching the great Odin to deliver unto them. Characters fighting each other was great and all, but all that did was determine which single person was stronger. What fans truly craved was a battle of *universes*, an all-encompassing smack-down between DC and Marvel, pitting scads of heroes against one another to determine, once and for all, which reigned supreme. Who was better? Marvel or DC?

After more than thirty years readers were about to find out.

The market downturn had made such a project not only possible but necessary, and hopes were it could prove to be a major fiscal shot in the arm. Also serving to grease the wheels was the ascendency of Mike Carlin at DC and Mark Gruenwald at Marvel to the executive editor positions.

Gruenwald was a former fanzine editor who had begun working for Marvel in the 1970s. His knowledge of the characters' histories was among the deepest on staff, and he served as a sort of "continuity cop." Carlin had gotten his start as Gruenwald's assistant back in the early eighties before jumping to DC and handling the Superman titles. The two were like brothers, and Gruenwald had hanging on his office wall an image of his face morphed together with Carlin's.

In 1995 Carlin and Gruenwald hatched a plan for the ultimate crossover, which was to be called *Marvel/DC: Super War*. As with past crossovers, the idea was to choose talent from both sides who was emblematic of each company—an interesting idea that set up the series as not just a clash of characters but of each publisher's style and expertise. The artists were to switch off, with each side drawing two of the four issues.

DC's initial choice to pencil the company's half was José Luis García-López, a longtime DC artist who drew the characters so on model, so perfectly within DC's house style that his work was often used for images on licensed products. He declined, and DC tapped Dan Jurgens, the penciler on "The Death of Superman," instead.

Marvel at first had problems securing an artist for the same reasons it did back in 1976.

"There was some reticence on Marvel's part to pull one of their A-list guys from one of their titles to do this thing that was only half of a Marvel project, so we went through a list of guys who ended up turning it down," Marz says.

John Romita Jr., the son of Marvel's longtime art director and the artist of *Spider-Man*, passed. As did Andy and Adam Kubert, the sons of former DC editor Joe Kubert and superstars in their own right. Marvel ultimately settled for Claudio Castellini, an Italian artist who had done very little work for them. In a way it perfectly summed up the companies. DC chose a seasoned veteran, Marvel went for a hot newcomer.

The writing duties were also to be tag-teamed. For its part DC selected Ron Marz, the *Green Lantern* writer and someone who, at age six, had penned a letter to Marvel (in crayon, no less) demanding that the Avengers fight the Justice League.

"Mike [Carlin] called me to ask if I wanted to write the crossover, and ten-year-old me had a head explosion," Marz says. "I fell off my chair. I thought, I actually get to do this?"

Marvel's contribution was Peter David, a former sales department employee who broke into writing and was known for his work on *The Incredible Hulk*.

The writers and editors began planning the series, but fearful that the details of the project would leak, they met in secret at Gruenwald's uptown Manhattan apartment. There they hashed out the basic plot. It involved two warring godlike brothers—one representing Marvel and the other DC—challenging each other to a proxy duel that would pit champions from each of their universes against one another to see which was superior. And the universe that lost "could cease to exist forever." (And if you buy that, we've got a super-bridge to sell you.)

"It was a popcorn story. It was an excuse to have these characters meet and fight, which was what everybody wanted," Marz says. "We knew we weren't doing Shakespeare."

The list of one-on-one battles came together pretty easily, as most DC characters had a reasonably obvious counterpart. Marvel's scrappy, violent Wolverine would fight DC's scrappy, violent Lobo. Marvel archer Hawkeye would battle DC archer Green Arrow. Aquaman would square off against the Sub-Mariner. The four issues would contain eleven battles in total—an odd number to ensure there would be no tie. The first six contests would end in stalemates. But the outcome of the final five would be determined by a fan vote, cast through email or regular mail. Those match-ups—Batman vs. Captain America, Hulk vs. Superman, Superboy vs. Spider-Man, Wolverine vs. Lobo and Wonder Woman vs. Storm—were carefully chosen to avoid a drubbing by either side.

"We knew who'd win based on popularity and which character was more well known," Marz says. "Batman and Superman were going to win. The only one we didn't know was Wonder Woman and Storm."

For the record the X-Men's Storm triumphed. But somewhere out there is a page in which Wonder Woman emerges victorious. Because of the tight production schedule, two different pages had to be drawn to cover both possible outcomes of the vote.

The Storm win sealed Marvel's victory for the whole event. Despite the loss, the DC universe was spared. At the end of issue #4 the cosmic brothers shake hands and agree that both universes have value—and, presumably, merchandising potential.

Marvel wasn't quite as good of a sport. The company later ran a house ad in some of its comics crowing about the victory. "We won!" the page read in massive red type. The ad was quickly discontinued because the contract between the two companies forbade either side from publicly declaring themselves the victor.

The spirit of cooperation between the two companies extended further than just the four issues that comprised *Marvel versus DC*. The real surprise of the crossover came with the announcement that for one month between the third and fourth issue of the miniseries the companies would be creating new, hybrid characters by combining one from each company. The temporary line—it was to last for one month only, publishing twelve titles—was to be called Rival Comics. That was later changed to Amalgam, due to trademark issues.

At a DC meeting each editor and assistant was asked to write down five ideas for the proposed line. The titles and concepts were to come first, with the stories determined later. *JLX* mashed up DC's JLA (Justice League of America) and Marvel's X-Men. *Doctor Strangefate* combined the two occult heroes from both companies, Marvel's Doctor Strange and DC's Doctor Fate.

"One idea that didn't make it was *Giant-Sized Man Servant*, which was some sort of combo between [Batman's butler] Alfred and [Avengers butler] Jarvis with growing powers," says Chris Duffy, the assistant editor on *DC versus Marvel*.

The initial twelve Amalgam titles landed on shelves in February 1996, leaving the fanboy community trembling with joy at seeing the universes mashed up. If readers only knew how far the original plans extended. The initial proposal called for one particularly unprecedented piece of cooperation: The publishers would actually exchange characters for a year. Someone from the Marvel universe—She-Hulk was given as an example—would appear in DC's publications, and someone from the DC universe would cross over into Marvel's.

"That didn't happen," Duffy says. "I imagine that was just too complicated to figure out how they could reprint that material."

Marvel versus DC and the Amalgam experiment were, for many, among the high points of the 1990s—a decade known more for its unnecessary titles, flashy art, sloppy writing, and cash-grab gimmicks. The projects certainly marked an apex for Marvel.

The company, once stable and small, had grown increasingly chaotic since its new corporate overlords assumed control. It cycled through executive leadership, with some honchos lasting just a matter of months. At a 1996 editorial retreat writer Scott Lobdell joked to the assembled crowd, "Don't worry if you haven't met the new president, Scott Marden. Wait a few weeks and you can meet the new one."

Marvel continued to struggle with slowing sales and mounting debt. In December 1996 Perelman filed for bankruptcy protection. For longtime comic book readers the news was akin to being told Strawberry Shortcake had cancer, an unwelcome intrusion of harsh reality into a beloved fantasy world. The bankruptcy also helped, once and for all, to kill the myth that Stan Lee had cultivated for so many years, painting Marvel as a rollicking, carefree place staffed by the wacky bullpenners who did it for the love of superheroes and the pursuit of far-out ideas. In the end Marvel had no special magic. It was just like every other business—all about dollars and cents and vulnerable to the cruel whims of capitalism.

The once-great publisher was in such dire straits that it literally sold the doors off its office. The glass entryway, etched with Marvel's characters, was snapped up by a collector.

The bankruptcy rightfully spooked many at DC. As much animosity as the companies might have had with one another, as much pride as the staff might have had that its company was better, Marvel and DC needed one another. If one were to disappear, it wouldn't be long until the other collapsed as well.

"There were no parties at DC about the Marvel situation," says former DC editor K. C. Carlson. "We were very concerned about the industry as a whole. We were aware this was not good times."

That sympathy only extended so far, however. Rumors began to swirl that Marvel might cease publishing its own books—similar to the whispers that had dogged DC in the seventies and eighties.

"DC was hoping to get the Fantastic Four publishing rights," says one insider who asked to remain anonymous. "If a few dominoes had fallen differently or a few people made minutely different decisions, the face of comics would look very different—and worse—today."

Marvel did continue to publish, though, and after a long, complicated (and boring) corporate battle among wealthy titans—few of whom had probably ever read a comic book—the company emerged from bankruptcy under the control of new ownership. Ike Perlmutter and Avi Arad, a bearish, Harley-riding Israeli who grew up reading comics in Hebrew, were now in charge. The two were determined to take Marvel in their own direction.

"Avi and [Marvel's CEO from 1996–1997] Scott Sassa would often team up and override Stan," former publisher Shirrel Rhoades says. "Stan would say, 'I was talking to David Schwimmer from *Friends*, and he'd like to get involved with us.' And they'd laugh and say, 'David Schwimmer?! That's not our image.'"

Perlmutter was a hardened veteran of the Israel Defense Forces who was rarely photographed and had developed a legendary reputation for thrift. While DC continued to enjoy its cushy corporate existence, Marvel was bent to Perlmutter's penny-pinching ways, compounding the misery many felt working in a dying industry.

"He called me in once to justify why [editor] Tom Brevoort was on the phone with [artist] Carlos Pacheco, who lived in Spain, for an hour?" says former editor Frank Pittarese. "Well, Carlos was drawing the *Fantastic Four*. 'They got to talk for an hour?!' he'd ask."

The staff was given key cards they were required to swipe when they entered and left the office, and Perlmutter would supposedly study the data to make sure no one was taking too long at lunch. As a joke, someone circulated a fake memo on official Marvel letterhead that demanded employees who needed to "go number two" should use the bathroom at the McDonald's downstairs.

The bankruptcy period also brought a new editor-in-chief. Marvel ousted Tom DeFalco in 1994, making way for Bob Harras in 1995. The choice was a clear indication where Marvel's priorities remained, as Harras was best known for launching the mega-selling *X-Men* #1 back in

1991 and overseeing an increasingly impenetrable X-Men family of titles popular with lifer readers.

Harras seemed to personify Marvel in the nineties, with his sensibilities meshing with the flashy art and superficial storytelling that had come to define the decade. He was also no fan of DC, believing the company's talent to be inferior. (Which is ironic because Harras became DC's editor-in-chief in 2010.) When Marvel managed to poach Grant Morrison, the heady Scotsman who had produced the best-selling *Arkham Asylum* graphic novel for DC, Morrison was put on a low-profile miniseries called *Skrull Kill Krew.*

"It was considered a real get to land Grant," says Glenn Greenberg, the assistant editor on *Skrull Kill Krew.* "But the best that Grant could do was *Skrull Kill Krew* because, coming from DC, he wasn't valued."

Morrison quickly returned to DC, where he helmed a much-lauded relaunch of the Justice League in 1996. He took a little revenge on Marvel in the series' first issue. The book included a scene in which aliens executed a group of villains, and among those meeting a fiery end—you had to squint to see them—were two characters who looked an awful lot like Marvel's Doctor Doom and Wolverine.

Morrison must have had clout, or perhaps none of the higher-ups at DC noticed. As the companies became even more corporate, the cheeky, in-book digs and homages to the competition once the currency of the rivalry were becoming less frequent.

"We got in trouble for that stuff," says former DC editor Dan Raspler. "Paul [Levitz] was nervous about getting sued. I think he thought if it was a general policy of allowance, somebody would cross a line and just put Wolverine in the comic and we'd get sued."

"I never liked it," Levitz says. "When I was twelve, I got a kick out of it, but was never a fan past twelve."

One of the more blatant homages came with the introduction of the Extremists in a 1990 issue of *Justice League Europe*. The team of villains were clearly modeled after Marvel's most iconic baddies. Dreamslayer, a magical demon, was based on Doctor Strange foe Dormammu, the armored Lord Havok a stand-in for Doctor Doom, and Gorgon for Doctor Octopus.

"Marvel did this group based on the Justice League, Squadron Supreme, so we thought, turnabout is fair play," says Extremist cocreator

Keith Giffen. "We just threw it in there and thought, let's have some fun with this. We never heard from Marvel. If they'd come to us and said anything, we'd go, 'What about [the Squadron Supreme]?'"

"I got to DC in 1992, and it was the kind of thing where some young punk like myself who was a fan would say, 'Hey, wouldn't it be great if we used the Extremists?'" former DC editor Ruben Diaz says. "And someone would go, 'Yeahhh, that's probably not a good idea.'"

Marvel writers, too, were under strict instructions not to include cameos of DC characters.

"Walt Simonson had had [Superman's alter ego] Clark Kent show up in *Thor* [#341 in 1984], and DC was not happy with that," says Marvel writer Peter David.

Despite the ban, David pulled off a stealth crossover of his own in 1994 when he had Death, Dream's sister from Neil Gaiman's *Sandman* series, briefly appear in an issue of *The Incredible Hulk*. David sought and received the blessing of Gaiman as well as Paul Levitz under two conditions: Neither Death's face nor her trademark ankh necklace could be shown.

One of the most costly intercompany jabs came in 1999 with issue #5 of *The League of Extraordinary Gentlemen*, published through a DC imprint. The series teamed classic Victorian literary characters and was written by Alan Moore, the bearded Brit genius behind the most influential series of the 1980s, including *Watchmen* and *Swamp Thing*.

Each issue of the series reprinted real ads from the 1800s in the back of the comic, and issue #5 contained a rather unfortunate notice for Marvel brand "whirling spray," a "vaginal syringe." The implications were pretty clear: Moore was calling Marvel douches.

Deeming the visual barb vulgar and fearful that it would lead to retaliation from Marvel, DC decided to pulp the run and alter the ad to read "Amaze" instead of "Marvel" in a reprinted edition.

The recall cost DC tens of thousands of dollars and delayed the release of issue #5 by several months, but it was consistent with the company's conservative attitude. Marvel tended to be scrappier, ballsier, and more willing to poke its competition in the eye, while DC continued to hold on to its self-image as the gold standard of comic book publisher—a leftover from the 1960s. Even when given the chance to take a gentle dig at its competitor, DC opted to take a loss instead.

"It's classy to take the higher road," DC editor Dan Raspler says. "The attitude was, 'We're not going to do the gutter-sniping, playful, childish bullshit. We're going to be classy gentlemen.'"

DC had better Bubble Wrap its china and stow its pocket square, because its genteel disposition was about to be severely tested. Mud was set to fly between the two companies like never before, marking the nastiest era in the Marvel-DC rivalry to date.

12

The War Gets Uncivil

"My general sense was that when Jemas was around,
that was a low point in the rivalry."

—*Deadpool* artist Scott Koblish

"**R**ivalries," writer Peter David says, "derive from who's in charge, and depending on who was in charge at Marvel or DC at the time, we either got along swell or there was hostility."

Mark down the early twenty-first century as one of those hostile periods.

The days of two best friends being in charge at both companies were gone—Marvel's executive editor Mark Gruenwald had died suddenly in 1996—and toward the end of the 1990s the Marvel-DC rivalry grew coarser, eerily mirroring the shift happening generally in society. It was a time in America when civility was dying. The political discourse reached a new level of nastiness with the election of George W. Bush. The growing prevalence of the Internet and its culture of online commentary made it easier and cheaper than ever to disseminate trollish criticism. In entertainment reality TV personalities hurled insults at one another for our amusement.

Following the 1996 bankruptcy filing Marvel had endured several depressing years of staff layoffs, belt-tightening, and low morale. Its very survival teetered on the brink as various vultures attempted to swoop in and pick the carcass clean—including Stan Lee, who claimed to have joined forces with Michael Jackson in an unsuccessful bid to buy the company.

With more important issues to worry about, the rivalry was put on the back burner for a few years.

"Marvel didn't really affect us that much then," says Tom Palmer Jr., a former DC editor and the son of the legendary inker. "It was almost like the person you were fighting against wasn't really there. You got the impression that things weren't that organized at Marvel. They were trying to get their footing back."

The company emerged from bankruptcy at the end of the century, and with its new lease on life came a management shake-up. In January 2000 Bill Jemas, a former Marvel executive, returned to the company to serve as the new president, initiating an era of enmity between the longtime rivals, the likes of which had not been seen before.

Jemas was a Harvard-educated tax attorney who'd once worked for the National Basketball Association. He'd first come to Marvel in the early 1990s through card company Fleer, which Marvel had purchased.

"Bill Jemas had been brought over from trading cards, and when I got there [in 1996] there was really nothing for him to do," says former publisher Shirrel Rhoades. "He was playing around with children's products, like coloring books, that didn't go anywhere. He was kind of restless and left shortly thereafter."

Jemas went to work at Madison Square Garden in 1997, organizing special events and working with merchandising. From there he was recruited to return to Marvel and run it.

"I remember being in the bullpen when Jemas came in," says artist and former Marvel assistant editor Gregg Schigiel. "It was like the fourth president in my time there. They announced Jemas, and there was a rumble in the bullpen like, 'Oh, boy,' because everyone knew who he was. There was a bit of like, 'This isn't going to go well' vibe in the air."

Jemas admitted that he had never read a comic before working for Marvel, and he had a brash, in-your-face personality that rubbed some the wrong way.

"He was enthusiastic, he was passionate, and some of it was tough love and some of it was tough humor," says Bob Greenberger, a former DC editor whom Jemas brought to Marvel in 2001. "There were some staffers he would just ride. He gave people nicknames. And he thought it was funny, and he never stopped to realize these people were suffering."

Shortly after being handed Marvel's reins, Jemas cut editor-in-chief Bob Harras loose and promoted Joe Quesada. Quesada was a Queens-born, Mets-loving artist who had worked for both Marvel and DC. He was a casual presence, with a doughy build; an earring; spiky, bleached hair; and a wardrobe that favored T-shirts over suits. He'd been hired in the midst of Marvel's bankruptcy woes to run a nearly autonomous new imprint called Marvel Knights that offered edgier, creator-driven takes on some of the company's then-stagnating heroes. Quesada recruited *Clerks* filmmaker Kevin Smith in 1998 to write *Daredevil* and tapped Irish-born Garth Ennis to provide a wonderfully vulgar take on vigi-lante the Punisher.

Quesada and Jemas came out swinging, determined to return Marvel to greatness by dragging it out of the financial morass it had been stuck in and shaking off the creative inertia that had dogged the company for years. Marvel would once again become the scrappy, cutting-edge pub-lisher it had been back in its 1960s heyday.

And one important aspect of their plan was to rekindle the rivalry with DC to a blistering, openly antagonistic level that hadn't been seen since the days of Stan Lee sniping at "Brand Echh." Marvel comics were the best in the world, and Jemas and Quesada were going to let everyone, including those unfortunate souls at DC, know it.

If *Survivor* and *The Real World* and other popular shows at the time have taught us anything, it's that conflict equals audience engagement.

"I liked it when the two companies hated each other," Quesada said in 2002. "It made it better for the fans. You know, if you like DC, then you hated Marvel. If you like Marvel, then you hated DC."

"Bill had come from sports, and he had that instinct of team rivalry," says Stuart Moore, a former DC editor who went to Marvel in 2000. "He wanted to stir up the fans to root for one side or the other. And he really liked to tweak the DC people, who had a tendency to take themselves a bit seriously. He loved to taunt them. He was into causing trouble."

Unlike previous presidents who preferred to remain behind the scenes, Jemas saw himself as the public face of the company. He quickly became the industry's latest answer to P. T. Barnum—a loudmouthed carnival barker who was quick with a boast or attention-grabbing sound bite. He held regu-lar press conferences, penned an online fan question-and-answer column, and generally did his best to thump his chest about the company at every turn. And one of his favorite ways to do it was to take a poke at the "Distinguished Competition." He seemed to have a put-down for every dollar of his $505,000 salary.

He regularly referred to DC, whose parent company Time Warner had recently been acquired by an online giant, as "AOL" simply because he knew it irked them.

He regularly ribbed his rival for the poor sales and quality of its titles, once saying, "Somewhere somebody wrote down this rule that comic books are supposed to suck, and the vast majority of what is published by our competition . . . closely adheres to that rule."

Upon seeing the original 2002 *Spider-Man* movie, he proclaimed it so good that "DC could do a Spider-Man comic and it wouldn't hurt the character."

In 2001, when DC censored issues of writer Mark Millar's *The Authority*, an ultraviolent, R-rated look at superheroes, Jemas publicly offered to publish the banned comics, generously offering DC a 10 percent royalty. He later clarified that he'd meant to say 10 cents.

Jemas imagined his antics harkened back to the days of Stan Lee, but his tone was harsher, more fit for the blunter twenty-first century. His swipes seriously ticked off the more sensitive employees of DC.

"Stan did it with class. Stan did it in such a way that you couldn't take offense," says former Marvel editor Glenn Greenberg. "I know for a fact that the DC folks were taking it really seriously and personally, and there were a lot of bad feelings and they were really hurt. I know that at the senior level people were taking it personally."

Jemas was especially exuberant in his antagonism of Paul Levitz, who in 2002, after some thirty years at the company, had ascended to become DC's president and publisher, following Jenette Kahn's departure. Levitz was an intense, cerebral figure who didn't suffer fools. He had a reputation for conservatism and loathed gossip and the airing of the industry's dirty laundry—in other words, the perfect foil for Jemas's sophomoric shenanigans.

Jemas penned a taunting foreword to *Marvel 2000–2001 Year in Review: Fanboys and Badgirls, Bill and Joe's Marvelous Adventure*, a worshipful, 2002 hardcover detailing the first year under the company's new regime. In it he took a flamethrower to Levitz and his management of DC.

"Those who love him say it's because Levitz wants to shield his creators and characters from the commercial exploitation and corruption that could come from mass media exploitation," Jemas continued. "Those who loathe him say Levitz is a man with teeny talents, who keeps the industry tiny to protect his own power over truly bright and talented creators."

Jemas's masterstroke of childish antagonism came with a satirical 2002 limited series he wrote called *Marville*. The comic was little more than a vehicle for a series of gags aimed at DC and its parent company.

The story concerned a Superman-like character—the title *Marville* was a play on the DC TV series *Smallville*—whose parents send him back to our era from the year 5002. The boy, whose name was KalAOL (Superman's real name is Kal-El), struggled to make his way in our world, his only possession an AOL DVD with one hundred free minutes.

The series took personal shots at everyone from Time Warner executive Ted Turner to Levitz—a shocking breach of protocol in an industry where the competition had always been fierce but rarely nasty. *Marville* #1 opened with a text page introduction that read in part, "Marvel's Distinguished Competition (DC Comics) is run by a man named Paul Levitz who fights a never-ending battle to keep his business obscure. This is no small feat as DC owns Batman and Superman."

"Because it was Jemas, everybody thought, oh it's just Bill being Bill," says former Marvel editor Greenberger. "We were more dismissive or more embarrassed than angry by it."

Not the case at DC.

"Jemas was a real terror for DC," says former DC editor Raspler. "He sort of broke the rules, the gentleman's agreement. He crossed lines, which was thrilling for his supporters and scandalous for his targets. We all talked about it."

Even though Jemas's antics rubbed many in DC the wrong way and they were dying to respond, the staff was forbidden from retaliating publicly. No one, they were told, was to speak to the press about the feud. When one DC staffer asked about Jemas's provocations, Levitz just shrugged his shoulders and said, "What are you gonna do?"

Jemas and Quesada's methods may have turned off some in the industry, but much like Simon Cowell hurling nasty put-downs on *American Idol*, readers seemed to eat them up. The new management began pulling Marvel out of the bankruptcy doldrums, helping the comic book business as a whole, which, in recent decades, had been overly dependent on Marvel. One year after Jemas and Quesada came to power, the industry reversed seven straight years of decline to register modest growth. Marvel in 2001 opened up a six-point lead in direct market share over DC after the two were locked in a near dead heat in 2000. By 2002 the lead was eleven points.

"[Jemas and Quesada's pugilistic style] may well have helped them. They were scrappy at a time when a lot of folks might have been willing to write them off," says former DC editor and writer Brian Augustyn. "It certainly rallied fans. Jemas was looking to create kind of the exclusivity of, 'You belong to a rare club.'"

The product undeniably got better under the new leadership. Early in their tenure Jemas and Quesada wrote up a twenty-page publishing plan detailing the changes they hoped to bring to Marvel. It called for less reverence for the status quo and a demand for higher quality.

The duo looked to recruit new creators and to make Marvel's comics more accessible to readers. Jemas felt that Marvel's editors and creators were too beholden to their fanboy sides, producing insular, self-referential storylines that required decades of knowledge to read—"comics about comics" Jemas called them.

He lamented the fact that many of Marvel's core heroes had been allowed to grow up and change. In the days of *Amazing Spider-Man* #1, Peter Parker was a nerdy high school loser who couldn't catch a break. Now he was in his twenties, long out of college, and married to a supermodel, Mary Jane. Jemas joked that soon they'd probably be publishing a story arc about his prostate issues.

Part of the solution was to launch a brand-new line of comics called Ultimate, aimed at unburdening the characters from decades of continuity. The stories would start over at the beginning, feature younger versions of the heroes, and officially take place outside the canon Marvel universe. *Ultimate Spider-Man* #1, released in September 2000, retold the hero's origin with a modern sensibility. *Ultimate X-Men* followed, as well as *The Ultimates*, a contemporary take on the Avengers by writer Mark Millar that served as a blueprint for 2012's *The Avengers* film.

Jemas and Quesada also pushed the editorial department to take more chances and to tell stories that Marvel had been afraid to tell previously. At the time one of the biggest mysteries in the Marvel universe was the origin of Wolverine, the ultra-popular, virtually indestructible member of the X-Men. Only fragments of his backstory had been revealed over the character's twenty-five-year history, in part because no one knew what it was. (An unproduced 1984 X-Men screenplay by Roy Thomas and Gerry Conway said Wolverine had been given his metal skeleton after a car accident.) Editorial was also fearful that telling the story would ruin the character. All it took was a financial shortfall to change all that.

"One time one of our financial guys came into me and Jemas, and he said a couple projects had fallen off the table," former Marvel publishing operations director Greenberger says. "He said, 'We're going to have an $800,000 shortfall this year if we don't do something.' That's when Jemas said, 'Well, I guess it's time to do Wolverine's origin.'"

The six-issue miniseries called *Origin* appeared in 2001 and revealed that Wolverine—aka Logan—had been born James Howlett to a wealthy Canadian family. He was cast out into the wilderness following the murder of his father. The gamble to finally tell the tale paid off. The series was a big hit, finishing near the top of the charts for the year.

The new Marvel regime also opened up its pages to more mature content. In 2001 the company launched Max, an imprint for adults that included *Alias*, writer Brian Michael Bendis's hard-boiled series about a female detective that was turned into the hit 2015 Netflix series *Jessica Jones*. (The series was so spicy that Marvel's Alabama-based printer refused to print it.)

Jemas also made the controversial decision to remove Marvel from the Comics Code Authority—the censoring body that had been policing content since the 1950s. Marvel management resented paying an outside body to monitor its books and considered the Code irrelevant for the twenty-first century and Marvel's increasingly older readers. It was also inconsistent. In April 2001 the governing body had asked Marvel to remove certain words from one of their comics but had allowed them in an issue of *Superman*.

Jemas decided it was time for Marvel to pull out.

The other major publishers—DC, Archie, and Dark Horse—were opposed to Marvel's decision, and a meeting was called at Marvel's office.

Code meetings were held regularly, and often one or two representatives attended from each company. In this case Paul Levitz and executive editor Mike Carlin represented DC, while Michael Silberkleit repped Archie.

As for Marvel's contingent, Jemas had a surprise in store. To tweak DC's nose, he decided to pack the conference room with the various Marvel employees he'd recently poached, despite the fact that none had ever attended before and that the extra bodies had no business being there. Jemas dragged Bob Greenberger, Stuart Moore, and former Vertigo editors Jennifer Lee and Axel Alonso into the room.

"He put us there to basically be the peanut gallery," Greenberger says. "Bill was having the time of his life. He thought it was hysterical."

"It irritated the DC people," Moore says. "It was a strange meeting, a little uncomfortable."

When questioned why Marvel had brought the unnecessary staffers, Jemas contended that the number of people from each company was in direct correlation to sales.

The sides also began arguing over the Code, with DC and Archie advocating for staying in it. Abandoning the Code, they argued, might draw unwanted attention and force the government to step in. Silberkleit at one point produced a thick file containing clippings from the 1950s anticomics crusade and warned it could happen again. Levitz cautioned that senators might be coming for the industry again.

"Quite frankly, Paul," Jemas replied, "I'm more scared of sentinels than senators," referencing the killer robots from the X-Men comics.

Marvel began using its own in-house ratings system, and as has happened so often in this business, DC—at first so violently opposed to Marvel's progressive stance—eventually came around. It likewise abandoned the Code in January 2011, long after everyone had ceased to care.

The antagonism between the companies would only grow, but before it got to the point of no return, Marvel and DC had been able to play nice long enough to finally negotiate the publication of one of the greatest unfinished projects in comics history, the white whale of fandom, *JLA/ Avengers*. The series had been started then ultimately abandoned back in 1983 after the two sides had been unable to agree on a plot and creative direction. Fans never gave up hope, and through the years rumors that it would finally be completed would trickle out, but no firm announcement ever came, even after Marvel and DC began cooperating on a new round of crossovers in the mid-1990s.

Finally, in March 2001, it became official. The announcement was made at an Orlando, Florida, convention that *JLA/Avengers* was back on track and was scheduled to hit shelves the next year. It was to be drawn by its original artist George Perez and written by Kurt Busiek, an *Avengers* scribe and the cocreator of *Marvels*, an acclaimed and influential 1994 miniseries that offered a realistic, ground-level view of the Marvel universe through the eyes of its nonsuperpowered inhabitants.

Through the years DC and Marvel had spoken occasionally about restarting *JLA/Avengers*, but circumstances always conspired to prevent it.

"People think about [the delays] as Marvel and DC are mad at each other, and it's not usually something like that," Busiek says. "What it was about is that these companies are owned by larger corporations and these larger corporations interact."

In one case a potential *JLA/Avengers* deal was tabled after Marvel and Time Warner squabbled over some petty international deal involving, of all things, sticker licensing. One of Marvel's European publishing companies subsequently bought an Italian company that had a license to produce DC stickers, meaning the company never did produce the DC stickers. Bickering between the two parties over money ensued.

"Literally, sticker licensing derailed *JLA/Avengers*," Busiek says. "But then the skies cleared. I think it was Joe Quesada who called DC and said, 'No one is mad at anyone at the moment. Let's do it.'"

Because the series had been so anticipated, the creators involved were determined to do it justice and make it richer than your typical Marvel-DC crossover.

"When we originally sat down to talk about the story, one of the first things we agreed on is that we didn't want to do the standard kind of crossover where you have to have the exact same number of villains per universe, and each side has to have the exact number of panels, and all fights have to end in a draw," Busiek says. "It's about doing a square dance where everything balances rather than doing a story that has drama and surprises. And everybody flat out said yes."

The plot involved two godlike entities who, in a bit of cosmic gameplay, send each team on an interdimensional scavenger hunt, tasking the heroes with collecting twelve powerful artifacts. The heroes travel to each other's universes in search of the booty and, because this is a comic book, eventually come into conflict during the pursuit.

Unlike the earliest Marvel-DC pairings, *JLA/Avengers* came after decades of similar crossovers, and seasoned readers had become familiar with the format and the industry's tropes. That familiarity allowed the creators to have a little fun, adding a layer of sly, meta-commentary about the fundamental differences between the DC and Marvel universes.

"We played off the old sixties reputations of the two universes, where in the Marvel universe, the heroes have to struggle, and once they win the day, people throw things at them," Busiek says. "And over in DC Superman is a citizen of every country in the world, the Flash has a museum. They're practically a pantheon."

When the Avengers arrives in the DC universe for the time, they're dismayed by the city's clean modernity and the way the public idolizes the heroes.

"This is quite some world," Marvel's mutant speedster Quicksilver notes while taking a look around the Flash museum. "Heroes are respected, not hounded."

Meanwhile Superman and the Justice League are disappointed that the Avengers, with all their power, have failed to usher in a utopia.

"I'm not impressed," Superman growls. "Not with their world, not with their achievements."

The creators included other knowing winks for fans. The best line went to Hawkeye, who noted the Justice League's similarity to a certain team of Marvel heroes that had been created as an homage.

"These losers—they're nothing but a bunch of Squadron Supreme wannabes," Hawkeye cracks.

Perez, who'd been waiting nearly twenty years to finally tackle the project, went nuts. When Busiek asked him which of the dozens of characters who'd been members of the Avengers and Justice League over the years he'd like to draw, Perez replied, "All of them." He didn't disappoint. He peppered the series with detailed pages filled with so many figures that they were downright Where's Waldo–esque in their awe-inspiring clutter. His cover to issue #3 contained a whopping 208 heroes. It was such a big job that it literally gave the artist tendinitis and delayed the release of #4 by a few weeks.

The series ended on a hopeful note, with the DC and Marvel characters acknowledging the regard they have for one another before being returned to their respective universes. "Perhaps we should do this again someday," the final page reads.

But it was not to be. Unbeknownst to readers and the staffs at the time, *JLA/Avengers*, released in September 2003, was to be the final Marvel-DC crossover. Not that there wasn't a push for more.

After the companies had managed to play nice on *JLA/Avengers*, the prospect of future cooperation seemed hopeful. Why couldn't the companies work out a deal where they partnered to release a slate of team-ups, as they'd done back in the late 1970s?

In the spring of 2001, shortly after *JLA/Avengers* had been announced, Marvel's Greenberger brokered a lunch between the two sides. DC's executive editor Mike Carlin and sales and marketing chief Bob Wayne sat down with Marvel's editor-in-chief Joe Quesada, president Bill Jemas, and Greenberger in an attempt to kickstart the crossovers. It did not go well.

"I think they wanted to take each others' temperature to see if they really could work together, and one lunch later they knew they couldn't," Greenberger says. "It was like two rival countries that were never going to see eye to eye. They just didn't like each other. Bill was mocking everything about DC, and Bob Wayne was bristling. It was just not a comfortable lunch."

Even with Greenberger proposing a springboard for a crossover that had villain Lex Luthor, who at the time had been elected president in the DC universe, declaring war on Latveria, the stronghold of Marvel's Doctor Doom, nothing came of the meeting. The two sides parted ways grumpy and without agreeing to any future team-ups. The worst acrimony was, unfortunately, yet to come.

Of Marvel's two public faces, Quesada had generally been more well behaved than Jemas, preferring to play good cop to the boss's bad. Like Jemas, he had a cocky, showman quality to him and became a regular media presence, but his musings rarely rose to the inflammatory, DEFCON-1 level that Jemas's did.

That all changed in April 2002.

The interview Quesada gave to the *New York Observer* was supposed to be little more than a puff piece promoting Marvel's plans in conjunction with the upcoming *Spider-Man* movie. Instead it became arguably the most damaging single provocation in the rivalry's history. In the interview Quesada let rip with a series of digs at DC that would drive a nearly irreparable wedge between the companies and chill relations—perhaps for all time.

"What the fuck is DC anyway?" Quesada railed in the *Observer* piece. "They'd be better off calling it AOL Comics. At least people know what AOL is. I mean, they have Batman and Superman, and they don't know what to do with them. That's like being a porn star with the biggest dick and you can't get it up. What the fuck?"

As expected, DC and Paul Levitz declined to comment in print, but privately the feeling inside the company was that these comments represented a new low, a breaking point in the increasingly hostile relationship between the two rivals.

"To be compared to a porn star to begin with would drive Levitz mad, and then to be compared to one who can't get it up and is wasting all these great characters, it's like the long, dark night of the soul," former DC editor Raspler says. "He was just tormented by this horrible shit. He was wound pretty tight."

"The relationship between the companies has not been warm ever since," says then-Marvel-editor Stuart Moore.

Relations got so frosty at the time that a rumor circulated, claiming DC had killed off Azrael, the Batman replacement cocreated years earlier by Joe Quesada, in an attempt to punish the Marvel editor-in-chief and to avoid paying him royalties for the character. Great story, but not true. Azrael's solo series was canned and the title character snuffed in 2003 due simply to low sales.

Adding more juice to the rivalry was the 2002 hiring of Dan DiDio as DC's vice president of editorial. DiDio was a native New Yorker with a bald head, a graying goatee and a brash, fuhgeddaboutit attitude that was closer to Marvel's traditional persona than DC's, leading one online commenter to label him "Bill Jemas Lite." DiDio's addition gave DC an aggressive, passionate public voice who, unlike Paul Levitz, was less likely to take the high road. (The wall outside DiDio's office bore a dent from his fist when he once got upset.)

"Jemas and DiDio are much more inclined to get up in your face and say mean things," says former Marvel staffer Gregg Schigiel. "Post-*JLA/ Avengers*, things went poof. The rivalry became very antagonistic. It almost became like dueling fraternities."

And like his Marvel counterpart, DiDio was an outsider to the industry. He'd previously spent his career working in TV, including soap operas and animation. And as an outsider, he, like Jemas, was less likely to bow to the industry's unspoken customs or to do things a certain way simply because that's the way they'd always been done.

DiDio set out to put his stamp on DC and to fix what he thought was wrong with it. The solution, as usual, meant moving it closer to Marvel, attempting to make DC's fantastical universe and square characters more realistic, gritty, and relatable. It was the same problem DC had been grappling with since the 1960s.

"Our characters were created in the 1940's and 50's and 60's," DiDio said in 2005. "There's a lot of elements where we've had a disconnect with the reader base of today."

One of DiDio's first big projects was *Identity Crisis*, a 2004 miniseries written by novelist Brad Meltzer that took grim and gritty to new heights and soon become one of the more controversial titles DC has ever published. The story found members of the Justice League investigating the brutal murder of the Elongated Man's wife, Sue Dibny. That investigation soon uncovered dark secrets from the past, including that a villain had once raped Dibny aboard the JLA's orbiting satellite headquarters. The heroes ended up giving the perpetrator a psychic lobotomy, and when Batman tried to interfere, they wiped his mind too.

"*Identity Crisis* was this flashback to the Justice League's satellite days [during the 1970s], this magical time, but it was really dark and sinister," says former DC editor Frank Pittarese. "DC kept overcompensating. It wasn't like they were Marvelizing DC. They Marvelized it then added this layer of Quentin Tarantino over it. This gore factor started to creep in, this sexuality. That's after Dan stepped in."

In 2005 a villain named Maxwell Lord was shown graphically shooting wacky hero Blue Beetle through the head. Wonder Woman later murdered the killer by snapping his neck. Hey, kids! Comics!

DiDio and Jemas would not have long to match wits against each other, however, when Jemas's contract was not renewed.

"Jemas eventually got cast out," says former Marvel publisher Shirrel Rhoades. "Some have likened it to God casting Satan out of heaven."

During his tenure Jemas had increasingly run afoul of retailers, instituting policies that the store owners thought were damaging their business. He ordered that the stories in the monthly comic be written at a length and pace to ultimately be collected in trade paperbacks, and in

2001 Marvel started printing to order, meaning that once an issue had sold out, a retailer would be unable to order more.

"Fuck that guy in the neck, man," Comix Experience owner Brian Hibbs says. "Jemas was the first executive at any publishing company that I've ever encountered who seriously did not give a fuck about what was going on with the market or whether the market was healthy or what he was doing was sustainable or logical. It's someone coming in throwing bombs and stirring up shit and not really caring about the long-term ramifications of what his actions are."

The Marvel executive also began meddling more in editorial, leading some creators to gripe about being micromanaged. Mark Waid, a fan-favorite writer, was fired in the midst of a well-received run on the *Fantastic Four* after he balked at Jemas's orders to suddenly transplant Marvel's first family to the suburbs and turn the magazine into a wacky dramedy.

By October 2003 Jemas had alienated many within Marvel and was on his way out. The move delighted those at DC, who had been praying for Jemas's departure nearly from the day he got there. His exit, however, was not enough to completely reset relations between the companies. Quesada was still there, and as long as he remained, relations would remain chilly.

DC's animosity was laid bare at an August 2004 convention in Chicago. There superstar Marvel writer Brian Michael Bendis was hosting a panel about his upcoming work when he mentioned his dream project, a potential team-up between Batman and Daredevil. Bendis asked the audience's help in convincing DC to change its mind regarding intercompany crossovers.

"We went to Marvel, and Marvel said yes," Bendis told the crowd. "Then we went to Paul Levitz. Paul Levitz said no."

Suddenly a voice called out from the audience.

"Actually, that's not entirely correct, Brian," a man said, emerging from the back of the room.

The man turned out to be Bob Wayne, DC's head of marketing. He and Bendis began arguing, to the shock—and delight—of the assembled fans.

"I asked personally [Paul] to reconsider," Bendis told Wayne. "The reason he gave me for the no was a personal reason, that his relationship with Joe Quesada wasn't one that he liked. And I said that I thought that it shouldn't matter, that it was not a good reason."

"We expressed our interest in doing Batman and Daredevil," Wayne shot back, "and we said that we would be able to do it as soon as Joe Quesada is not at Marvel Comics. It's a very simple request."

"We're down to one person we want to see gone from Marvel—there used to be two," said Wayne, referencing the recently departed Jemas. "If there's anything you can do to speed Joe out the door, we'll be happy to get this on the schedule."

Bendis reiterated that the fans and retailers were calling for the book and that there was no good reason not to do it. "You guys are just mad that Joe kicks your ass," he said.

"The problem is the type of behavior that Joe exhibited in interviews like the one that ran in the *New York Observer* when he was completely over the line from what was appropriate behavior," Wayne said shortly before stepping aside, ending the public argument. Bendis was left to jokingly lament that he'd never work for DC now.

With the competition heating up between the two companies, so did the competition for talent. Marvel, emboldened by its emergence from bankruptcy, set about poaching several of DC's top employees, including Vertigo editor Axel Alonso in 2000 (he became Marvel's editor-in-chief in 2011) and editor Stuart Moore, among others.

"It was a bold move," says former DC editor Tom Palmer Jr. "It was a little frustrating because it seemed nothing was done about that. There was no, 'Oh, we'll grab some of those guys from Marvel.' They were kind of like, 'Oh, okay, they're gone.' We kind of moved on."

The race to sign top talent to exclusive contracts heated up as well. The contracts locked down a freelance writer or artist for a particular period of time, keeping them out of the hands of the competition. In exchange the creator often got medical coverage and other perks as well as a signing bonus.

Exclusive contracts had been around since the industry's early days, but they became more common as the years went by.

One of the first went to Irv Novick in the mid-1960s. Novick had been drawing DC war books edited by his friend Bob Kanigher, but he had left to take a job in advertising.

"Kanigher was really upset to lose Novick on his books," historian Mark Evanier says.

DC was able to lure the artist back to comics by crafting a contract that paid him regularly and guaranteed him a certain amount of work.

Marvel began offering more attractive deals to creators in the 1980s. Select freelancers were given medical benefits and vacation, and their travel expenses to conventions were covered. Some artists got a continuity bonus, earning an extra $500 if they completed a certain number of issues in a row.

The dollar figures ramped up in the early 1990s, when the industry exploded and began to increasingly recognize that talent, as opposed to characters, drove sales. With just two major companies in the field, the talent could play them off one another to land the best deal.

"There was such competition for talent, especially after the defection of the Image guys, it became like a war of escalation between Marvel and DC," former Marvel editor Bob Budiansky says.

"Around 1990 we really we started to bang against each other at both companies in trying to lock up talent with exclusive contracts," says former DC editor Brian Augustyn. "Both companies were in a feeding frenzy for talent."

The incentives for top creators had always been juicy. John Byrne, the architect of the mid eighties Superman reboot, was in part lured from Marvel with the promise that DC's sister company, Warner Books, would publish his prose horror novel. And rumor has it that one creator had a single request to seal his defection in the 1970s: an Asian hooker.

The 1990s took the incentivizing to new heights. Talent was being wined and dined and offered exorbitant sums. Instead of paying by the page, as was the tradition, a company might guarantee an artist a flat sum—say, $5,000—per issue. And the superstars made more—much more.

"I was paying [X-Men artists] Andy and Adam Kubert each of them about a million dollars a year under a superstar contract," says former Marvel publisher Shirrel Rhoades. "The artists that were big names, the Jim Lees and Kuberts, they demanded big money and got it."

The problem DC had was that it simply couldn't match its rival's money. Marvel titles sold far more copies than DC, making it a more attractive destination to freelancers, who could make bank on the royalties.

"We were casting for *The Flash* after Greg LaRocque left [in 1993], and Steve Skroce had come in and he had shown his portfolio around. We gave him the gig," recalls former DC editor Ruben Diaz. "Then he left the office, and unfortunately he stopped at Marvel and showed his stuff. We got a call a couple hours later that they offered him the *Cable* series, to which he then declined *The Flash* offer. He might have done better work on *The Flash*, but he was undeniably going to make more money on *Cable*."

The battle for talent led the companies to institute a certain amount of secrecy. In the days before email was commonplace, phone calls were often how talent was lured. Phone numbers became like currency.

"I wanted to hire [DC artist] Frank Quitely for a [1999] variant cover of *Avengers Forever*, and I could not find this guy's phone number anywhere," says former Marvel editor Gregg Schigiel. "Then [editor] Marie Javins, who had gone back and forth between the two companies, had the DC Comics phone list, the talent list. Anyone who'd come from DC had it. That was a resource that we didn't have at Marvel. DC was always the more professional organization. They had a phone list. Marvel was like, 'Whatever. Here's a Rolodex card. Scribble your number down.' So Marie was the one who knew Frank Quitely was not his real name. His name is Vincent Deighan, and I was able to call him and get him to do the cover."

"DC was very tight-lipped about sharing contact info," says artist Joe St. Pierre. "I did a Batman job with an inker I liked named Ray McCarthy. I asked the Batman office, 'Hey, could I get Ray's number, because I want to tell him what an awesome job he did?' They were like, 'Uh, we'll tell him for you.' I was working at Marvel at the time, so it wouldn't have been past me to say, 'Hey, let's get Ray for the next miniseries.' DC was probably being protective."

Marvel's mid-1990s troubles cooled the talent wars somewhat, but by the early 2000s the contest grew hot again. Marvel was healthier financially, and on the other side DC's Dan DiDio was determined to become more aggressive and proactive.

In 2003 DC stole away Grant Morrison, the Scotsman who was then writing Marvel's *New X-Men*. They also locked up writer Jeph Loeb and artist Tim Sale, the team behind an acclaimed 1996 Batman miniseries, *The Long Halloween*.

Marvel brought Chris Claremont back into the fold in 2003. The writer had been removed from his X-Men book shortly after Quesada became editor-in-chief.

"One of Ike [Perlmutter's] guys noticed that I was actively looking for work at DC, and the attitude was, the creator of Marvel's biggest franchise is pitching himself to our competitor?" Claremont says. "And the next thing I knew, I was negotiating a contract at Marvel."

Claremont reportedly remains under contract to this day and is forbidden from working for any company besides Marvel, despite the fact that he rarely produces new work for the publisher.

One person DC was able to poach during the decade was the biggest Marvel name of them all: Stan Lee. It came as quite a shock to readers and the industry when it was announced that the man who had been synonymous with Marvel for some sixty years was finally crossing over to write a special project called *Just Imagine . . .* to be released in late 2001. The series would be composed of thirteen stand-alone issues, allowing Lee to rework the origins of DC's top heroes, including Batman, Superman, Wonder Woman, and Green Lantern.

The idea had come from Michael Uslan, the producer of the 1989 *Batman* film and a former DC writer. While at the film's June 1989 premiere Lee and Batman cocreator Bob Kane had been good-naturedly ribbing each other about their various successes, with Lee insisting Batman would have been better if he'd had a hand in it and Kane claiming Spider-Man would have been more successful had he drawn it. The argument got Uslan thinking: What *would* Batman have been like if Lee had created him?

The idea remained on the back burner for several years until Marvel's bankruptcy provided an opening.

"The reason Stan was able to go over to DC was because [Marvel boss Ike] Perlmutter decided to save money," former Marvel publisher Shirrel Rhoades says. "When I was there I was paying Stan a million dollars a year, and I had it on good authority that Perelman's people were paying him a separate million dollars a year that wasn't on our books. Perlmutter canceled the contract to save money."

The cancelation left Stan Lee, after some sixty years at Marvel, free to work for other companies. Uslan phoned Lee to float the idea.

"It would be great to get your take on how you would have done these characters if you were creating them," Uslan told Lee.

"Hell, of course it would be interesting to do, but I have as much chance of doing those characters as a snowball in hell," Lee replied.

Uslan contacted DC, and a couple of weeks later, the deal had been arranged. Lee was coming to DC. The man who cocreated the Marvel universe was going to be writing for the Distinguished Competition. To make up for the money Lee lost when his Marvel contract was canceled, DC agreed to pay him a million bucks for the series.

It was a big get for DC and made for some sensational headlines. But it's up for debate how much the then-seventy-eight-year-old Lee actually contributed beyond his name.

"Was he that involved with them?" asks artist Jerry Ordway who drew *Just Imagine Stan Lee's JLA*. "Ehhh."

"We had a story conference with me, Stan Lee, editor Mike Carlin, and Michael Uslan," Ordway says. "We spent two hours on the phone talking over what was going to happen, and then the phone call is ending and Stan says, 'You got enough there to work with? You don't need me to write anything do you?'"

Carlin gave Ordway notes from the phone call, and he laid out and drew the story. Lee later dialogued it.

The *Just Imagine* . . . series didn't impress critics and sold modestly, with each issue moving around thirty to forty thousand in the direct market. Some inside DC were also underwhelmed.

"It was a stunt, frankly," says former DC editor Joan Hilty. "There was nothing organic about Stan Lee imagining Aquaman. We thought it was strange around the office. It was a fun, brief idea, but I don't know exactly what the motive was. I think you could argue that it did have the effect of subconsciously saying to the editors, 'Your ideas aren't good enough. We need Stan Lee.'"

Marvel was also displeased to see its public face working for the competition, and the company quickly drafted a new contract to recapture Lee. Marvel had a more pressing reason to regain its editor emeritus, beyond just PR.

"Stan's contract implied that his employment gave Marvel rights to the characters he created, so by canceling the contract, there was a legal argument that the characters reverted to Stan," Rhoades says. "They eventually hired him back. I think they gave him $500,000 a year and required only 10 percent of his time."

The *Just Imagine* line quickly faded from memory, ending up little more than an interesting footnote in comic book history, and it appears that DC would rather it be forgotten as well. Many of the characters Lee created for the series were shown being slaughtered by murderous cyborgs in DC's 2015 event called *Convergence*. Which seems about right, considering how relations had gone between the two companies in the twenty-first century.

Superhero Movies and TV Shows Take Over the World

> "It's all there in the source material. Our success means that people can stay true to the source material. I think history has shown that the closer you stay to the spirit of the comics, the better. Comics fans are passionate for a reason: because the material is pretty darn good."
>
> —Kevin Feige, president of Marvel Studios

"Fuck Marvel!"

The words echoed across New York's Beacon Theatre, eliciting gasps and cheers from the thousands assembled for the August 2016 premiere of *Suicide Squad*.

Director David Ayer had taken the stage moments earlier to introduce the highly anticipated Warner Bros. Batman spinoff and had begun by saying the experience of making *Suicide Squad* had been "the best of his career." He was moving on to the requisite Hollywood platitudes—thanking production president Greg Silverman—when it happened. An overzealous member of the audience, perhaps jacked up from being moments away from seeing Margot Robbie in tight shorts, screamed out, "Fuck Marvel!"

On stage Ayer paused, then gripped the microphone and hollered back, "Fuck Marvel!" to cheers and bemused laughter.

At the time Ayers's outburst appeared ill advised. When the negative reviews for his movie started flooding in (aggregator Rotten Tomatoes awarded it an anemic 26 percent), it looked downright stupid. But foolish or not, Ayers's declaration gave public voice to one of the most high-profile—and lucrative—battles in Hollywood. Superheroes, in case you haven't noticed, have taken over pop culture, and with their ascension the long-simmering rivalry between Marvel and DC has been taken to another level.

Just like in print, this new billion-dollar battle plays out with each company bringing to the table various institutional strengths and weaknesses as well as oppositional philosophies.

Marvel does things one way, DC does things another, and viewers are left to vote with their dollars, euros, and (increasingly) their yuan as to which vision, characters, and universe they prefer. This is where the battle is playing out most fiercely nowadays—on the movie and TV screens around the globe. And the shift in arenas came not a moment too soon.

Monthly comic books are becoming an increasingly endangered product, catering to a smaller and smaller group of hardcore hobbyists. For superheroes to survive, they were going to need to find another outlet. Writer Grant Morrison theorized that paper comics were simply a step in a long journey for the concept of superheroes, a "first-stage rocket" that had to be jettisoned to reach greater heights.

"The definition of a *meme* is an idea that wants to replicate," Morrison told *Rolling Stone.* "And [superheroes have] found a better medium through which to replicate."

The answer was movies.

Superhero movies have definitely brought these characters to another stage. They're now the hottest thing going, with a popularity that shows few signs of diminishing. The genre raked in some $1.9 billion in 2016 alone and accounted for nearly 17 percent of movie market share (compared to just .3 percent twenty years earlier). There are now so many superhero movies that characters who can barely sustain their own print comic book are being tapped to launch potential film franchises. As recently as 2005 a big-budget Aquaman movie was considered so absurd that the makers of HBO's behind-the-scenes Hollywood comedy

Entourage turned it into a running joke for the whole season. Now it's going to be a reality.

This newfound domination by costumed characters is a truly shocking turn of events. Growing up as a comic book fan in the 1980s and 1990s meant existing in a state of simultaneous optimism and frustration, as big-time projects were announced, before inevitably fading into oblivion without any explanation. Fanzines, including *Comics Scene*, ran regular columns devoted to short updates on the scads of comic book adaptations in development. A 1988 edition lists in the works a tantalizing array of never-consummated deals, such as a Sgt. Rock movie starring Arnold Schwarzenegger, a Thor sitcom, and a Silver Surfer live-action film.

These projects all seem plausible now, but back then the idea of high-profile projects based on comic books was almost inconceivable.

Even less so for Marvel properties.

"I smell a lot of Marvel bitches up in here!"

**—Dwayne "The Rock" Johnson at the 2016 MTV Movie
Awards**

"We were trying to pick a DC vs Marvel fight. But Marvel's brilliant successes kicks our ass."

—Dwayne "The Rock" Johnson later on Twitter

When it came to film and television the company had suffered so many failures and misfires that it was not considered a particularly premium brand. Its ignominious track record had left Marvel pulling up the rear behind DC—in spite of Stan Lee's best efforts. He'd left New York for California in 1980 and devoted himself almost exclusively to kindling Hollywood's interest in film and TV projects. But he had little success. Marvel was such a failure when it came to conquering other media that Batman cocreator Bob Kane took to teasing that "Batman was a big deal on television and in movies, and we at Marvel had done nothing," Lee once recalled.

Until the late 1990s Kane was dead right. Marvel's Hollywood dreams had remained largely unrealized. Science-fiction ace Harlan Ellison was working on a Black Widow TV series in the early 1980s. A Doctor Strange movie was in development in 1986, but after Eddie Murphy's *The Golden Child* fizzled, the studio canceled it.

"The studio said, 'Well, that had magic in it and it bombed, so magic must not sell,'" says Carl Potts, then the editor of *Doctor Strange*.

Of the projects that did make it to the screen, Marvel probably wished they hadn't.

Howard the Duck, released in 1986, was Marvel's first modern-day big-screen adaptation, and the title earned just $16 million domestically against a $36 million budget. It was such a spectacular loser that it supposedly led to a fistfight between two Universal executives over who was to blame.

The Punisher cast Swedish lunkhead Dolph Lundgren as the gun-toting vigilante for a 1989 dud that went straight to video.

Also skipping theaters was 1992's *Captain America*. The bargain-basement thriller—sorry, "thriller"—from director Albert Pyun got hustled into production following the success of *Batman*, but he didn't have the budget (a reported $7.5 million) or script to do the story justice.

Fantastic Four was the perhaps the biggest black eye of all. A German company had optioned the property in the mid-1980s, and it was put into production more or less because the option was set to expire in 1992, dashing Marvel's hope of reacquiring the potentially valuable property in the wake of *Batman*'s success.

In the contract Marvel had failed to specify a minimum budget, so executive producer Bernd Eichinger went ahead with a rock-bottom level of reportedly just $1 million. The cast, which included Jay Underwood and Rebecca Staab, was paid a measly $3,500 a week, and the on-set catering consisted of little more than bologna sandwiches. The special effects budget was just as skimpy. Mr. Fantastic's stretching was accomplished in one shot by attaching an empty glove to a pole and pulling.

The finished product was so embarrassing that Marvel bought the movie back so it would never be released. Bootleg copies have trickled out on VHS and DVD.

From its early days Marvel flirted with producing its own material. The company had launched a production studio in 1980 (it later became an animation entity) and founded a subsidiary called Marvel Films in

1993. However, its M.O., more often than not, was to license properties to others, leading to less control over the finished product—as well as a complicated tangle of rights.

"Marvel had licensed that stuff so much in the seventies and eighties that stuff was still hanging out there in pieces and parts all over the place," says former Marvel president Terry Stewart. "We couldn't get anything done because we couldn't get back our rights. At the same time, we felt the characters couldn't be done right with the technology available. We worried we'd have to spend a gazillion dollars for something that might fail and might not live up to standards. We didn't want to put the characters in that position. That's why we did the cartoons."

The studio produced popular X-Men and Spider-Man animated series in the 1990s. But live-action success eluded them.

Beyond the special effects problem, one of the issues both Marvel and DC faced was that comic book movies for a long time weren't particularly respected in Hollywood. The idea of comics as kids' stuff was deeply entrenched.

"Studios were behind the curve in terms of the growing popularity of comics, and not just their growing popularity, but also the age of the comic-book reader," DC's former president Jenette Kahn said in 2012. "They found it impossible to believe that the average age of our reader was 28 years old. And if I told them it was 28, they would say, 'Oh, well, he's clearly a dope.'"

That outdated perception began to change when younger executives and producers began moving into positions of power in Hollywood. These were people who'd read *The Dark Knight Returns* and *Watchmen* growing up and were hip to how cool and sophisticated comic books could be. They respected the medium and were eager to mine it for all its worth. Many directors were also comic fans, including Steven Spielberg, who used to hang around the DC offices when he was twelve.

No one had to explain to these people that comic books didn't necessarily equal trash.

Comic books also garnered more respect when they consistently began to generate the thing Hollywood respected most: money.

Batman had been a global sensation, but like *Superman* before it, its increasingly terrible sequels offered diminishing returns. By the time the embarrassing *Batman & Robin* hit screens in 1997, the franchise deserved to be tossed in the bottom of the Batcave, reinforcing the alarming notion that even the most iconic comic book properties had a limited lifespan on film. Comic book movies couldn't possibly become a Hollywood mainstay, could they?

The comic book adaptation that kicked off the modern-day obsession is a movie that many don't even realize is from a comic book. *Men in Black*, the 1997 Will Smith–Tommy Lee Jones blockbuster, was adapted from an obscure black-and-white comic published in 1990 by indie press Aircel. Aircel was later acquired by Malibu, which was then bought by Marvel in 1994.

"Don't ever forget that the movie that changed everything was a black-and-white pick-up," artist Steve Bissette says. "That changed the paradigm away from all Marvel being able to get was a Hulk TV series and an awful Dr. Strange TV movie. Everything they'd been aching to do with movies for decades was suddenly possible, and it was possible because of something they had accidentally acquired."

Malibu founder Scott Rosenberg began trying to sell *Men in Black* in the early 1990s. He encountered resistance.

"I touted it as a comic book, but the studios were thinking that there was a correlation between the success of a comic in print and box office," says Rosenberg, now the head of Platinum Studios. "I was explaining that was not the case. I was turned down by every studio two to three times at least."

The property eventually landed at Sony, and the movie's success opened many people's eyes to the rich opportunity comic books presented. Hollywood began delivering more properties based on funnybooks.

New Line Cinema's *Blade* followed the next year. The vampire-hunter character played by Wesley Snipes was plucked from a relatively obscure Marvel magazine called *Tomb of Dracula*, and like *Men in Black* the year before, Blade did not seem like a typical superhero film. The main character didn't sport a colorful costume, and many who bought tickets were probably ignorant of the Marvel connection.

The real game changer would come in 2000.

Marvel and its various partners had been trying to adapt its most successful print property, the X-Men, into film for nearly two decades. Comic writer Chris Claremont had written an outline in 1982, and Gerry Conway and Roy Thomas had taken a crack at a screenplay in 1984 for Orion

Pictures. Like so many proposed adaptations before them, they simply sat in a drawer.

"The closest we came was the meeting with James Cameron [in the late 1980s]," Claremont says. "Stan [Lee] and I went out to meet with him. We'd been through *Superman* and Tim Burton's *Batman*. This was Marvel's way to get on the bandwagon and do it in a uniquely Marvel style, which was to find a visual storyteller who was the cinematic equivalent of [comic artists] Dave Cockrum, John Byrne, and Paul Smith on the *X-Men*."

During the meeting Lee and Cameron, a big comic book fan, got sidetracked talking about another Marvel property—Spider-Man—and it quickly became clear that X-Men wasn't Cameron's priority anymore.

Marvel explored deals with other partners, including Columbia, before ultimately optioning the rights to 20th Century Fox in 1993.

"From Marvel's perspective, the only films they'd done were *The Punisher* and *Blade*," Chris Claremont says. "They weren't awful, they weren't great. They were just B-List. That was the expectation Fox had for *X-Men*. But from Marvel's perspective, it was, 'Wow, 20th Century Fox, a real studio, wants to make a movie! Cool!'"

The conventional wisdom since has been that Marvel made a terrible deal for the property—a mistake that was only magnified over the years as the *X-Men* under Fox went on to unimaginable financial success. But the price—$1.5 million and 5 percent of the gross receipts per movie, according to a copy of the deal dated July 1993—was reasonable. At the time comic book properties were commanding around $100,000 to $200,000.

The problem for Marvel came with the contract's language. Rights contracts are usually written with ridiculous specificity to try to define exactly what the buyer is getting. The language in this particular contract, according to sources, was too broad and ended up transferring a larger-than-expected swath of Marvel's intellectual property to Fox. In short, instead of a limited number of X-Men, the movie studio ended up landing the rights to all things mutant in the Marvel universe in perpetuity. That windfall includes not just the X-Men we all recognize, such as Professor X and Wolverine, but also dozens of other characters from Marvel's numerous X titles.

A character such as the time-traveling Cable—not technically an X-Men but related to the universe—wasn't part of that original deal, but the contract basically granted Fox rights if Cable was mentioned in another film. (He's set to appear in Fox's *Deadpool 2*.)

"They were good deals at the time, in that they got us into the movie business. We didn't have the money or the expertise to do it," says Marvel's former publisher Shirrel Rhoades. "Now, they're bad deals because Marvel is doing so well with *The Avengers* and the other stuff. The people running Marvel wish those deals had never been made, but back then it got our foot in the door."

X-Men was hardly a sure thing in the 1990s. The comic book sold millions of copies a year, but it was far from a household name. When, in 1996, director Bryan Singer was hired to direct it, trade bible *Variety* botched the movie's title in a headline, running a banner that read, "Singer to Direct Fox's 'Men.'"

Singer had the page framed and hung it on his office wall—a humorous reminder of a time when comic book movies got no respect.

The script went through several permutations, and originally the studio was thinking of *X-Men* as just another superhero story. Luckily Fox sought counsel with Marvel over its various drafts. Claremont, then Marvel's editorial director, offered one particularly important critique.

The question was, What made the X-Men different? The thing that separated them from other superheroes was that they were outsiders, shunned by society for being different. That was the crux of what made them interesting, and that aspect was made central in the final script. The movie wasn't about costumed do-gooders saving the world. Instead, the X-Men and the persecution they suffered for being mutants was an allegory for the mistreatment of every marginalized group in society. If you were gay, a minority—even a comic book reader who'd been made fun of—you saw yourself in the X-Men.

The director wisely made the decision to dispense with any hint of camp and treat the movie as deadly serious. One of the concessions to this dark worldview was to dispense with the group's colorful spandex costumes and instead outfit the team in black leather tactical get-ups. The move disappointed some diehards.

"I remember when the first photos of the X-Men suits came into the office," says Ruben Diaz, a former Marvel editor. "We all looked at them and said, 'These aren't the X-Men's suits.' It was identifiable as the X-Men, but they weren't being true to canon with the costuming."

Heretical or not, in the end *X-Men* cleaned up. The cast (which included a ripped Hugh Jackman as Wolverine and Patrick Stewart as Professor X) and the story really connected with audiences around the world. The movie rang up a massive $54 million opening weekend that shocked the industry, including Fox Studio, which had been estimating something closer to $35 million. *Variety* characterized the numbers for an adaptation of a lesser-known property with no marquee stars as "x-plosive" and "stupefying."

Fox immediately started planning sequels, and the movie's runaway success also helped jumpstart other films based on Marvel characters, including *Daredevil* at Fox and a long-gestating *Hulk* movie at Universal.

But it was to be a movie based on another Marvel character that would become the genre's biggest hit to date: 2002's *Spider-Man*. The fact that the movie ever saw the light of day remains a minor miracle. The movie had been caught in a tangled web of legal red tape for years and was subject to so many rumors, changes of ownership, and stops and starts that it grew to almost mythological proportions.

Spidey was optioned in 1985 for a reported $225,000 by the Cannon Group, a B-movie company run by two Israeli cousins. Cannon was best known for churning out forgettable action movies in the 1980s, including *American Ninja* and Sylvester Stallone's *Cobra*. The company tried for several years to get the movie up and running, but it lacked a clear understanding of the character. Early treatments hewed closer to schlocky monster movies than the story of adolescent angst that Spider-Man required. A parade of script rewrites and attached directors followed.

"The Spider-Man movie has been the longest on-going disaster you have ever heard of," Stan Lee said at a 1989 sales conference. "Cannon has had 10 scripts done already, each one worse than the one before. . . . Every year you'll read in the trades, 'Coming soon Spider-Man, don't miss it.' Miss it, please, until we get a good script."

Cannon soon went into bankruptcy and another studio acquired Spider-Man setting off years of lawsuits among the players who had bought into the original production. Untangling the mess dragged on for years. Ultimately the delay might have been a good thing.

"I worked on every Spider-Man movie except the ones that got made," says former Marvel editor-in-chief Tom DeFalco. "I think people bought the rights because they thought there might be something there, but then the technology wasn't there yet for the special effects. So ultimately they ended up watering it down to the point where it wouldn't have been the big-scale film we think of. One of the Spider-Man treatments I worked on, we could have done for $2 or $3 million dollars. It would have essentially been a crime movie. Besides the web-swinging, it was not a big special effects film. It was more the human drama."

The rights were finally sorted in the late 1990s, and Spider-Man ended up at Columbia. The movie was fast-tracked for production with Sam Raimi at the helm and Tobey Maguire as the hero. Raimi not only conquered the technological challenges—he convincingly showed Spider-Man swinging through the canyons of New York—but also presented a story that captured the lovable awkwardness of Peter Parker and his quixotic pursuit of girl-next-door Mary Jane (Kirsten Dunst).

Spider-Man opened in May 2002 and smashed box office records, raking in an unbelievable $115 million domestically. The number obliterated the all-time box office record by 26 percent.

"Invent a new word, because it's better than great," an executive from research firm ACNielsen gushed in 2002. "It's so big, the mind has trouble comprehending how great a record they've set."

Marvel's success was in contrast to DC, which arguably hadn't had a universally acclaimed hit since 1989's *Batman*. Instead, the company gave audiences 1997's *Steel*, starring basketball lug nut Shaquille O'Neal in a suit of armor.

DC still strongly believed in its characters' abilities to translate into other media. As early as the 1980s DC's president Jenette Kahn began spending less of her time on the day-to-day operations of comic book publishing and more out in Los Angeles trying to broker television and film deals.

"I remember editorial meetings where Jenette had returned from LA and told us that Warner Bros considered DC 'a garden of characters.' We were excited by that," says former editor Michael Eury. "By that point it was clear that these characters were ripe for multimedia exploitation."

The time was so ripe that after DC's parent company, Warner Communications, announced a merger with media giant Time Inc. in 1989, DC was placed under the control of Warner Bros.' movie division, not its publishing.

Several hits and misses followed in the decade. (The Wachowskis, the siblings behind *The Matrix*, worked on a treatment for Plastic Man in the mid-1990s, but it went nowhere.) It quickly became clear that DC was going to have to get more aggressive if it hoped to counter Marvel's success with *X-Men* and *Spider-Man*.

"It wasn't until Marvel started making superhero movies that Warner Bros, our chief engine for turning DC properties into movies, began to think, 'Wait, maybe there is a treasure trove at DC, and maybe it's not just Superman and Batman,'" Kahn said in 2012.

Warner Bros. worried that without successful movies featuring its characters, it was set to lose a whole generation of fans—fans who would be indoctrinated into Marvel's world instead.

"We're not going to let that happen," Warner Bros. exec Kevin Tsujihara said in 2003, insisting that the studio was set to begin hiring writers to exploit DC properties.

While Marvel remained a relatively nimble company, with Perlmutter and Arad in charge, DC remained part of a plodding corporate behemoth, and the bureaucracy made it difficult to get movies made.

What followed Warner Bros.' newfound early-aughts commitment to DC characters was—with one exception—a string of misguided films that didn't make much of a dent in the box office. In 2004 Halle Berry played a woman who gains superpowers after being resurrected by a cat. Critics roundly trashed *Catwoman*, and the only positive to come out of it was the opportunity for entertaining cat-pun takedowns in newspaper headlines. "Far from Purrr-fect," read one. "Should Be Fixed," read another. *Constantine*, a Vertigo comic about a chain-smoking British mage, opened with a woefully miscast Keanu Reeves in 2005. *V for Vendetta*, released in 2006, didn't make a particularly strong case for watching the movie versus reading the original Alan Moore and David Lloyd series.

Warner's one true home run came with its latest interpretation of Batman. After the critical drubbing the previous two films took, 1995's *Batman Forever* and 1997's *Batman & Robin*, the studio was determined to move in a new direction. No more Batnipples, no more awful Arnold Schwarzenegger "cold" jokes. The new take would aim to reposition the Batman franchise and move it away from the camp that had crept in, in the same way that Tim Burton's 1989 film had obliterated the memory of the goofy 1966 TV series.

The studio needed a director capable of treating the material in a respectful fashion that would get viewers of all ages excited about Batman again.

Brit Christopher Nolan had made a name for himself with the trippy *Memento* and the noir drama *Insomnia*. When he heard that Warner Bros. was in search of a new direction for Batman, Nolan walked into studio president Alan Horn's office and said, "'Look, this is what I want to do in the movie."

In just fifteen minutes the director laid out a detailed vision that included everything from what the Batmobile would look like to the body armor that the hero would wear. Horn basically committed to Nolan right there in the room.

Richard Donner's *Superman* inspired Nolan the most. As with that movie, Nolan wanted to tell a unique origin story.

"What I wanted to do was to tell the Batman story I'd never seen, the one that the fans have been wanting to see—the story of how Bruce Wayne becomes Batman," Nolan has said. "There were also a lot of very interesting gaps in the mythology that we were able to interpret ourselves and bring in our own ideas of how Bruce Wayne and Batman evolved specifically."

Batman Begins starred Christian Bale in the titular role and provided an in-depth look at how young Bruce trains and develops his superhero persona. Along the way he battles the Scarecrow (Cillian Murphy) and former mentor, Ra's al Ghul (Liam Neeson).

Before the film's release in June 2005 the studio's marketing department set out to impress upon potential ticket buyers that this new chapter had no connection to the Joel Schumacher movies from a few years before and that it represented a different, cooler new take on Batman.

Batman Begins was screened for DC employees, and president Paul Levitz provided an introduction.

"He said this is one of the movies where they got it right. 'You can be proud of this movie,'" says former DC editor Tom Palmer Jr. "That kind of made everyone feel good to see that there are people out there that get it."

The film opened to respectable, if not record-breaking, returns. It pulled in some $49 million in its opening weekend. Its most significant contribution may not have been to Warner's bottom line, however. What *Batman Begins* did do was successfully establish a new tone for DC's movies.

Nolan's world was not the optimistic, colorful world of Richard Donner's *Superman*. It was a dark, violent, and monochrome place filled with corrupt cops and heroes who spoke with a guttural growl—much of it borrowed from Frank Miller's 1987 "Year One" story arc.

The "grim and gritty" tone that had permeated comic books since the 1980s had taken hold in the movies, and it soon became the prevailing aesthetic. Woe unto those who gave audiences something different. When *Superman Returns* opened the next summer, audiences and critics generally rejected it for too closely aping Richard Donner's *Superman* films. The reboot was directed by Bryan Singer, who'd quit the X-Men franchise after a dispute over money to defect to DC. *Superman Returns* opened just a month after *X-Men: The Last Stand*, and Marvel partisans were happy to gloat that the mutant film opened to double what Superman did.

About the only victory *Superman Returns* did score over the competition was when ads for it appeared in Marvel comics, a rare breach of protocol that angered some Marvel zombies. Stan Lee had caught a similar kind of flak back in 1966 when Marvel comics carried an ad for CBS's Saturday morning cartoon lineup that included Superman. He was forced to pen an explanation that ran in Marvel's books.

By 2008 Nolan was back. And the darkness with him. *The Dark Knight* presented a crime-ridden world where a violent, almost fascist hero in heavy body armor lays down the law. It was a sophisticated take on the genre, and to many it represented the height of the increasingly popular superhero genre. The film was anchored by a head-turning performance from Heath Ledger as the psychotic Joker—a role that earned him a Best Supporting Oscar, making him the first actor to ever win for a superhero film.

Around the time that DC was reinventing its superhero world with *Batman Begins*, Marvel was set to take bold steps of its own to gain more control of its properties and change the superhero game forever.

Since the founding of Marvel Studios, the company's Hollywood arm, in 1993, Marvel had been mostly in the business of licensing its characters to other studios, content to sit back and collect a chunk of the merchandising money that often flowed in as a result of a theatrical film. The returns from the films themselves were certainly modest. Marvel reportedly took in a piddly $25,000 from *Blade* and earned just $62 million for the first two Spider-Man movies.

In 2003 David Maisel had an idea. Maisel was a Harvard-educated Hollywood insider who'd worked with former Disney head Michael Ovitz and superagent Ari Emanuel, the basis for Jeremy Piven's pushy character on *Entourage*. Maisel reached out to Marvel with a promise to improve their bottom line, and he was given a meeting with Ike Perlmutter, who, along with Avi Arad, was in control of Marvel at the time.

Maisel's pitch was simple: What if Marvel Studios owned and produced its own movies, making and releasing them in a time and manner of its own choosing? And the kicker would be that all the movies would take place in the same cinematic universe, with each subsequent film building on the previous—sort of like George Lucas had done with *Star Wars*. It would be the cinematic equivalent of the tightly woven Marvel print universe, where the mantra was, "If you see thunder clouds in one comic book, it would be raining in the next."

The thrifty Perlmutter and Marvel's conservative board were skeptical, but in early 2005 they gave the plan a green light. The company soon arranged a financing deal with Merrill Lynch that offered $525 million to make ten films over the next eight years featuring, basically, the characters Marvel hadn't already licensed to others. Even to longtime comic book fans, the list was somewhat underwhelming. Who's Shang-Chi again? And who cares about Hawkeye, a guy whose power is something kids learn at summer camp? And Nick Fury? Hadn't they tried that already, and the result was a terrible 1998 David Hasselhoff TV movie?

Disappointing or not, the deal allowed Marvel to chart its own course and with little risk for the company. The only thing it put up for collateral was the rights to these supposedly B-list characters.

Luckily for Marvel, the repo man never came for their heroes. Marvel's first self-produced movie, *Iron Man*, outperformed even the most optimistic predictions and launched the studio on a nearly unbroken string of successes that continues to this day.

Marvel had reacquired the rights to the armored character from New Line in 2005 and made it the debut film in part because head of the studio Avi Arad loved the character when he was growing up. Hopes were not high for a character who few outside of the comic book industry knew. Those hopes got even lower after Robert Downey Jr., an actor best known at the time for his stint in rehab, was picked to star.

"Don't worry. We'll be very happy if this breaks even and we can sell more toys," a Marvel board member told David Maisel.

But fewer decisions in Hollywood have been smarter. Downey, along with director Jon Favreau, brought a lightness to the film about a cocky munitions titan who builds his own personal hi-tech suit of armor.

The amusing tone immediately set *Iron Man* apart from other super-hero films, especially those from its rival.

"Marvel figured out that we'd rather hang out with flawed charac-ters who were nonetheless spiritually uplifting heroes rather than the dark, self-loathing, and haunted DC characters," says Jeff Most, a Hol-lywood producer whose credits include the comic book adaptation *The Crow*. "That DC pathos intrigues us to a point, but wallowing in darkness is never as satisfying as a good laugh in a popcorn flick with a lighter tone."

Robert Downey Jr. was also firmly in the Marvel camp. He had a few choice words for *The Dark Knight*, which happened to be going head to head with his *Iron Man* in the summer of 2008. Downey slagged off the competitor for its pretentious, operatic tone.

"That's not my idea of what I want to see in a movie," Downey said. "This is so high-brow and so fucking smart, I clearly need a college educa-tion to understand this movie. You know what? Fuck DC Comics. That's all I have to say, and that's where I'm really coming from."

Iron Man, with its unique mix of thrilling action, engaging characters, and winking humor, finally fulfilled the dream that Stan Lee had been chasing for some thirty years; it was able to capture that special formula that made Marvel comics great, and it stayed faithful to what had already been established in print. Iron Man looked and acted like he did in the comics. His origin was the same. His supporting cast was kept intact. (One concession: Stark's human butler, Jarvis, was turned into a disem-bodied computer over fears he was too close to Batman's Alfred.) It was a far cry from Marvel's previous licensed efforts, which often ignored the source material. *The Punisher* had jettisoned nearly everything recogniz-able about the character, including the costume, and turned him into a generic action hero. The 1992 *Captain America* turned Nazi villain Red Skull into an Italian, for some reason.

From *Iron Man* forward, every Marvel movie has attempted to cap-ture the essence of the character and to remain true to its print origins. Marvel trusted its comics. The studio brought in editors and writers from the various comics to consult on the scripts, smartly figuring that those who are in the trenches with the characters every day know them best. Marvel publishing has functioned like an R&D lab for more than fifty years, testing ideas and honing concepts, and it would be foolish to ignore that information.

Captain America: The First Avenger nailed the hero's Boy Scout charm and wisely set the story during World War II, over the objections of some at Marvel who thought a period movie would alienate young viewers. The company even managed to find a take on thee-and-thou-spouting Thor that didn't have audiences laughing it out of the theater.

For better or worse—and judging by the box office returns, it's for better—Marvel Studios is like a factory, stamping out movies like GM churns out cars. Each is built to similar specifications, and audiences know what they will be getting.

It's a top-down approach, similar to the way rival DC produced comics back in the 1960s, and it can be limiting for filmmakers. Directors are brought in to execute Marvel's vision, not their own. The look and feel of Marvel movies can vary only so much, and each has to fit comfortably within the universe the company has established.

As with its comics line back in the early days, the result is that the Marvel brand itself has become a powerful draw. If you liked the previous Marvel offering, you'll probably like the next. Simply the fact that a movie is being released by Marvel is now enough to guarantee ticket sales.

"Stan once told me [in the 1970s] was what he had in mind for Marvel was what he called an 'advertising agency,'" says former Marvel writer and editor Denny O'Neil. "If he had a chance to rewrite that, he might have called it 'synergy,' where everything supports everything else. So you don't go to see a superhero movie; you go to see a Marvel movie. It's not the same with DC. With DC, you go see a Batman movie, not a DC movie. With Marvel, you go see a Marvel movie."

DC, however, is not strictly beholden to a single interpretation of its characters and allows far more variety. As a result, a character such as Batman can simultaneously exist in different iterations across various media. He's the harmless caped crusader on Saturday morning cartoons, the sarcastic wisecracker in *The LEGO Batman Movie*, and the violent avenger from Nolan's *Dark Knight* trilogy.

"It isn't just about a single approach to everything," Diane Nelson, president of DC Entertainment, said in 2014. "It's the right character matched with the right talent in the right medium."

The downside to the approach is that DC's brand is not as strong or cohesive as Marvel's. If you went to see, say, *Catwoman* and loved it (assuming there was something very wrong with you), you really had nowhere to go from there. All you could do was wait for the next DC superhero movie and hope that the director and tone established was to your particular liking.

The scattershot approach was great when the character and a filmmaker's particular vision meshed and you got something like *Batman Begins*. When it didn't, you got misfires such as the 2011's *Green Lantern*, which someone at Warner Bros. thought would be best served as a silly action yarn.

Marvel has also been much more disciplined with its planning than DC. On the heels of *Iron Man*'s success the studio confidently announced that four more movies were in the works—each with a release date as far as three years out. (That schedule has since been revised multiple times to run through 2019.)

"I think Marvel has led the way there," says Hugh Jackman, who played Wolverine. "The more you plan, the more payoff there is."

Payoff is right. Partly driven by the success of its movie slate, Marvel announced in August 2009 that it was being acquired by Disney for an astounding $4 billion dollars. For comparison's sake, the company was valued at $400 million as recently as 2003. At the time some in the financial world thought Disney was crazy for spending so much on a company whose top properties, such as the X-Men, were in the hands of others. Disney's stock fell when news of the purchase hit.

But Disney—and Marvel—believed in the prospects for the huge number of characters Marvel still had left. A group of interns was tasked with going through Marvel comics and counting them. They came up with more than eight thousand.

Regardless of whether any of those characters are as good as Spider-Man, the Marvel purchase put the marketing and merchandising might of Disney behind the company and ended its dependence on other studios to distribute its films. A good thing was about to get better.

The sale caught Warner Bros. and DC off guard and forced the entertainment giant to think about ways to catch up to Marvel. DC had been thinking about a reorganization to coincide with the company's seventy-fifth anniversary in 2010, but the Disney sale forced it to accelerate its plans.

One month after the Marvel-Disney announcement Warner Bros. dropped some fairly significant news of its own. It announced that Warner Bros. was tightening its control over DC Comics, moving the publishing company into a new division called DC Entertainment, which had been created "to maximize the potential of the DC brand." With the re-structuring, DC Comics was eventually moved from New York after three-quarters of a century to new digs in Burbank, California, forcing staffers to make the difficult decision about whether to uproot themselves and their families and go west.

"It would have been disingenuous for us to suggest that we had not been thinking about [the Marvel sale]," Warner chairman and CEO Barry Meyer said in 2009. "[The announcement] reconfirmed in us our strong belief in how valuable DC really is."

Translation: We've got hundreds of characters sitting there that we better start exploiting, because we're getting left behind.

Fans and industry watchers worried that DC's latest reorganization didn't exactly appear to lead to a coordinated effort when it came to its film slate. It looked to all the world that the company's strategy amounted to frantically chasing Marvel without a well-reasoned plan in place.

"Here's the problem: Marvel's slate of movies is by and large a very carefully coordinated endeavor," says writer Peter David. "Everything interconnects to everything else. I am not remotely convinced that DC is putting any kind of that detailed thought into the movies they're doing. It's possible that they are, but I wouldn't necessarily bet the farm on it."

Part of the reason Marvel Studios has remained so disciplined is that it has someone overseeing it all, president of production Kevin Feige. He's less of a stuffy executive than a geek in a suit. Feige is a *Star Wars* and comic book nut who owns an action-figure collection so large that he's forced to house it in a shed he built in his backyard. He worked on *X-Men* in 2000 before being hired by Marvel. In 2007 he was named the studio's head at just thirty-three years old. He quickly began managing the studio's plans and building Marvel's cinematic world.

By contrast, DC had no single guiding voice; various executives throughout Warner Bros. managed its superhero films. DC was also stuck without a defining gestalt for its superhero universe after Christopher Nolan concluded his stand-alone Batman trilogy and moved on to non-superhero projects. Marvel had established its world, some of its characters, and the tone of its films from its very first entry, *Iron Man*, but DC still did not have a movie that would serve as the foundation for every project moving forward.

That would change with 2013's *Man of Steel*, the Superman reboot from director Zack Snyder that polarized audiences and critics alike.

Some found the dark, broody, monochrome take on the classic hero refreshing. Others wanted no part of Snyder's repellant and violent vision and took to nicknaming his world the DC "murderverse."

In spite of the lukewarm reception, Warner Bros. opted to forge ahead with Snyder's vision (probably because they had no time to find a new one and another reboot would be embarrassing). In October 2014 the studio announced an ambitious slate of superhero flicks, all the way through 2020, flowing out of the cinematic world established in *Man of Steel*. Snyder was now the de facto creative head of the DC universe. Audiences would get movies starring the Flash, Aquaman, and Wonder Woman, among others.

The announcement looked like a desperate attempt to copy Marvel's success—but with one glaring difference: instead of introducing the heroes one by one in their own solo movies, as Marvel had done, the studio decided to rush out a pairing between Batman and Superman for its very next movie and follow it up with a gigantic team-up of all its major heroes in *Justice League*—both directed by Snyder. It basically appeared that DC was hastily backing into a cinematic universe.

"People make an assumption that we're going to mirror Marvel's strategy, for example with *Avengers*," DC Entertainment president Diane Nelson said in 2010. "We do have a very different attitude about how you build a content slate. And it isn't necessarily about connecting those properties together to build into a single thing. We think we've got great stories and characters that will lend themselves to great stand-alone experiences, and that's the way we're focusing on it."

Not everyone was buying it.

"The cinematic universe is a perfect example of the rivalry, where they say, 'We've got to do the same thing, but we can't *look* like we're doing the same thing, because it will look like we're copying,'" says industry analyst Milton Griepp. "DC couldn't start with a minor character and expand it out, like Marvel did with *Iron Man*, so they start with their two biggest characters because they want to build a cinematic universe, but they're going to do it differently than Marvel."

To Marvel, however, its success was responsible for DC's plan.

"I don't think they'd be doing it if we hadn't succeeded, so I like the acknowledgement that we've succeeded," Kevin Feige says of DC's slate. "That's always nice."

DC, on paper at least, remained confident. In one particular case of propaganda DC responded to a seventh grader who'd written a letter asking how DC planned to compete against Marvel when "Marvel seemingly dominates."

DC's December 2013 reply claimed Marvel was ahead because it had the freedom to work with numerous distributors and DC was stuck with one: Warner Bros. "We don't like to toot our own horn (well actually we do)," the letter concluded, "our movies by far exceed all of Marvels in sales."

"I feel like Batman and Superman are transcendent of superhero movies in a way, because they're Batman and Superman. They're not just, like, the flavor of the week Ant-Man—not to be mean, but whatever it is."

—*Batman v Superman* director Zack Snyder in 2015

"Do I want to fire some shots at DC right now, at Zack Snyder? I read some of those comments . . . and I was like, 'Oh thanks, Zack. That's great. Way to do something original.' But I would say we're still making something very original in our own way. . . . [We're] not trying to mimic a better Christopher Nolan movie or something like that."

—*Captain America: Civil War* star Sebastian Stan in 2015

It was a weirdly defensive boast, especially in response to a neg from a preteen named Spencer, but DC was free to believe what it believed. Its next movie would test that claim of superiority in a way that none of its releases had before.

Batman v Superman: Dawn of Justice was originally intended to be a straight *Man of Steel* sequel, but following the lukewarm reception for the first one, the subsequent film was basically changed into a new Batman movie with Superman costarring. Following delays, the studio announced the movie would hit theaters May 6, 2016.

The date put DC's movie on a collision course with Marvel, which had claimed that opening weekend way back in June 2013 for a then-unnamed film. The situation got even rockier for Warner Bros. when Marvel revealed that the untitled movie would in fact be *Captain America: Civil War*, the anticipated follow-up to the well-liked second movie, *The Winter Soldier*. The DC-Marvel game of chicken sent fans into a tizzy.

For months neither side backed down.

"We had the flag there first," Marvel's Feige told *Empire* at the time. "What other people do and where has always been less of our concern. It's about keeping our head down and doing what we would believe would be cool for an audience to see."

DC admitted that when they had squatted on the release date, they were gambling that Marvel would not have its movie ready for release. When it was clear that Marvel was moving ahead with the third Captain America, Warner Bros. caved, shifting *Batman v Superman* up a few weeks to March 25, 2016.

"Maybe our reconnaissance wasn't great," admitted Warner Bros.' president of domestic distribution Dan Fellman in 2014.

Score yet another one for Marvel.

But for Warner Bros. all the delays and shifts and adjustments would be worth it because—in the words of Warner CEO Kevin Tsujihara—it was crucial that *Batman v Superman* got "the foundation right on DC." *Man of Steel* had been a bit of a bust, causing the studio to rejigger its universe plans, and if the sequel also underperformed, what then? Warner Bros. and DC would be left with a long slate of promised movies stretching years into the future and no viable creative direction in which to take them. If you can't even get Batman right, how in the hell do you tackle Aquaman?

Unfortunately for Warner Bros., *Batman v Superman* didn't come close to living up to expectations. It used Nolan's template from the previous three Batman movies as a starting point, then bolted on all of Zack Snyder's polarizing trademarks, including gratuitous slo-mo and more gratuitous slo-mo. The tone was humorless and coal-black, the story nonsensical, and the big showdown between the two heroes a bore. This was a movie that used Lex Luthor's urine, known affectionately as "Granny's peach tea," as some sort of plot point. A movie with a plan from its villain so complicated that it immediately crumbles under the barest scrutiny. A movie in which Batman and Superman stop trying to kill each other because they discover their mothers have the same name.

The beating it took in the press was far worse than either one of its titular heroes suffered in the movie itself. "A stink bucket of disappointment," Vox wrote. "It's about as diverting as having a porcelain sink broken over your head," the *New York Times* sniped. The flick earned a hefty eight 2016 Razzie nominations, the annual awards celebrating the most putrid in film.

Not helping the film's case was all the hype over its showdown with Marvel's *Captain America: Civil War*. Even though Warner Bros. had backed down on releasing it the same day, the movies couldn't help but be tied together. Nearly every article and review compared the two, which didn't do Warner any favors. The audience found itself being forced to weigh Marvel and DC's outputs and probably concluding it preferred Marvel's.

Civil War told a ripped-from-the-headlines tale of superheroes lining up on opposite sides after disagreeing on a government regulation policing their actions. It asked questions about the limits of heroism and the power of government. The hint of political resonance wasn't particularly overt or deep, but in comparison to *Batman v Superman*, it made *Civil War* look like Chaplin's *The Great Dictator*.

Having its heroes violently opposing one another was a risky direction for Marvel to take, and as with so many other great moments in this long rivalry, Marvel's decision was due in part to DC. After Warner Bros. announced *Batman v Superman*, *Civil War* directors Joe and Anthony Russo became determined to do something beyond just another superhero adventure. They began lobbying Kevin Feige to do something different with the third Cap movie.

"After they announced *Batman v Superman*, [Feige] said, 'You guys are absolutely right,'" Joe Russo said in 2016. "We needed to do something challenging with the material or we were going to start to lose the audience."

Losing the audience was a real danger, and the main cause was likely to be boredom. By the time *X-Men: Apocalypse* (from Fox) limped into theaters in May 2016, audiences had been under almost continuous assault by superhero movies for more than a decade, with one arriving nearly every two months. Fatigue became a threat, and any movie that looked like just another spandex origin story ran the risk of being ignored by audiences, convinced they'd been there, done that already. (To wit: *The Amazing Spider-Man 2*.)

Fox's *Deadpool*, released in February 2016, was the perfect antidote for tired superhero flicks. The story about a sarcastic, sword-wielding assassin capitalized on the ubiquity of comic book movies, taking advantage of the viewers' familiarity with the tropes to perfectly send up the genre. It was nearly impossible to sit through another self-serious superhero film after watching Deadpool cackle as he ran over a bad guy with a Zamboni.

DC felt the wind shift, but by the time of its next release, it was too late. *Suicide Squad*, an edgy team-up of Batman villains Harley Quinn, Killer Croc, Deadshot, and others, was set to arrive some four months after *Batman v Superman*. Warner Bros. executives were reportedly spooked at the drubbing the previous film took and began desperately scrambling to lighten the tone of *Suicide Squad* in hopes that it wouldn't land with the same kind of thud as *Batman v Superman*.

The film was in disarray in part because of the tight timetable. Writer-director David Ayer, the man behind the 2014 Brad Pitt tank drama *Fury*, finished the *Suicide Squad* script in just six weeks. A release date had to be met, and promotional deals had to be honored. Once again it felt that, unlike Marvel, DC lacked firm control over its product.

"Feige's success boils down to getting the tone right at the script development stage," says producer Most. "The development factory nurtures its scripts and doesn't back into distribution dates before a script is ready to go into production. A common refrain from the filmmakers working on DC films has been they've had to adhere to a distribution date circled on a calendar and back into such, even when the script may not be fully ready to go."

Suicide Squad turned out to be Warner's second critical disaster of the year (though it did respectably at the box office). Critics and bloggers absolutely hated what they saw, their rage magnified by the frustration of being served yet another DC lemon. No story, no character development, an equally dark tone as *Batman v Superman*. The pile-on in the days leading up to the movie was absolutely brutal.

"*Suicide Squad* is bad," *Vanity Fair* wrote. "Not fun bad. Not redeemable bad. Not the kind of bad that is the unfortunate result of artists honorably striving for something ambitious and falling short. *Suicide Squad* is just bad."

Superhero fans, who had pegged the film as the one that might finally right the fast-sinking DC ship, were dispirited. Discouraged DC partisans lashed out at review aggregator Rotten Tomatoes, creating a petition to shut down the site over its harsh reviews and spreading a ridiculous rumor on social media accusing Disney of paying off critics to trash non-Marvel movies.

Ayer initially defended *Suicide Squad*, saying on Twitter, "I love the movie and believe in it." A few months later in January 2017 he tweeted a more revealing postmortem on the movie, admitting the movie had "flaws." He said that he wished he had a time machine so he could go back and make the Joker (in a cameo appearance by Jared Leto) the main villain and "engineer a more grounded story."

Too little too late. The backlash from the failure of *Suicide Squad* was becoming harder to ignore. In September 2016 a former Warner Bros. employee calling herself "Gracie Law" wrote a widely read open letter to Kevin Tsujihara, blasting the CEO for mishandling the DC universe. The anonymous employee called *Suicide Squad* a "trainwreck" and a "disservice to the characters." The letter questioned how Zack Snyder, the man behind two stillborn superhero movies, was still not being punished for his failures, while rank-and-file employees were being laid off.

The studio soon took action, making its umpteenth attempt to finally get the DC cinematic universe on the right footing. The studio quietly demoted Zack Snyder's upcoming *Justice League* epic, originally announced as two movies, to one and tried to move away from the depressing "murderverse" vibe by tweaking the script.

In September 2016 Warner promoted Geoff Johns, DC's chief creative officer and former assistant to Richard Donner, to a more powerful role overseeing DC's film output. Johns, a prolific writer, had been responsible for many of DC's more popular comic book story lines during the past few years, including ones that sparked a resurgence in the popularity of Green Lantern and Aquaman. Warner paired Johns with production executive Jon Berg, making the duo the first full-time team overseeing DC's movies. DC, like Marvel, finally had its guiding voice.

"Mistakenly in the past I think the studio has said, 'Oh, DC films are gritty and dark and that's what makes them different.' That couldn't be more wrong," Johns told the *Wall Street Journal*. "It's a hopeful and optimistic view of life. Even Batman has a glimmer of that in him. If he didn't think he'd make tomorrow better, he'd stop."

It remains to be seen whether DC's changes will save its superhero universe from a slow, sad descent into irrelevance. (One good sign: the movie script for one of Johns's signature characters, the Flash, was ordered completely rewritten in early 2017.) In the meantime Marvel marches on, continuing its historic run. It may be that there's room enough for both companies to succeed.

"I may be naive, but I think there's some data to suggest they don't compete with each other," says Simon Kinberg, producer of *Deadpool* and *X-Men: Days of Futures Past*. "I think that they build off each other. I think the reason they're the biggest genre right now is because they've been good. The interest continues to grow and building beyond the comic book base into the mainstream audience. As long as they make good ones, it'll be beneficial."

For DC, making good films has been problematic—and may remain so without a more drastic course correction than the many they've made over the last few years. But one area where the company's heroes have flourished is on television.

Beginning in 2012 with the CW's *Arrow*, DC has built a cozy little broadcast universe that has grown in recent years to include *The Flash*, *Legends of Tomorrow*, and *Supergirl*, among others.

DC has enjoyed modest success in the past on television, with the 1990s hit *Lois & Clark: The New Adventures of Superman* and a syndicated *Superboy*, but now its properties have never been more in demand on the small screen.

The reasons are simple. The characters have built-in name recognition—an asset that's becoming increasingly important in Hollywood where, on that basis alone, someone green-lit *The A-Team* movie.

Technology has also caught up. In years past it would have been impossible to offer cinema-level effects on a TV budget. *Smallville*, the long-running series about a young Superman, famously instituted a "no tights, no flights" rule and instead chose to tell more grounded stories about its hero. Now, however, most effects are within reach. *The Flash*, for example, accomplishes many shots of its lightning-quick hero by seamlessly inserting a computer-generated double.

Supergirl, *The Flash*, *Arrow*, and *Legends of Tomorrow* are all interwoven and act like a mini-DC cinematic universe. The shows have a similar tone—fun, light, and reliant on shocking cliffhangers. The characters all exist in the same world and occasionally cross over with one another.

But as with DC's overall strategy, they have nothing to do with the movies. *The Flash* who appears on the CW every week is not the one who first showed up on the big screen in *Batman v Superman: Dawn of Justice*. And the world portrayed in Fox's *Gotham* each week also has no connection to the movie. The DC tent is large enough to accommodate multiple interpretations, and it may be better off for it. Audience members who are turned off by Snyder's cinematic murderverse can simply switch on the TV for versions of the characters they might like more.

The approach provides more flexibility to tell different kinds of stories. It also makes it easier to switch up something that isn't working.

Meanwhile Marvel has taken the exact opposite approach, opting to set all its TV and film projects (except the licensed ones) within the same universe. The company is hoping that if you enjoyed *The Avengers*, then you'll tune in to *Agents of S.H.I.E.L.D.*, the ABC series starring Clark Gregg, the actor who also plays Agent Phil Coulson in the movies.

The show got off to a decent start when it debuted in 2013, fueled by a halo effect from the blockbuster films. The pilot drew some 12.1 million viewers. But by the second episode ratings fell some 30 percent and continued to decline.

The disinterest exposed the problems with Marvel's single-universe strategy. By tying *Agents of S.H.I.E.L.D.* into its films, the TV show just felt small by comparison. (And the production budgets on the first season didn't help.) When Coulson references events from *The Avengers* or Samuel L. Jackson shows up in a brief cameo, as he's done in two episodes, viewers are probably left wishing they'd watched a DVD of a Marvel movie instead.

Marvel's subsequent attempts would be more successful. Back in 2013 the company had struck a deal with Netflix to produce five shows featuring its more street-level characters Daredevil, Jessica Jones, Iron Fist, and Luke Cage.

The idea began with Jeph Loeb, a former DC and Marvel writer who's now head of Marvel TV. While watching the climatic battle in *The Avengers*, Loeb wondered what was going on in other parts of New York City. He pitched a concept to Netflix, and the resulting deal would follow the Marvel movies template. The characters would be introduced in solo adventures before coming in a mega-crossover, here called *The Defenders*.

The Netflix series were surprisingly adult and gritty and drew critical acclaim for their smart writing and brutal fight choreography.

"I think the other part that separates us from, let's just say, our distinguished competition is that we take place in a very real, grounded world," Loeb told *Entertainment Weekly*. "We've always said that there is a fifth Defender, and that is New York."

Comics books are everywhere, and all the success in TV and movies has allowed some geeks to declare victory. After years of being ridiculed for their love of superheroes and having the culture remain on the periphery, superheroes are now mainstream. They're globally popular and big business, to boot. But as has often been the case in the superhero industry, it's unclear whether the creators behind all of these great characters are benefitting as they should.

Both Marvel and DC pay their talent a fee when one of their creations is used in a movie or television series, though the money handed out differs from project to project, character to character, and creator to creator.

Keeping track of who did what over all those years and comics is now a vital issue in an age when even a minor supporting character can play a major role in a blockbuster film. A few years ago DC hired a staffer to go through every comic book it had published and identify the first appearances of every character in order to correctly identify the creators behind them. It took the staffer literally years.

Many in the comic book industry find Hollywood's new obsession with their work exciting—but they find the business end confusing. Checks will arrive in the mail for various sums with almost no explanation of what the money is for. A toy? Lunchbox profit sharing?

The amounts can be both exciting and disappointing.

"When the *Green Lantern* movie came out and [my cocreation] Kilowog was in it, the guy in charge of royalties at DC said to me, [writer] Len Wein got $500,000 for Lucius Fox [played by Morgan Freeman] in the Batman movies, you'll get a check somewhere in six figures for this," says writer Steve Englehart. "Then the movie tanked, so I ended up getting something like ten thousand bucks."

"The most I ever got was a portion of the option for the *Constantine* feature film," says Steve Bissette, cocreator of Constantine. "I got a check for $45,000."

In some cases talent have seen their share decrease with the rising popularity of comic book properties. A character's appearance that would pay $500 in the 1993 series *Lois & Clark: The New Adventures of Superman* now might pay $300 for an appearance in the CW's *Supergirl*.

The drop could be attributed to DC Entertainment consolidating its production in house instead of using outside companies.

"One hand doesn't have to pay the other hand as much as they would if there was a third hand—an independent company—and so it's beneficial to DC obviously," says one artist.

In another case a character's appearance in *Superman Returns* rewarded its cocreator 5 percent of a $1 million licensing fee that the movie studio paid DC, or $50,000. By the time *Man of Steel* rolled around, the licensing fee had apparently fallen to $760,000 because the cocreator's share was $38,000.

But these payments are for characters created after the revenue-sharing agreements of the 1980s. Artists and writers whose creations first appeared before those contracts aren't often as lucky. Many are entitled to nothing, although some are paid an honorarium. Swamp Thing cocreator Bernie Wrightson got just $2,000 when his creature starred in a feature film.

David Michelinie, who cocreated James Rhodes, aka War Machine (played by Don Cheadle in the *Iron Man* and *Avengers* movies), says he was fully aware he was "entitled to get nothing, either money or credit" for use of some of his characters.

"But no one put a gun to my head and forced me to create new intellectual properties," he says. "I was an adult, I knew what I was doing, and I have no legal right to complain. Characters I created later on—[Spider-Man villains] Venom, Carnage—were done with revenue-sharing contracts, and I did receive a portion of earnings from T-shirts, action figures, and so forth."

Marvel and its new owner, Disney, appear to be fully aware of the value of its library of characters. A few years ago the conglomerate began attempting to buy creators out of their share of ownership for a flat fee.

"Within the last decade Marvel has gone back and revisited a lot of those agreements so that the creators had no ownership," writer Ron Marz says. "If I owned 1.5 percent of something in a movie, there would be difficulty with the rights. So there were new contracts and payments. It's all very obvious in the new contract: you get this much if a character becomes an action figure and this much if it appears in a TV or movie. It gave a framework to everything."

Other creators weren't so eager to sign the new deal.

"Marvel contacted me around 2010. They didn't offer much," Ann Nocenti says. "I was just at a Comic Con, and I asked [another writer], 'Are you getting these letters?' and they said, 'Yeah, don't sign 'em.'"

The Rivalry Moves from the Comic Rack to the Corporate Boardroom

"They're the competition! They're not supposed to talk good about us and what we're doing. And vice versa."

—Marvel's Tom Brevoort on DC

Much has changed at both Marvel and DC since the 1960s. The comics business, for better or worse, has grown up. Long gone are the days when Marvel and DC were mom 'n' pop businesses left to pursue any crazy idea they could crank out before the impending deadline. Corporate is now the word. Today both Marvel and DC are cogs within multinational corporate machines, valued less for their publishing profits than for their vast intellectual property libraries.

DC has abandoned New York—its home since the days when the publisher bought Superman from two Cleveland kids for $130—and moved to the West Coast to be better integrated into the Warner Bros. entertainment empire. Marvel has gone from a single-office operation down the hall from a skin mag publisher to a subsidiary of Disney valued at more than $4 billion. To put that valuation in terms comic book collectors will understand, that's 14,337 near-mint copies of *Fantastic Four* #1.

One thing that hasn't changed is the conflict between the two biggest names in superheroes. The employee poaching, the competing events, and the marketing gamesmanship still feature prominently. With these characters becoming global icons worth billions, if anything, the stakes are higher now than ever before.

"To me the rivalry is as strong as it's ever, ever been," says Milton Griepp, an industry analyst and CEO of ICv2. "The competition is really visible and strong, and when you talk to the management, you can feel it. It's in the DNA at these companies so strong. It's bigger than one person."

The comic book fanbase, who began to cleave in the 1960s with the emergence of Marvel, may have become more polarized than ever before. That schism that manifested itself decades ago via playground arguments is now being taken to a new level online, where social media makes it easier than ever to throw stones at the opposition. And the success of the movies has added a very high-profile impetus to pick a side. Once again an important question has become: Are you a Marvel, or are you a DC?

"There are people on Facebook and Twitter who say, 'If you like Marvel movies, you can't like the DC movies,' or, 'If you like the DC movies, you can't like the Marvel movies,'" says artist Jerry Ordway. "It's like this weird polarity that you're getting in the entire world with politics and everything else in what should be fun entertainment."

Despite the corporate takeovers, the company's personas remain as they have been. Marvel is the eternal hipster, while DC remains the classy, conservative uncle, forever on a quest to make itself more youthful and relevant.

But the corporate ownership has changed both company's products and the way they do business. The relentless, Wall Street–driven pursuit of quarterly earnings has, in a declining periodicals markets, forced Marvel and DC to give in to their worst tendencies. Now nothing is out of bounds in the quest for the all-important short-term profit.

"The biggest difference at DC really came when Paul Levitz was kind of forced out [in 2009, he chose to leave after 35 years. Warner Bros gave him an option to stay but in a different capacity]," Ordway says. "Paul was the last link to—and I hate to say this—DC being a stand-up company."

"Paul kept corporate at arm's length and from exploiting the properties to the nth degree," retailer Brian Hibbs says. "I think that he knew that if you let the corporate guys, who don't really give a shit, get in, they were just going to fuck it all up. They were going to look at DC as a bank account, which is clearly what's going on right now."

In years past, the corporate masters generally ignored the publishing business and might have gotten involved only when big changes were afoot—say, if Superman were getting a new costume. But the realization that anything—even a goofy talking raccoon—could potentially be worth billions has tightened the oversight. The assets must be protected.

"Now they see money in everything. Anything could be a cartoon or a TV show," says former DC editor Frank Pittarese. "When I was there back in 2014 or 2015 we got an email once from [DC Entertainment president] Diane Nelson or her team. It was like, 'Hey guys, it's great to be embarking on this adventure. Yay, comics. Please remember comics are a springboard for other media like video games. That's why you're here.' That infuriated me because comics are an art form all their own. Don't tell me that I'm just an element in your thing."

Both companies now operate under editorial-driven systems, much like the 1960s heyday of DC's Julie Schwartz and Mort Weisinger. Gone are the days when Marvel writers in the 1970s could write a story under the influence of some strange hallucinogenic substance, and it would run as long as it got turned in on time.

"There's more top-down involvement, shall we say," writer Ron Marz says. "When I took over *Green Lantern* in the mid nineties, I was left to my own devices to come up with the new Green Lantern [Kyle Rayner]. That wouldn't happen now. There would be somebody way up the corporate ladder, at least having pretty severe involvement. There are a lot more people looking over your shoulder in what used to be a job where you could do whatever you wanted."

What's forgotten is that most of the billion-dollar characters the corporations are so desperate to safeguard were created by artists flying by the seat of their ink-stained pants, just throwing out cool stuff. Today industry news reports are filled with tales of friction created by editorial meddling, with numerous big names walking off DC books after interference ground them down.

"The current regime at DC is far more strict," says writer Peter David. "People have to do far more rewrites. Things are approved, then subsequently disapproved. It is not the best place to be a creator these days. I don't know why they're so concerned with the status quo. My guess is that they've been around for seventy-five years or so, and you have concerns that the guy who's working with them is going to screw them up."

"It was generally well known that DC paid better, had better insurance, and had nicer offices than us," says one Marvel editor. "There was a general consensus that the trade-off for better pay at DC was that you had to deal with Dan DiDio running the DCU, which wasn't a good thing."

Marvel appears to have also embraced the top-down structure that defined DC in the 1960s.

"Marvel has imposed a corporate structure over the friendliness of the thing. It's the old [Julius] Schwartz model now, where the editors are in charge and the writers are filling in the blanks," writer Steve Englehart says. "You tell us what you want to write, we'll tell you what you can write, you tell us what you're going to do for the first twelve issues, then we'll tell you what you're going to have to change, then you can go write it."

The need for strict oversight is essential, in part, due to the increasing number of events. Once considered an annual novelty back in the 1980s, events now run almost continuously (at least at Marvel), with one bleeding into the other and each promising more spectacular repercussions than the last.

In 2014 alone Marvel gave readers—among others—*Original Sin*, which promised to "reveal shocking secrets about every major Marvel character!" *Axis*, which the company trumpeted would "change everything!" and *Death of Wolverine*, "the single most important X-Men event of the decade."

That same year DC had *Superman: Doomed* ("the super-event you have been waiting for") and *Futures End*, which the company boasted would "forever alter the direction" of the DC universe.

And back and forth Marvel and DC go, releasing overhyped, dueling sagas, almost always at the same time—and occasionally with suspiciously similar premises.

DC ran a 2016 Batman epic called "Night of the Monster Men." Marvel soon announced a 2017 event called "Monsters Unleashed."

The most insane similarities came with the publishers' 2015 events. That summer both DC and Marvel ran heavily promoted, mega-storylines involving a powerful villain building a single world out of various parts plucked from different dimensions. DC's, called *Convergence*, debuted in April, while Marvel's, *Secret Wars*, was released in May. The similarities were not lost on readers. *Tech Times* ran an article entitled, "Are Marvel's 'Secret Wars' and DC's 'Convergence' the Exact Same Story?"

Yeah, pretty much.

"When DC did *Convergence* I was also talking to Marvel about a *Secret Wars* mini that ultimately didn't come off," says writer Ron Marz. "I had signed [nondisclosure agreements] for both things, and I realized, 'These are the same story!' To my knowledge it was dumb luck. I was like, 'I'm not gonna say anything, but I guess they don't know they're doing the exact same story.' There were a few of us out there that were involved with both places, and no one was saying anything."

"There's no bad idea, so if someone comes up with one, everyone's going to do it," says longtime writer and artist Keith Giffen. "Marvel does Civil War, DC does something else. It's that good-natured rivalry."

The companies' 2011 event battle was especially fierce due to a brazen Marvel marketing promotion that took direct aim at DC's offering. That summer Marvel was in the midst of *Fear Itself,* a major crossover storyline that led out of the previous major crossover storyline, *Siege.* DC was pushing *Flashpoint,* a big event centering on the Flash that was running neck and neck with *Fear Itself* on the direct-sales charts. As per usual, both storylines unfolded in a main miniseries but were supplemented with tie-ins in the companies' regular comics—an attempt to gently nudge customers to try titles they were not currently reading.

It was these tie-ins that Marvel targeted. The publisher made retailers an interesting offer: it would send them one rare, variant edition of *Fear Itself* #6, which could presumably be marked up and sold well over cover price, in exchange for every fifty covers of Flashpoint tie-ins the retailers ripped off and mailed in. Marvel was actually encouraging retailers to destroy its competitor's product.

"In these tough economic times, [we] feel it's our duty to help," Marvel's publisher David Gabriel said sarcastically in a press release.

Marvel had tried something similar the previous year, offering a *Deadpool* variant in exchange for fifty stripped DC covers—an effort to blunt its rival's "Blackest Night" crossover. Marvel claimed retailers had sent in "tens of thousands" of covers during that promotion, seemingly drawn from massive piles of unsold DC comics sitting in stock rooms.

"I think it's hilarious and a perfect demonstration of the fact that these companies still hate each other and that they'll poke each other in the eye at every opportunity," Griepp says. "Marvel's goal wasn't to send out this limited edition comic or to give the retailers something to sell. What they were trying to do was demonstrate DC's failure, and yes, I did think it put an exclamation on that. Marvel was trying to show that DC's product is so terrible that retailers have cases of it sitting around, and we're trying to help them out because we support the market. That was particularly inspired."

In another equally inspired though more scatological marketing scheme, Marvel poked fun at DC's plan to offer fifty-two different variant covers for *Justice League of America* #1 (April 2013) featuring the flags of all fifty states plus Washington, DC, and Puerto Rico. The same month that issue hit, Marvel released a special cover of *Uncanny X-Men* #1 showing every state bird . . . crapping all over Deadpool.

"You have to remember that if there's a guiding light over at Marvel, it's that you want to do the Puck-ish thing," says Marvel artist Scott Koblish. "Marvel enjoys being a little bit of pranksters. The way of handling things has been sort of passed down. You don't want to take things too seriously."

In their bid to capture more dollars from a shrinking pool of customers, Marvel and DC have also gone overboard with relaunches and reboots. Titles are started over so often with a new #1 that the number has basically lost its currency. Wolverine, Marvel's popular mutant hero, has had his title restarted three times since 2010 alone.

DC has taken that gimmick to the next level, and instead of rebooting individual titles, it's decided to take the drastic step of rebooting its entire universe—twice within just five years.

The first revamp came in 2011 and was dubbed "The New 52" after the number of titles the company planned to release. The month prior DC canceled every one of its comic books before starting them over again, often with updated origins, in an attempt to freshen up and make the heroes younger or give them a younger vibe. (Yes, that again.) The new volume of *Action Comics* #1 introduced a young Superman who was at the beginning of his crime-fighting career. Its cover showed Superman streaking through Metropolis wearing a tight-fitting, S-logoed T-shirt and blue jeans.

The initiative angered many longtime readers because it seemed to wipe out some seventy years of history, essentially saying that many of the stories that had come before, stories that readers had loved and cherished, had not happened.

Despite some grumbling, the hype made the New 52 among the most successful industry initiatives in recent memory. The initial launches of the new titles sold in huge numbers and reportedly brought many lapsed readers back into comic book stores. The early months of the relaunch allowed DC its first win in a long time in terms of direct-market share. DC edged Marvel by 5 percent in September 2011. That lead swelled to 20 percent the following month.

Marvel, on top for so long, remained unfazed—at least publicly. Joe Quesada, who'd by then been promoted to chief creative officer, claimed the DC relaunch was "a response to *everything* Marvel's been doing. . . . You don't set fire to your entire house for no good reason," he said.

Marvel's senior vice president of publishing, Tom Brevoort, also took a poke at his rival's new direction on an online forum. He advised DC to stop "trying to be a bad Marvel clone—because they're not even getting bad Marvel right."

DC quickly fired back. John Rood, the company's sales chief, posted a statement on DC's website in August 2011 praising the New 52 and castigating Marvel for its aggressive business practices and reliance on publishing gimmicks, including a February 2011 statement by one Marvel executive that the company planned to kill off a character every quarter to fuel sales.

"To be clear—DC is not a market-share-chaser," Rood wrote. "If we were, we would not be creating a quality lasting direction across a controlled number of titles. We would instead be flooding the market with over 200 titles a month, changing your prices with abandon, killing off a character every quarter or so, and/or randomly announcing decimal-pointed event-ish thingies. We haven't."

Marvel soon announced a soft relaunch of its own revamp called Marvel Now! A mysterious house ad promoting the endeavor showed fifty-two red slashes on a black background, which appeared to be some sort of cheap slap at DC's New 52.

"Marvel Now! starts with the creators, so don't expect writer shake-ups across the line by the fourth or fifth issue, or half the titles to get cancelled and replaced by a new #1," Marvel editor-in-chief Axel Alonso said, piling on the New 52 in a 2012 online interview. "We aren't throwing shit at a wall, seeing what falls off and then replacing it with more shit. We're building books we expect to last."

Marvel Now! would restart series at #1, but the reboot would not wipe out what had come before. Marvel's precious continuity, which had remained intact since its modern-day superhero universe was founded in 1961, would soldier on.

"DC has this obsession with rebooting its universe every few years," Pittarese says. "DC would say every few years, 'Everything you knew didn't happen, or it happened differently.' Marvel was ashamed of nothing. So if you liked the fact that [Fantastic Four member] Johnny Storm was married to a Skrull who laid an egg and a monster came out of it, then they're not going to say that didn't happen."

It didn't take long for DC's New 52 to stumble. Instead of cleaning up continuity, it managed to muddy it even more. The quality of the books was also uneven, as creative teams came and went seemingly on a whim.

"DC completely reconfigured their timeline to try and tailor the characters and the stories for a twenty-first-century audience, and they had some initial success," says Robert Lyons, owner of Connecticut store Legends of Superheros. "But then they kind of lost their way. The sales started trailing off, and Marvel was quick to take advantage."

DC's New 52 continued to slump, and by 2015 Marvel had a commanding lead once again in the direct market, dominating with 42 percent to DC's 27. DC's drop-off revealed the diminishing returns of reboots and laid bare the Big Two's dangerous reliance on marketing-driven inventions instead of good, simple storytelling to sell titles.

"Any publisher can sell #1s and #2s, but can they sell #12s and #18s?" asks Bill Schanes, a former comic book distributor. "That's when all the gimmicks are over and you should have your core consumers in."

With New 52 fading, what was DC to do? The solution came in a cryptic February 2016 tweet from DC copublisher Jim Lee showing an image of a theater curtain with the headline "Rebirth" across it. A message below read, "It's not a reboot . . ."

Turns out it was a reboot.

The company announced it was launching an initiative to be called "Rebirth," basically taking a mulligan on the whole New 52 thing. The latest reboot would start most titles over yet again with #1s and try to capture the essence of the DC universe by "putting the highest priority on the direct market," in a sense catering more heavily to the aging fanboy demographic, who had been alienated by DC's jarring New 52. Rebirth was to return the DC universe to basically where it was before the New 52 disappointment, bringing back some fan-favorite characters and elements from the past.

To promote the launch DC allowed retailers to begin selling its first batch of Rebirth comics Tuesday at midnight—a relaxation of rules that generally forbade selling the week's new releases until Wednesday morning. Marvel promptly countered by also allowing retailers to sell its comics the night before.

As this was DC's second line-wide reboot in just five years and was being orchestrated by the same executives and much of the same talent who had screwed up things so badly the last time, Rebirth was met with skepticism. A website, hasdcdonesomethingstupidtoday.com, kept track of the company's perceived blunders, and readers—weary from the endless events and reboots as well as the sunny promises that always accompanied them—took to the Internet to complain.

"DC compulsively reboots more times than Windows 7," artist Jules Rivera wrote on Twitter.

DC had woken up to the fact that its core readership, the die-hard fanboys to whom the industry was exclusively catering, cared about the company's legacy, cared about continuity. It mattered to them whether the Batman they were reading about that month was the same Batman who had begun calling himself "The Batman of Zur-En-Arrh" after a mental break a few years earlier. It mattered that the Flash (technically the second Flash, Barry Allen) had perished during *Crisis on Infinite Earths* before being miraculously resurrected in 2008's *Final Crisis*. Rebirth marked a return to that original continuity.

The corporate culture manifests itself in the offices as well. Years ago Marvel was a place where impromptu silly-string fights would break out and the staff celebrated paddle ball day. A staffer played a joke on editor-in-chief Tom DeFalco by secretly changing the name on every one of his business cards to "Tom DeFatso."

It was a place where staffers and freelancers could hang out and swap industry gossip and ideas. Nowadays just getting through the door is a problem.

"Steve Ditko and other artists used to come by and hang out in my office. I think that's pretty much gone," says former Marvel editor Ann Nocenti. "You can't walk into Marvel or DC anymore without some kind of hall pass or pre-approval. Even then you get taken by someone through a labyrinth of offices to the exact spot where you're supposed to be, then escorted back out again."

DC is now out on the West Coast, marking the first time in the illustrious history of the medium that the major superhero publishers aren't operating out of New York. The move means there's less camaraderie between the staffs and less overlap.

Marvel-DC crossovers have also become a thing of the past, even with Bob Harras, a former Marvel editor, as DC's editor-in-chief, and Axel Alonso, a former DC guy, in charge of Marvel.

"I've talked to people from both companies who are convinced we'll never see another crossover again, and the reason is entirely about corporate stuff," says writer Kurt Busiek. "There will never be a point where things are exactly even, so right now the people at Disney are going, 'Marvel movies are doing better than DC. Why should we give them a foot up?' And at some point in the future people at Warner Bros. might be going, 'You know, DC TV is doing better than Marvel. Why should we give them a foot up?'"

Add that to the fact that with a crossover—no matter how successful—DC and Marvel will receive only half of the profits. It's a deal the corporate masters are unlikely to make.

The corporate rivalry has also affected the monthly comic books. Marvel canceled *Fantastic Four* in April 2015 amid rumors that the company was trying to punish movie-license holder Fox ahead of the Josh Trank–directed movie's arrival that summer.

"The relationship was fine until Disney bought us," says Chris Claremont. "There was no problem between Marvel and Fox and the X-Men and Fantastic Four as long as Marvel was an independent company. The minute Marvel became a subsidiary of a rival studio, that changed the whole parameters."

When Marvel licensed the Fantastic Four to Fox years ago, the studio argued that a successful movie would drive comic book sales, so Fox demanded a royalty on sales of Marvel's *Fantastic Four*, according to artist and Image cofounder Erik Larsen. Marvel opted to cancel the book, preferring not to pay Fox and to promote a rival studio's property.

Perhaps the biggest threat to superhero comics is sales. The characters have become global icons at the box office and on TV, but that increased exposure hasn't boosted monthly comic book sales much. Marvel and DC

"I think Marvel has figured out a way to make those movies accessible to the public that DC hasn't. I don't know what that is. I don't know why you can't get Batman and Superman or people to get as juiced up to be a part of that."

—Samuel L. Jackson in 2015

"I ain't afraid of Sam, I ain't afraid of you! You don't think we know you got a lazy eye up under that patch, bitch, you lazy eye-patched bitch!"

—Kevin Hart at the 2016 MTV Movie Awards

have seen their circulation numbers dwindle considerably over the decades to the point at which they're now turning out product for a niche audience consisting of a handful of aging, hyper-devoted readers. Where popular titles once sold in the hundreds of thousands or even millions, many DC and Marvel books are lucky to break fifty thousand. Plenty of titles sell a paltry twenty thousand copies, meaning that the estimated twenty-five hundred comic shops in America order just eight copies each. Eight.

Both companies have responded to the drought by once again flooding the market with more than eighty comics a month each as well as publishing popular titles twice as often in an attempt to capture more dollars from whatever readers they have left.

Unfortunately for Marvel and DC's future publishing prospects, the comic book industry is changing. Superhero comics aren't even mainstream anymore. The irony is that the push to improve superhero comics over the years—with *The Dark Knight Returns*, *Watchmen*, and other revolutionary leaps forward—helped open the general public's eyes to the possibilities of the medium and went a long way toward making comic books an accepted and respected art form. Civilians were no longer embarrassed to be seen reading them. Those changes opened up the medium to different kinds of material, which has since shunted the superhero genre aside.

Marvel and DC are no longer the leaders when it comes to graphic fiction. That honor belongs to offerings from traditional publishers that move far more units than the average issue of *Superman*. Scholastic's *Diary of a Wimpy Kid* series has sold more than 164 million copies, and cartoonist Raina Telgemeier's autobiographical books aimed at a younger audience have topped the *New York Times* best-seller list. The breadth of material now stretches from kiddie to crime, manga to memoir.

"I think comics are in the best spot they've ever been in the entire history of the medium," retailer Hibbs says. "There's not a person who walks in my store that I can't find something that they will enjoy. That's phenomenal. But I don't think that those things are the Marvel and DC superhero universes anymore. Marvel and DC used to be 90 percent of our sales, and now they're 70 percent. They're not the conversation that's happening anymore."

Lucky for superhero fans, the genre's diminishing publishing prospects hasn't put a damper on the conflict between the Big Two.

"There's still a rivalry, but it's more of a corporate rivalry," says former Marvel editor-in-chief Gerry Conway. "There's always going to be a competition between them. They're the two big dogs, and they're going to keep fighting."

And we, the readers, will gladly go along for the ride.

Epilogue

$\mathcal{S}$o who won?

It's the question that gets asked most often when it comes to this or any other rivalry, and it's only natural that onlookers would demand a victor. No one wants to invest their precious time and attention in a competition only to walk away unsure who came out on top. This isn't a soccer match.

But in the case of Marvel and DC, declaring a winner can be complicated because not everyone may agree on what the rules of the game even are. What are the yardsticks for "winning?"

In terms of sales Marvel is clearly the victor. The company's titles generally dominate the direct market and have for decades. When it comes to the box office it's pretty clear that the films from Marvel Studios have been better received than those of its competitor, and in terms of lifetime box office Marvel owns DC ($8.9 billion to DC's $4 billion). In the crucial area of licensing revenue Marvel now also comes out ahead.

But then there are the intangibles—those factors that can't be quantified with simple numbers. Superheroes are almost always discovered during youth, and as a result these characters have a powerful emotional connection. Superman, Spider-Man, Wonder Woman, and the rest remain forever wrapped in a comfy blanket of nostalgia and bathed in the golden hue that seems to color everything from childhood. They are gateways to another time.

To read a Superman comic book or to watch a Batman movie is to experience the character in the now but also to relive the fond memories of the character in the then. That is a power that both Marvel and DC have, and it's far more valuable than money.

In the end declaring a winner maybe isn't all that important. The winner is whichever means more to you. It can't be measured, argued, or debated.

Can't we just celebrate the extraordinary achievements of both companies? The artists, writers, and editors who've worked for Marvel and DC over the years have given us a rich cast of characters who have endured for decades and are now recognizable around the globe. And the companies have survived for some eighty years, through recessions and wars, changing tastes and shifting habits, by finding new techniques to freshen their properties and new ways to deliver them to an audience. That's a remarkable run for companies in an industry in which every one of its contemporaries, aside from Archie, has long since died. Let's just tip our hats to their accomplishments and thank them for the entertainment they've provided over the decades—and for entertainment yet to come.

These characters aren't going away anytime soon. Superheroes are now as lasting a part of culture as Odysseus or Sherlock Holmes, and they'll likely be with us for years to come—maybe forever. It's all a matter of what form they will take. Stories about the great heroes of antiquity were passed down orally and survived long enough to be written down. The great superheroes were born on newsprint and have made the jump to movies and television, avoiding being dragged into obscurity by the decline of print media.

But when the current superhero movie boom ends, as it inevitably will, what then?

When it's no longer profitable to publish a monthly paper comic book, what then?

And what will become of the Marvel-DC rivalry? For rivalries to matter, they require opposing entities with easily identifiable traits and characteristics that fans can latch onto. And they also require that something of value is at stake, be it money, position, or prestige. As Marvel and DC continue to lose the unique identities that were built in the New York publishing business over the decades and continue to become subsumed within larger corporate entities, what then?

What happens when Stan Lee is gone and the face of Marvel becomes some executive VP of publishing? What happens when the culture moves on and a whole generation of children decide that Superman holds no interest for them, no matter how much his costume is darkened or his personality tweaked?

We're at the end of an era. Marvel and DC, the companies we've all grown up with, are changing. And so is their rivalry. It's moving from the battlefield where it was born and has been defined for more than fifty years—print—and is heading in new, uncertain directions. In the coming decades Marvel vs. DC may no longer hold the same meaning it once did. But as Death, the Gothish Grim Reaper from Neil Gaiman's *Sandman* series, once said, "It always ends. That's what gives it value."

ACKNOWLEDGMENTS

*T*hanks to everyone—the comic book artists, writers, executives, and fans—who were kind enough to speak to me. Without their generosity and insight, this book would not have been possible.

Thanks to my agent, Byrd, for finding it a home. Thanks to Dan for his editorial guidance. Thanks (and apologies) to my wife for reading it along the way.

And thanks to all the superhero fans whose passion made this a worthy topic for a book.

NOTES

INTRODUCTION

xvi "**good, intriguing covers were about all that mattered**": Shirrel Rhoades, *A Complete History of American Comic Books* (New York: Peter Lang Publishing, 2008), 46.

xvii "**It didn't make any difference in the sales**": Stan Lee, interview, *Comics Scene* 3, no. 1 (May 2000).

xix "**I think the Marvels are great for a very conceited reason**": "As Barry Jenkins, Ohio '69, Says: 'A Person Has to Have Intelligence to Read Them,'" *Esquire*, September 1966, 116–117.

CHAPTER 1

1 "**All of a sudden it hits me**": Otto Friedrich, "Up, Up and Awaaay!!!" *Time*, June 24, 2001, http://content.time.com/time/magazine/article/0,9171,148856,00.html.

1 "**They could have been any kind of office**": Todd Klein, "Visiting DC Comics in the 1960s Part 3," Todd's Blog, http://kleinletters.com/Blog/visiting-dc-comics-in-the-1960s-part-3.

2 "**The editors had this great little gentleman's club**": Jon B. Cooke, "Orlando's Weird Adventures," *Comic Book Artist* #1, Spring 1998, 19–26.

3 **The stories of his abuse number in the dozens**: 4. Todd Klein, "Visiting DC Comics in the 1960s Part 1," Todd's Blog, http://kleinletters.com/Blog/visiting-dc-comics-in-the-1960s-part-1.

3 "**His brother was worse**": Alan Moore, Jon B. Cooke, and George Khoury, "Alan Moore and the Magic of Comics," *Comic Book Artist* #25, June 2003.

6 **Action Comics and Superman sales**: Jerry Franken, "Superman Crushes Steel But Never Hits a Lady," PM, July 29, 1940.

7 "**material that no respectable newspaper would accept**": Sterling North, *Chicago Daily News*, May 8, 1940.

10 "**I pointed out that the average comic book reader**": Julius Schwartz, *Man of Two Worlds: My Life in Science Fiction and Comics* (New York: Harper Paperbacks, 2000), 87.

11 "**The Flash jump-started the whole superhero business again**": Carmine Infantino with David Spurlock, *The Amazing World of Carmine Infantino: An Autobiography* (Lebanon, NJ: Vanguard Productions, 2001), 54.

CHAPTER 2

13 **"The fact is that Marvel Comics are the first comic books"**: Sally Kempton, "Super Anti-Hero in Forest Hills," *Village Voice*, April 1, 1965.

13 **"We were a company of copycats"**: Stan Lee with George Mair, *Excelsior!: The Amazing Life of Stan Lee* (New York: Fireside, 2002), 64.

14 **"We tried to outdo Superman"**: Roy Thomas and William Schelly, eds., *Alter Ego: The Best of the Legendary Comics Fanzine* (Raleigh, NC: TwoMorrows Publishing, 2008), 174.

14 **"If you get a title that catches on"**: Blake Bell and Michael J. Vassallo, *The Secret History of Marvel Comics: Jack Kirby and the Moonlighting Artists at Martin Goodman's Empire* (Seattle: Fantagraphics, 2013), 45.

16 **Without the new distribution deal, Marvel would have likely died**: Lou Mougin, "Roy Thomas," in *Comics Interview* #66, 1989, 5–32.

16 **"We didn't want the competition"**: Jack Liebowitz, unpublished memoir, quoted in Larry Tye, *Superman: The High-Flying History of America's Most Enduring Hero* (New York: Random House, 2012), 184.

17 **"[Goodman] said, 'Hey, maybe there's still a market"**: David Anthony Kraft, "The Foom Interview: Stan Lee." *FOOM* #17, March 1977, 13.

17 **"Martin felt in those days that our readers"**: "Stan Lee's Amazing Marvel Interview: Two Extraordinary 2005 Audio Sessions with the Man Who Spearheaded Marvel Comics," *Alter Ego* #104, August 2011, 26.

19 **"We tried to inject all kinds of realism"**: Stan Lee, 1968 interview with WBAI-FM, transcribed in Danny Fingeroth and Roy Thomas, *The Stan Lee Universe* (Raleigh, NC: TwoMorrows Publishing, 2011), 40.

19 **"These are real people who just happen to have superpowers"**: John Byrne, "John Byrne: Anatomy of a Phenomenon," *Comics Feature* 1, no. 27 (January–February 1984), 24.

19 **"I doubt you can imagine the sheer impact"**: Alan Moore, The Untold Story, http://seanhowe.tumblr.com/post/32172785745/alan-moores-lost-stan-lee-essay-1983-part-1-of.

20 **"A good influence"**: Dr. Lauretta Bender, "Testimony of Dr. Lauretta Bender, Senior Psychiatrist, Bellevue Hospital, New York, N.Y.," www.thecomicbooks.com/bender.html.

22 **"How can a character as hopelessly healthy"**: Sally Kempton, "Super Anti-Hero in Forest Hills," *Village Voice*, April 1, 1965.

25 **"Only a few short months later"**: Alan Moore, The Untold Story.

26 **"The thing that appealed to me"**: Peter Sanderson, "Peter B. Gillis," *Comics Interview* #27, 1985, 7–23.

26 **"It's a simple thing"**: Stan Lee, interview, *Comics Scene* 3, no. 1 (May 2000).

26 **"Marvel is a cornucopia of fantasy"**: Stan with Mair, *Excelsior!*, 3.

CHAPTER 3

28   **"We were looking at this Marvel stuff"**: Bob Haney, "Bob Haney Interview by Michael Catron Part Two (of Five)," *Comics Journal*, January 6, 2011, http://classic.tcj.com/superhero/bob-haney-interviewed-by-michael -catron-part-two-of-five/2.

28   **"We do $100 million a year"**: Bob Haney, *Comic Reader* #196, November 1981.

28   **"What was happening was the Marvel revolution"**: "Bob Haney Interview by Michael Catron Part Two (of Five)."

29   **"Marvel was doing very well"**: Will Murray, "The Legendary Carmine Infantino," *Comic Book Marketplace* #75, January 2000, 39.

30   **"They've got problems too"**: Marc Svensson, "My Greatest Adventures: A Candid Conversation with Arnold Drake, Co-Creator of Deadman and The Doom Patrol," *Alter Ego* #17, September 2002, 3–20.

31   **"I decided I want a superhero"**: "Talking to Arnold Drake," *Newsarama*, http://web.archive.org/web/20071011174524/http://newsarama.com/general /ArnoldDrake/DrakneInterview.htm.

31   **"Don't get your bowels in an uproar"**: Jim Amash, "Arnold Drake Talks about the X-Men, His Time at Marvel — and the Doom Patrol!" *Alter Ego* #24, May 2003, 15–17.

32   **"Not unless someone was looking"**: Lou Mougin, "Arnold Drake," *Comics Interview* #16, 1984, 5–17.

32   **"I [initially] reasoned that there wasn't enough"**: Arnold Drake, interview, *Alter Ego* #24, May 2003.

32   **"Brotherhood of Evil"**: John Wells, *American Comic Book Chronicles: 1960–1964* (Raleigh, NC: TwoMorrows Publishing, 2013) 207.

32   **"The last thing in the world I wanted"**: Roy Thomas, "Stan Lee Talks to Roy Thomas about the Early Days of the X-Men — and Even The Doom Patrol," *Alter Ego* #24, May 2003, 3–5.

34   **"In those days comics were"**: Jon B. Cooke, "Donenfeld's Comics: A talk with Irwin Donenfeld, 1960s DC editorial director," *Comic Book Artist Collection*, vol. 2 (Raleigh, NC: TwoMorrows Publishing, 2002), 67.

34   **"It was the stupidest idea we ever heard"**: Rhoades, *A Complete History of American Comic Books*, 91.

35   **"[Marvel] succeeded for two reasons primarily"**: Arnold Drake, memo, reprinted in "A Memo to DCs Publisher," *Alter Ego* #17, September 2002, 21.

35   **"You're as full of shit as a Christmas turkey"**: Arnold Drake, *Alter Ego* #17, September 2002.

39   **"I don't want anybody to know who *you* are"**: Jim Shooter, interview, Silver Age Sage, www.wtv-zone.com/silverager/interviews/shooter_1.shtml.

41 **"Don't bother trying to fool me"**: Clifford Meth, *Marvel Presents: The Invincible Gene Colan* (New York: Marvel Comics, 2010).

43 **"I was . . . watching these jerks"**: Jim Amash and Eric Nolen-Weathington, *Carmine Infantino: Penciler, Publisher, Provocateur* (Raleigh, NC: TwoMorrows Publishing, 2010), 110.

CHAPTER 4

45 **"Change had to come"**: Amash and Nolen-Weathington, *Carmine Infantino*, 113.

46 **"They were hamisha [comfortable] people"**: Jack Liebowitz, unpublished memoir, quoted in Larry Tye, *Superman: The High-Flying History of America's Most Enduring Hero* (New York: Random House, 2012), 188.

46 **"They made me all kinds of promises"**: John Wells, *American Comic Book Chronicles: 1965–1969* (Raleigh, NC: TwoMorrows Publishing, 2014), 192.

46 **"I went into Jack Liebowitz's office"**: Amash and Nolen-Weathington, *Carmine Infantino*, 104.

46 **"Marvel was kicking the hell out of DC"**: Carmine Infantino, "From There to . . . Infantino," *Back Issue* #1, November 2003, 86.

47 **"I like you a lot"**: Amash and Nolen-Weathington, *Carmine Infantino*, 92.

48 **"Because they're a bunch of spoongroins over at DC"**: Clem Robins, "Here Comes Captain Relevant!," Treasure Keeper, www.dialbforblog.com/archives/493.

48 **"The cover sells that month's issue"**: Arnold Drake in Jim Amash, "Arnold Drake Talks about the X-Men, His Time at Marvel — and the Doom Patrol!" *Alter Ego* #24, May 2003, 15–17.

50 **"When I went to DC, they wanted me to respond"**: Jon B. Cooke, "Along Came Giordano," *Comic Book Artist* #1, Spring 1998, 30–40.

50 **"Wear a tie"**: Gary Groth, "The Joe Kubert Interview," *Comics Journal*, www.tcj.com/the-joe-kubert-interview/3.

51 **"It was like walking into a bank"**: Paul Levitz, "The Many Worlds of Joe Orlando," *Amazing World of DC Comics* #6, June 1975, 2–13.

54 **"What happened with DC was they ran out"**: Gary Groth, "An Interview with Gil Kane," *Comics Journal* #38, February 1978, 34–46.

55 a series of **"weak and ill at ease impressions"**: Grant Morrison, *Supergods: What Masked Vigilantes, Miraculous Mutants, and a Sun God from Smallville Can Teach Us About Being Human* (New York: Spiegel & Grau, 2011), 146.

56 **Sell-through of the rebooted issues jumped**: Jon B. Cooke, "Director Comments," *Comic Book Artist* #1, Spring 1998, 6–14.

57 **"Everybody was happy that Bob Kane was gone"**: Amash and Nolen-Weathington, *Carmine Infantino*, 103.

57 **"Don't you know what you got here"**: *Comic Book Artist Collection*, vol. 2 (Raleigh, NC: TwoMorrows Publishing, 2002), 25.

61 **"Well, OK. We'll miss you. Bye.":** Amash and Nolen-Weathington, *Carmine Infantino*, 124.

61 **"You squeeze them until there's no juice left":** Lou Mougin, "William Woolfolk," *Comics Interview* #29, 1985, 7–15.

CHAPTER 5

63 **"Carmine was trying to beat Marvel":** Jon B. Cooke, "'Thank You & Good Afternoon!' Talkin' with Dick," *Comic Book Artist*, http://twomorrows.com/comicbookartist/articles/01giordano.html.

64 **"They're sensational":** Spurlock, *The Amazing World of Carmine Infantino*, 110.

64 **"It was that simple":** Ibid.

64 **"I used to wonder why he left":** Les Daniels, *Marvel: Five Fabulous Decades of the World's Greatest Comics* (New York: Harry N. Abrams, 1993), 145.

64 **"At DC, I'm given the privilege":** Jack Kirby, interview, *Rocket's Blast Comicollector* #81, 1971.

65 **According to Kirby, Infantino had initially asked him:** Interview, *Comics Scene* 1, no. 2 (March 1982).

65 **In Infantino's telling, however, Kirby lobbied:** 7. Infantino, "From There to . . . Infantino," 87.

66 **"We didn't enjoy changing an artist's work":** Spurlock, *The Amazing World of Carmine Infantino*, 111.

66 **DC editor Mike Sekowsky once told Kirby's assistant:** Greg Stump, "Infantino Raises Questions About CBG Letters Policy Following Kirby Controversy Flare-Up," *Comics Journal* #191, November 1996, www.tcj.com/infantino-raises-questions-about-cbg-letters-policy-following-kirby-controversy-flare-up-by-greg-stump.

71 **"I know Stan Lee, I know you well":** Amash and Nolen-Weathington, *Carmine Infantino*, 129.

73 **A price war was what Goodman wanted:** Stan Lee, *Stan Lee: Conversations* (Jackson: University Press of Mississippi, 2007), 147.

74 **"[The distributors] were throwing our books":** Jon B. Cooke, "From Art Director to Publisher: The Infantino Interview," *Comic Book Artist*, http://twomorrows.com/comicbookartist/articles/01infantino.html.

75 **"Screw them":** Christopher Irving, "Carmine Infantino's Final Interview? No Way," Graphic NYC, http://graphicnyc.blogspot.com/2009/07/carmine-infantinos-final-interview.html.

76 **"My books sell, so I'm not pulling":** Jon B. Cooke, "Director Comments," *Comic Book Artist* #1, Spring 1998, 6–14.

76 **"You know that I will not in any shape":** Lawrence Van Gelder, "A Comics Magazine Defies Code Ban on Drug Stories," *New York Times*, February 4, 1971, 37, 44.

79 create a "resurgence of the comics industry": *Comic Book Artist Collection*, vol. 1 (Raleigh, NC: TwoMorrows Publishing, 2000), 61.

79 **Marvel was understandably none too pleased**: Sean Howe, *Marvel Comics: The Untold Story* (New York: Harper, 2012), 87.

CHAPTER 6

83 **"And if you think that's gonna be a battle"**: Stan Lee, "Stan's Soapbox," April 1976.

84 **"After a while, I began to feel"**: Stan Lee, *Origins of Marvel Comics* (New York: Simon & Schuster, 1974), 73.

93 **Although Len Wein was then in charge**: Daniel Best, "Superman vs. Spider-Man: The Secret Artist Revealed," *Back Issue* #11, October 2013, 26–32.

96 **"You lost a million dollars last year"**: Amash and Nolen-Weathington, *Carmine Infantino*, 131.

CHAPTER 7

99 **"a little like quitting comics"**: Roy Thomas, *Alter Ego: Centennial* (Raleigh, NC: TwoMorrows Publishing, 2011), 20.

100 **"I have next to nothing favorable to say"**: David Anthony Kraft, "Fear and Loathing with David Anthony Kraft," *Comics Journal* #35, June 1977, A-7.

101 **"of another generation"**: Jenette Kahn, interview, *Comics Journal* #37, December 1977, 54.

103 **The company's sexual politics had always been**: Rhoades, *A Complete History of American Comic Books*, 61.

103 **Whit Ellsworth was tasked with "de-sexing" Lois Lane**: Larry Tye, *Superman: The High-Flying History of America's Most Enduring Hero* (New York: Random House, 2012), 143.

103 **"a wish dream of two homosexuals living together"**: Fredric Wertham, *Seduction of the Innocent* (New York: Rinehart & Company, 1954).

103 **"We sort of give the idea"**: Stan Lee, 1970 WNYC radio interview, transcribed in *Stan Lee: Conversations*, 28.

107 **"warm body theory"**: Mike W. Barr, "You Can't Spell 'Implosion' Without 'I:' A Bottom-Rung View of One of DC Comics' Darkest Hours," *Back Issue* #2, February 2004, 72–82.

107 **DC's spokesperson, Mike Gold, admitted at the time**: "DC Announces Format Change 50¢ - 40 Page Books in June," *Comics Journal* #38, February 1978, 8–9.

107 **"Unless they do so well"**: "Stan the Man Raps with Marvel Maniacs at James Madison University," *Comics Journal* #42, October 1978, 45–55.

108 **"More market share for us"**: Mike W. Barr, *Back Issue* #2.

108 **"Comics are sort of beneath him"**: N. R. Kleinfield, "Superheroes' Creators Wrangle," *New York Times*, October 13, 1979, 25.

111 **Cockrum, who was then illustrating the Legion of Super-Heroes**: Jim Amash, "We Kicked the Whole Thing Around a Lot," *Alter Ego* #24, May 2003, 34–47.

111 **he "was very conservative"**: *Alter Ego* #24, May 2003.

113 **"There's only two or three people"**: Kim Thompson, "Roy Thomas Leaves Marvel," *Comics Journal* #56, June 1980, 9–12.

113 **"If Gene Colan is being positioned"**: "Gene Colan Leaves Marvel," *Comics Journal* #63, April 1981, 11–13.

113 **"I don't really begrudge DC Marv"**: "Marv Wolfman Now at DC," *Comics Journal* #51, November 1979, 11.

114 **Wein and Wolfman assembled a team**: Keith Dallas, *American Comic Book Chronicles: The 1980s* (Raleigh, NC: TwoMorrows Publishing, 2013) 21.

114 **"three refugees from Shooter-land"**: Heidi MacDonald, "DC's Titanic Success," *Comics Journal* #76, October 1982, 46–51.

116 **"systematically kept people away"**: From *Chain Reaction*, quoted in *Marvel Age* #19, October 1984.

117 **"That doesn't really impress me"**: "Marvel Unimpressed with DC's Move," *Comics Journal* #53, January 1980, 10.

120 **They agreed to issue a joint press release**: Dick Giordano's "Meanwhile" column, January 1985.

120 **"In my view . . . the JLA/Avengers"**: Ibid.

120 **"unfounded and foolish"**: *Marvel Age* #19, October 1984.

CHAPTER 8

123 **"In a way, we were the laboratory experiment"**: Les Daniels, *DC Comics: Sixty Years of the World's Favorite Comic Book Heroes* (New York: Bulfinch, 1995), 174.

123 **"It began to be generally assumed"**: *Back Issue* #2, February 2004.

124 **DC's first leaps into another medium**: Bruce Scivally, *Superman on Film, Television, Radio and Broadway* (Jefferson, NC: McFarland, 2007), 25.

125 **"We have people now working"**: "Stan Lee at Princeton, 1966: Steve Ditko's Departure Announced," YouTube, posted December 28, 2013, www.youtube.com/watch?v=A73KehrmpOU5.

126 **"Getting this on television"**: John Romita Sr., "Off My Chest," *Back Issue* #5, August 2004, 57–60.

126 **"breakfast food" to "four, five, and six-year-olds"**: Stan Lee, speech at Vanderbilt University, 1972, transcribed in *Stan Lee: Conversations*, 33.

126 **Martin Goodman's son Chip made a terrible deal**: Jordan Raphael and Tom Spurgeon, *Stan Lee and the Rise and Fall of the American Comic Book* (Chicago: Chicago Review Press, 2004), 190.

126 **"I'd be happier if the shows hewed"**: Stan Lee, "Stan's Soapbox," November 1978.

127 **"I felt like an idiot"**: Jackson Ayres, "When Were Superheroes Grim and Gritty?" *Los Angeles Review of Books*, February 20, 2016, https:// lareviewofbooks.org/article/when-were-superheroes-grim-and-gritty.

127 **"It's not a 'comic book show,' the stars insist"**: *Us*, July 11, 1978.

127 **The elder Salkind referred to the character as "Mr. Superman"**: "Movie Might Have Been Different," *Dispatch*, December 23, 1978.

128 **"It's not a good property for a film"**: Ilya Salkind in Jake Rossen, *Superman vs. Hollywood: How Fiendish Producers, Devious Directors, and Warring Writers Grounded an American Icon* (Chicago: Chicago Review Press, 2008), 60.

128 **"When the script for the first Superman film"**: Spurlock, *The Amazing World of Carmine Infantino*, 124.

128 **"It's a movie for adults that children"**: Susan Heller Anderson, "It's a Bird! It's a Plane! It's a Movie!" *New York Times*, June 26, 1977, www.nytimes .com/1977/06/26/archives/its-a-bird-its-a-plane-its-a-movie.html.

129 **"We had a very expensive film"**: Al Jean Harmetz, "The Marketing of Superman and his Paraphernalia," *New York Times*, June 21, 1981, www.nytimes.com/1981/06/21/movies/the-marketing-of-superman -and-his-paraphernalia.html.

130 **"unhappy, unfunny, unexciting"**: Roger Ebert, "Supergirl," RogerEbert.com, www.rogerebert.com/reviews/supergirl-1984.

131 **"The first *Superman* movie had a lot"**: *Chaffey College Mountain Breeze*, October 10, 1987.

131 **Rumor has it that in 1966**: Vartanig G. Vartan, "Batman Fad Aids Stock Rise," *New York Times*, March 20, 1966, 148.

132 **"The method of producing"**: "The Dick Giordano Interview (Part One of Three)," *Comics Journal*, http://classic.tcj.com/superhero/ the-dick-giordano-interview-part-one-of-three/2.

CHAPTER 9

133 **"There are comic book readers who want to be sold"**: *Comics Scene* 1, no. 7 (January 1983).

139 **"Most of the complaints come from older readers"**: David Anthony Kraft and Jim Salicrup, "Marv Wolfman," *Comics Interview* #3, May 1983, 19–30.

141 **"We're not going to just sit there"**: Kim Thompson, "DC Creates New Royalties System for Freelancers," *Comics Journal* #69, December 1981, 16–17.

141 **"I didn't think they wouldn't follow"**: *Comics Journal* #69, December 1981.

141 **"It really cost us a fortune"**: "Marvel Offers Own Royalty Plan," *Comics Scene* 1, no. 3 (May 1982), 10.

142   **"Tell me what it is that you would really like to do"**: Jennifer M. Contino, "A Chat with Kahn," Sequential Tart, www.sequentialtart.com/archive/may01 /kahn.shtml.

143   **"*Ronin* provoked in me not only disappointment"**: Kim Thompson, *"Run of the Miller,"* Comics Journal #82, July 1983.

144   **"What's in it for Warner Com"**: Memo, JimShooter.com, http://jimshooter .com/2011/08/superman-first-marvel-issue.html.

CHAPTER 10

147   **"a Swedish movie with no subtitles"**: "Clash of the Comic Book Giants," *New York City Business*, February 11–22, 1985.

148   **"Don't put conflicting books on the stand"**: Jay Zilber, "An Interview with Martin Pasko," *Comics Journal* #37, December 1977, 37–46.

149   **"It was to get revenge"**: Keith Dallas, *American Comic Book Chronicles: The 1980s* (Raleigh, NC: TwoMorrows Publishing, 2013), 130.

149   **"When people think of DC"**: Mark Waid, "Beginnings and Endings," *Amazing Heroes* #66, March 1985, 23–30.

150   **"overlap the premiere of the DC series"**: "Clash of the Comic Book Giants."

152   **The reason for the purchase, he sheepishly admitted**: *Comics Interview* #20, February 1985.

152   **"Let's be honest. *Secret Wars* was crap"**: Paul Howley, "Paul Howley's Story: Parts 70–79," http://paulhowleysstory.blogspot.com/2009/12/part-70-79.html.

152   **"Each time [Marvel] puts out a book like that"**: Mitch Cohn, "Bruce Conklin," *Comics Interview* #28, 1985, 47–56.

152   **Besides sending a clear signal to the readership**: Kevin Dooley, "The Total Marv Wolfman Interview," *Amazing Heroes* #135, February 1988, 22–45.

153   **"stodgy *Wall Street Journal* image"**: Gary Groth, "Brushes and Blue Pencils: An Interview with Dick Giordano," *Comics Journal* #62, March 1981, 44.

153   **"A company with the resources of DC"**: Calum Iain Johnston, letter, *Comics Journal* #85, October 1983.

154   **"DC is Marvel and Marvel is DC"**: Martin Pasko, "Messages from a Curmudgeon," *Comics Scene* 1, no. 11 (September 1983), 38–40.

154   **"The reason [for hiring Byrne]"**: Dwight Jon Zimmerman, "Steve Gerber," *Comics Interview* #37, 1986, 6–17.

154   **"The modern audience now wants"**: Paul E. Akers, "Bring Back the Real Superman," *Washington Post*, December 31, 1988.

155   **"Nobody noticed, so they dropped it"**: Rita Kempley, "Superman," *Washington Post*, November 2, 1985.

155   **"If he fights, it's in a way that leaves"**: Abraham Riesman, "What We Talk About When We Talk About Superman and Batman," Vulture, March 2016, www.vulture.com/2016/03/batman-v-superman-c-v-r.html.

156 **"They hated it"**: Ethan Alter, "'The Dark Knight Returns' at 30: Frank Miller on His Comic Book Classic," Yahoo! Movies, January 15, 2016, www.yahoo .com/movies/the-dark-knight-returns-at-30-frank-miller-on-151604704 .html.

156 **"We'll probably copy every one"**: Dwight Jon Zimmerman, "Mark Gruenwald," *Comics Interview* #54, 1987, 5–23.

157 **"I think DC, sooner or later"**: *Chaffey College Mountain Breeze*, October 10, 1987.

157 **"Quality became the motivation"**: Mike Richardson and Steve Duin, *Comics: Between the Panels* (Milwaukie, OR: Dark Horse, 1998), 121.

158 **"DC Comics publishing something"**: George Khoury, *Kimota! The Miracleman Companion* (Raleigh, NC: TwoMorrows Publishing, 2001).

158 **At a 1985 Chicago Comicon panel**: James Vance, "R. A. Jones," *Comics Interview* #48, 1987, 47.

159 **"Such creatures were almost nonexistent"**: Mike Cullen, "Real Life Super-Villains," *Amazing Heroes* #186, December 1990, 6–8.

160 **"Marvel is a backward-looking corporate behemoth"**: Darcy Sullivan, "Marvel Comics and the Kiddie Hustle," *Comics Journal* #152, August 1992, 30–37.

160 **"It seems to me that Marvel is in the same place"**: Cory Strode, letter, *Amazing Heroes* #168, July 1989.

CHAPTER 11

162 *Batman* **was able to tap ancillary dollars**: Graeme McMillan, "Batmania—The Merchandise," io9, June 21, 2009, http://io9.gizmodo.com/5296771/ batmania—-the-merchandise.

166 **McFarlane was more of a jock**: "' . . . That's the Spice of Life, Bud': The Todd McFarlane Interview," *Comics Journal*, http://www.tcj.com/ thats-the-spice-of-life-bud-the-todd-mcfarlane-interview/2.

166 **"I mean, fuck, I didn't let"**: Ibid.

171 **He was soon earning $85,000 a month**: Alec Foege, "The X-Men Files," *New York Magazine*, http://nymag.com/nymetro/arts/features/3522.

171 **Grant Morrison, the Scottish writer behind the hardcover**: Lance Parkin, *Magic Words: The Extraordinary Life of Alan Moore* (London: Aurum Press, 2013).

177 *Newsweek* **wrote an influential article**: "Superfans and Batmaniacs," *Newsweek*, February 15, 1965.

182 **DC's contract was reported to have come**: Eric Reynolds, "The New Dynamics," *Comics Journal* #177, May 1995, 9–19.

188 **"We won!" the page read in massive red type**: Brian Cronin, "Comic Book Legends Revealed #461," Comic Book Resources, www.cbr.com/comic-book -legends-revealed-461.

CHAPTER 12

197 **"I liked it when the two companies hated each other"**: Sridhar Pappu, "As the $139 Million Spider-Man Debuts in Movie Theaters, Joe Quesada, the Trash-Talking Editor in Chief of Marvel Comics, Spins," *New York Observer*, April 29, 2002.

198 **"Somewhere somebody wrote down"**: "AICN Comics: Gray Haven Interview Bill Jemas of Marvel Comics!!!," Ain't It Cool News, August 17, 2001www .aintitcool.com/node/9897.

198 **"DC could do a Spider-Man comic"**: "AICN Comics: Don't Ask Bill Jemas!!," Ain't It Cool News, March 20, 2002, www.aintitcool.com/node /11806.

199 **"Those who love him say it's"**: Bill Jemas, "Introduction," in Jim McLaughlin, *2000–2001 Year in Review: Fanboys and Badgirls Bill & Joe's Marvelous Adventure* (New York: Marvel Comics, 2002).

206 **"What the fuck is DC anyway?"**: "As the $139 Million Spider-Man Debuts."

206 label him **"Bill Jemas Lite"**: "Topic: DC's Single Biggest Mistake?," Byrne Robotics, www.byrnerobotics.com/forum/forum_posts. asp?TID=18585&PN=0&TPN=1.

207 **"Our characters were created"**: George Gene Gustines, "Recalibrating DC Heroes for a Grittier Century," *New York Times*, October 12, 2005.

209 **Bendis was left to jokingly lament**: "Another Reason Why DC Sucks!," www.classicmarvelforever.com/phorum_archive/read.php?3,21658,21697; and CBR, www.comicbookresources.com/?page=article&old=1&id=4075.

212 **"It would be great to get your take"**: Tasha Robinson, "Stan Lee," A.V. Club, June 20, 2001, www.avclub.com/article/stan-lee-13719.

CHAPTER 13

216 **"The definition of a *meme*"**: Brian Hiatt, "Grant Morrison on the Death of Comics," *Rolling Stone*, August 22, 2011 www.rollingstone.com/music/news /grant-morrison-on-the-death-of-comics-20110822.

216 **The genre raked in some $1.9 billion in 2016 alone**: "Box Office History for Super Hero," The Numbers, www.the-numbers.com/market/creative-type /Super-Hero.

217 **A 1988 edition lists in the works a tantalizing array**: *Comics Scene* 3, no. 13 (1988).

217 **"Batman was a big deal on television"**: Kevin Melrose, "Stan Lee Wishes Bob Kane Were Alive to See Marvel's Film Success,"Bloomberg Television, April 3, 2014, www.cbr.com/ stan-lee-wishes-bob-kane-were-alive-to-see-marvels-film-success.

219 **"Studios were behind the curve"**: Robert Greenberger, "The Path of Kahn," *Back Issue* #57, July 2012, 3–38.

223 **Spidey was optioned in 1985 for a reported $225,000**: Janet Shprintz, "Spider-Man's Legal Web May Finally Be Unraveled," *Variety*, August 19, 1998, http://variety.com/1998/film/news/spider-man-s-legal-web-may-finally-be-unraveled-1117479641.

223 **"The Spider-Man movie has been the longest"**: "Stan Lee Discusses Marvel Screen Projects at Sales Conference," *Amazing Heroes* #167, June 1989, 15.

224 **"Invent a new word"**: Carl DiOrio, "Spidey's Webbed Feat Rewrites Record Books," *Variety*, May 5, 2002, http://variety.com/2002/film/markets-festivals/spidey-s-webbed-feat-rewrites-record-books-1117866452.

225 **"It wasn't until Marvel started making"**: *Back Issue* #57, July 2012.

225 **"We're not going to let that happen"**: Ben Fritz, "Warner Bros. on a Caped Crusade," *Wall Street Journal*, April 27, 2014.

225 **Critics roundly trashed *Catwoman***: "Me-Ouch!," *Time*, July 28, 2004.

226 **"Look, this is what I want to do in the movie"**: Ben Child, "Christopher Nolan 'Took 15 Minutes' to Win Batman Begins Job," *Guardian*, September 23, 2013, www.theguardian.com/film/2013/sep/23/christopher-nolan-batman-begins-christian-bale.

226 **"What I wanted to do was to tell the Batman story"**: Laurence Maslon and Michael Kantor, *Superheroes: Capes, Cowls, and the Creation of Comic Book Culture* (New York: Crown Archetype, 2013), 283.

227 **Marvel reportedly took in a piddly $25,000**: Sean Howe, "Avengers Assemble!" Slate, September 28, 2012, www.slate.com/articles/business/the_pivot/2012/09/marvel_comics_and_the_movies_the_business_story_behind_the_avengers_.html.

228 **"Don't worry. We'll be very happy"**: Kim Masters, "Marvel Studios' Origin Secrets Revealed by Mysterious Founder: History Was 'Rewritten,'" *Hollywood Reporter*, May 5, 2016, www.hollywoodreporter.com/features/marvel-studios-origin-secrets-revealed-889795.

229 **"That's not my idea of what I want to see"**: "Robert Downey Jr on 'The Dark Knight': 'Fuck DC Comics,'" *Huffington Post*, September 17, 2008, www.huffingtonpost.com/2008/08/17/robert-downey-jr-on-the-d_n_119414.html.

230 **"It isn't just about a single approach"**: Ben Fritz, "Warner Bros. on a Caped Crusade," *Wall Street Journal*, April 27, 2014, www.wsj.com/articles/SB10001424052702303626804579505421209271680.

232 **"It would have been disingenuous"**: Edward Wyatt, "DC Comics Revamped Under a New President," *New York Times*, September 9, 2009, www.nytimes.com/2009/09/10/business/media/10warner.html,

233 **"People make an assumption"**: Diane Nelson, "DC: We're Not Marvel," IGN, September 21, 2010, www.ign.com/articles/2010/09/21/dc-were-not-marvel.

234 **"We don't like to toot our own horn"**: "My brother had to send a letter to a company for a class project so he picked DC Comics. He just got a reply today

thought you guys would be interested," Reddit, www.reddit.com/r/comic books/comments/1unxy2/my_brother_had_to_send_a_letter_to_a _company_for.

235 **"We had the flag there first"**: Brian Gallagher, "Joss Whedon and Kevin Feige Talk Avengers 2, Ant-Man and Thanos," MovieWeb, http://movieweb .com/joss-whedon-and-kevin-feige-talk-avengers-2-ant-man-and-thanos.

235 **"Maybe our reconnaissance wasn't great"**: Jeff Labrecque, "'Superman versus 'Cap': The Superhero Showdown that Everybody Won," *Entertainment Weekly*, August, 7, 2014, http://ew.com/article/2014/08/07/superman-versus -captain-america-the-superhero-showdown/?hootPostID=6381940b4456a21c e99819d9cad96d61.

235 **"the foundation right on DC"**: Stephen Galloway, "Warner Bros.' Chilly Summer Puts Execs in the Hot Seat (Analysis)," *Hollywood Reporter*, August 19, 2015, www.hollywoodreporter.com/news/ warner-bros-chilly-summer-puts-816176.

235 **"A stink bucket of disappointment"**: Alex Abad-Santos, "Batman v Superman Review: This Movie Is a Crime Against Comic Book Fans," Vox, March 23, 2016, www.vox.com/2016/3/23/11291550/ batman-v-superman-dawn-of-justice-review.

235 **"It's about as diverting"**: A. O. Scott, "Review: Batman v Superman . . . v Fun?" *New York Times*, March 23, 2016, https://www.nytimes.com/2016 /03/25/movies/review-batman-v-superman-dawn-of-justice-when-super -friends-fight.html?_r=0.

236 **"After they announced *Batman v Superman*"**: Patrick Brzeski, "'Captain America: Civil War' Director Joe Russo on the Film Industry's Chinese Future," *Hollywood Reporter*, April 22, 2016, www.hollywoodreporter.com /news/captain-america-civil-war-director-886842.

237 **"*Suicide Squad* is bad"**: Richard Lawson, "*Suicide Squad* Isn't Even the Good Kind of Bad," *Vanity Fair*, August 2, 2016, www.vanityfair.com/hollywood /2016/08/suicide-squad-review.

238 **a former Warner Bros. employee calling herself "Gracie Law"**: Gracie Law, "An Open Letter to Warner Bros. CEO Kevin Tsujihara About Layoffs, Zack Snyder, and Donuts," Pajiba, September 11, 2016, www.pajiba.com/think _pieces/an-open-letter-to-warner-bros-ceo-kevin-tsujihara-about-layoffs -zack-snyder-and-donuts.php.

238 **"Mistakenly in the past"**: Ben Fritz, "Warner Bros.'s New Strategy on DC: Lighten Up, Superheroes," *Wall Street Journal*, September 8, 2016, www.wsj .com/articles/ warner-bros-s-new-strategy-on-dc-lighten-up-superheroes-1473350000.

240 **"I think the other part that separates"**: Shirley Li, "The Defenders: Jeph Loeb on Whether the Show Will Connect to Marvel's Films," *Entertainment*

Weekly, January 13, 2017, http://ew.com/tv/2017/01/13/defenders
-marvel-cinematic-universe-crossover-jeph-loeb.

CHAPTER 14

243 **"They're the competition!"**: Vaneta Rogers, "Tom Brevoort Says 'Marvel
Better Off When DC Is Strong,'" Newsarama, September 7, 2011, www
.newsarama.com/8309-tom-brevoort-says-marvel-better-off-when-dc
-is-strong.html.

247 *Tech Times* **ran an article entitled**: Robin Parrish, "Are Marvel's 'Secret
Wars' and DC's 'Convergence' the Exact Same Story? We Look at the
Similarities," *Tech Times,* March 25, 2015, www.techtimes.com/articles
/42145/20150325/summer-event-comics-secret-wars-convergence
-exact-same-story.htm.

247 **"In these tough economic times"**: Jason Cranforoteague, "Marvel Bribes
Retailers to Destroy DC Comics," *Wired,* August 10, 2011, http://archive
.wired.com/geekdad/2011/08/the-great-marvel-comics-rip-off.

249 **"a response to *everything* Marvel's been doing"**: Jevon Phillips and Geoff
Boucher, "Marvel vs. Burbank-based DC Comics' 'New 52,'" *Glendale
News-Press,* March 13, 2012, http://articles.glendalenewspress.com/2012-03
-13/the818now/tn-818-0313-marvel-vs-burbankbased-dc-comics-new-52
_1_avengers-chief-creative-officer-dc-title.

249 **"Stop trying to be a bad Marvel clone"**: Sean T. Collins, "Quote of the Day |
Tom Brevoort: DC Is 'the Charlie Sheen of Comics,'" Comic Book Resources,
July 14, 2011, www.cbr.com/
quote-of-the-day-tom-brevoort-dc-is-the-charlie-sheen-of-comics.

249 **"To be clear—DC is not a market-share-chaser"**: John Rood, "Counting
Down to DC Comics—The New 52: A Note from John Rood," DC Comics
blog, August 29, 2011, www.dccomics.com/blog/2011/08/29/
counting-down-to-dc-comics-the-new-52-a-note-from-john-rood.

249 **"Marvel Now! starts with the creators"**: Axel Alonso and Kiel Phegley,
"Inside Marvel NOW," Comic Book Resources, www.cbr.com/inside-marvel
-now.

250 **"putting the highest priority on the direct market"**: DC press release, "DC
Entertainment Reveals First Details of 'Rebirth' to Retailers at Comics Pro
2016," DC Comics, February 18, 2016, www.dccomics.com/blog/2016/02/18
/dc-entertainment-reveals-first-details-of-%E2%80%9Crebirth%E2%80%9
D-to-retailers-at-comics-pro-2016.

251 **"DC compulsively reboots**: Jules Rivera (@julesrivera) on Twitter, https://
twitter.com/julesrivera/status/690717540490735616.

252 **Fox demanded a royalty on sales**: Erik Larsen (@ErikJLarsen) on Twitter,
https://twitter.com/ErikJLarsen/status/722319604597411840.

EPILOGUE

255   **When it comes to the box office**: Marvel Comics, Box Office Mojo, www
.boxofficemojo.com/franchises/chart/?id=marvelcomics.htm; and DC
Comics, Box Office Mojo, www.boxofficemojo.com/franchises/chart
/?id=dccomics.htm.

QUOTES

33   **"I don't know if their stuff has deteriorated"**: Paul Gambaccini, *Amazing Spider-Man* #7.

33   **"There is, however, one company which puts"**: Robert Wilczynski, *The Flash* #161.

49   **"Have you noticed the sorry mess"**: Stan Lee, "Stan's Soapbox," October 1965.

49   **"That's why everyone calls his magazines"**: Mort Weisinger, *World's Finest* #156, March 1966.

85   **"No competition Marvel winds"**: 3. "Marvel Is Better Than DC" Facebook page, www.facebook.com/Marvel-is-better-than-DC-163079197046288.

85   **"They can argue all they like"**: The "DC Is Better Than Marvel" Facebook page, www.facebook.com/DcIsBetterThanMarvel.

127   **"I could take my grandma and put her in a cape"**: Kevin Jagernaurth, "'I Could Take My Grandma and Put Her in a Cape . . . Anybody Can Do It' Says Jason Statham About Marvel Movies," I 400 Calci, June 5, 2015, www
.indiewire.com/2015/06/i-could-take-my-grandma-and-put-her-in-a-cape
-anybody-can-do-it-says-jason-statham-about-marvel-movies-263255.

127   **"It's Jason Statham"**: Kat Ward, "Mark Ruffalo Thinks He Could Take Jason Statham," Vulture, June 9, 2015, www.vulture.com/2015/06/mark-ruffalo
-thinks-he-could-take-jason-statham.html.

154   **"Spider-Woman has better hair"**: Graeme McMillan, "Why All the Wonder Woman Hate?" June 7, 2009, http://io9.gizmodo.com/5272808/why-all-the
-wonder-woman-hate.

154   **"I know this is part of the whole Marvel v. DC"**: Smith Michaels, "Stay Classy, Brian!," Blurred Productions, June 8, 2009, https://blurredproductions
.wordpress.com/2009/06/08/stay-classy-brian.

173   **"I'm going to speak frankly"**: Josh Wilding, "Geoff Johns Confirms DC's Lack of Plans for a *Justice League* Movie!," Comic Book Movie, October 8, 2010, www.comicbookmovie.com/justice_league/
geoff-johns-confirms-dcs-lack-of-plans-for-a-justice-league-movie-a23674.

173   **"dc sucks big hairy monkey balls"**: tony_von_terror, "Our Characters Are Bigger than Marvel's," IGN, October 8, 2010, www.ign.com/boards/threads
/our-characters-are-bigger-than-marvels.196547041/page-2.

217   **"I smell a lot of Marvel bitches up in here!"**: Lan Pitts, "The Rock Calls Out Marvel Stars on MTV Movie Awards," CB WWE, April 10, 2016,

http://comicbook.com/wwe/2016/04/11/the-rock-calls-out-chris-hemsworth
-on-mtv-movie-awards.

217 **"We were trying to pick a DC vs Marvel fight"**: Dwayne "The Rock" Johnson
(@TheRock) on Twitter, https://twitter.com/TheRock/
status/719321185499160577.

234 **"I feel like Batman and Superman are transcendent"**: Jen Yamato, "Zack
Snyder: Sorry Marvel, 'Batman v. Superman' Transcends Superhero Movies,"
Daily Beast, September 10, 2015, www.thedailybeast.com/articles/2015/09/10
/zack-snyder-sorry-marvel-batman-v-superman-transcends-superhero
-movies.html.

234 **"Do I want to fire some shots"**: Dave Trumbore, "'Captain America: Civil
War': Sebastian Stan Talks Winter Soldier, Returns Fire at Zack Snyder,"
Collider, September 18, 2015, http://collider.com/captain-america-3-sebastian
-stan-zack-snyder-comments.

253 **"I think Marvel has figured out a way"**: Russ Burlingame, Comicbook,
February 13, 2015, http://comicbook.com/2015/02/14/samuel-l-jackson
-says-marvel-has-figured-out-something-dc-hasnt-/.

253 **"I ain't afraid of Sam"**: Tom Cox, "Marvel 'Bitches' V DC Battle Triggered by
the Rock Dressed as Superman on MTV Awards," Movie Plot, April 22, 2016,
https://moviepilot.com/posts/3864294.

INDEX